Geronimo! U.S. Airborne Uniforms, Insignia & Equipment in World War II *Bill Rentz*. Explores the uniforms, insignia, and equipment of American Airborne, Glider, Troop Carrier, and Airborne Engineers in World War II. Detailed images of individual items, multi-side views of full combat rig, and over 100 World War II photos, most unpublished, showing the uniforms and equipment as worn by the troops. Also a comparative section with both British and German airborne gear. An important reference work for the airborne collector, reenactor, historian and veteran.
Size: 9"x12" • over 630 color and b/w photos • 192 pp. •
ISBN: 0-7643-0677-4 • hard cover • $59.95

Paramarine! Uniforms and Equipment of Marine Corps Parachute Units in World War II *Chris Mason*. *Paramarine*! is devoted to the Marines and Sailors of the Marine Corps parachute units of World War II. It explores in fascinating detail their unique, specially-designed uniforms, equipment, weapons and insignia. For the first time, over 500 photographs and images from World War II and modern collections have been assembled in one volume and combined with a wealth of facts and information about all aspects of Paramarine gear and training. *Paramarine* is the latest in Schiffer's series of studies on the airborne forces of World War II and is a must for historians and Marine Corps and Airborne collectors around the world.
Size: 9"x12" • over 500 color & b/w photos • 240 pp. •
ISBN: 0-7643-1924-8 • hard cover • $69.95

We are always interested in working with authors or collectors on wonderful book ideas. Contact us at **www.schifferbooks.com**, and page down to "For Authors – Submit a Book Proposal." Or call or write to us about your proposal.

Talk with your local bookseller. Their knowledge is one of the best tools in finding the correct book, and we all need to support them.

* *Peter Schiffer and Team* *

Designed & composed in America.

Printed in China.

Printed in China

FOREVER FORWARD: K-9 OPERATIONS IN VIETNAM

Forever Forward: K-9 Operations in Vietnam

Michael Lemish

Schiffer Military History
Atglen, PA

Book Design by Stephanie Daugherty

Library of Congress Control Number: 2009940197

Printed in China.
ISBN: 978-0-7643-3345-3

We are interested in hearing from authors with book ideas on related topics.

Published by Schiffer Publishing Ltd.
4880 Lower Valley Road
Atglen, PA 19310
Phone: (610) 593-1777
FAX: (610) 593-2002
E-mail: Info@schifferbooks.com.
Visit our web site at: www.schifferbooks.com
Please write for a free catalog.
This book may be purchased from the publisher.
Please include $5.00 postage.
Try your bookstore first.

In Europe, Schiffer books are distributed by:
Bushwood Books
6 Marksbury Avenue
Kew Gardens
Surrey TW9 4JF, England
Phone: 44 (0) 20 8392-8585
FAX: 44 (0) 20 8392-9876
E-mail: Info@bushwoodbooks.co.uk.
Visit our website at: www.bushwoodbooks.co.uk
Try your bookstore first.

This book is dedicated to the men and women
who have worked with honor in protecting our liberty.
And to the dogs that have served with them.

Contents

ACKNOWLEDGMENTS

Where does one begin when you need to thank those who have helped you along the way in seeing a book evolve over the years from an idea to publication? To just list names would be a disservice, because there will always be someone that was not mentioned, and as a consequence that person or organization may take offense, even though none was intended. I hope not to fall into that quandary.

My strongest supporter who has provided the greatest assistance and help is my best friend, who also just happens to be my wife. My biggest thanks go out to Susan, who helped to make it all possible. Without her support and assistance this project would never have been completed.

Another key component are the members of the Vietnam Dog Handler Association. The aid and support provided by everyone I have met or corresponded with over the years is overwhelming, and I thank everyone. Their names and actions are reflected within the pages of this book. On the other side of the world, members from the Australian Defence Force Trackers & War Dogs Association took time to contribute and in doing so displayed the human and canine bond that transcends a lifetime. Continued support from friends like SFC. Jesse Mendez, Columbus, Georgia and Robert Himrod in Yakima, Washington fielded every question tossed their way. Closer to home, Robert Kollar in Cumberland, Rhode Island was a constant supporter and delivered everything asked of him. I would also like to thank all those in numerous government agencies who have helped me along the way. The work provided by the men and women at the National Archives, Otis Archives, museums, and military organizations throughout the country has been overwhelming. I am grateful to folks I've met in this journey, like Nancy West, who kindly provided the foreword for this book

Sincere gratitude goes out to all the K-9 teams that have served and continue to work for our great country to protect our liberty and freedom every day. These are the individuals that need to be truly recognized, regardless of what conflict they served in. Without them, there would be no history to record.

FOREWORD

Dogs are everywhere in our popular culture these days. They bound across our television screens featured in ads selling everything from automobiles to perfume. Designer breeds adorn the covers of glossy magazines where they are carried like accessories on the arms of models and Hollywood stars. Increasing numbers of pooches go on puppy play-dates, are coiffed in chic grooming spas, and romp in parks designed for their exclusive use, replete with doggie water fountains and canine playground equipment. Dogs are our housemates, our soul mates, and even our surrogate children.

Yet, some human/canine relationships reflect back to ancient callings cultivated thousands of years ago when early man and the ancestors of *Canis lupus familiaris* first crossed paths. Whether these interactions were initiated by hunters who befriended wolves to track prey or by animals that approached flickering campfires seeking warmth and food in exchange for protection, these two species forged a lasting partnership. At the core of these intertwined roots is *service*, and it is grounded in trust and loyalty.

While all working dogs and their human companions are proof of this special bond, perhaps nowhere else is the ancient covenant better exemplified than between soldiers and their K-9 partners. One need only read Michael Lemish's fascinating book, *War Dogs – A History of Loyalty and Heroism,* to grasp the importance of man's best friend throughout military history. But it is the story of the handlers and dogs in Vietnam in particular that demands we stop and contemplate the invaluable deeds this unique relationship can produce.

Approximately 4,000 dogs served in the armed forces during the Vietnam War, and it is estimated they averted over 10,000 casualties. As with previous wars, there are no statistics to reflect the degree of security and comfort theses animals imparted to the soldiers who worked and lived alongside them. These benefits not only accrued to the individual handler, who often formed a deep attachment with his K-9, but to the other men in the unit or patrol who were fortunate enough to be with a dog team—if only for a short time. These combat troops generally reported less anxiety and better sleep patterns and appetite when accompanied by the ever-vigilant dogs.

Ultimately, the vast majority of these four-legged soldiers, not unlike their human comrades, did not return stateside to a hero's welcome. In fact, most Vietnam dogs never returned. Their fate has been a point of contention and anguish for those who have refused to forget the important part they played. In an effort to set the record right, groups of veterans and ordinary citizens work tirelessly to raise funds to erect war dog memorials both at home and overseas. It is the hope of many that a National War Dog Monument will one day grace Washington, D.C. to honor the thousands of military canines that have served the United States over the years.

Forever Forward is an important book that is long overdue. Michael Lemish has given the reader a rare insight into the Vietnam War through examining the extraordinary role of the K-9 teams. It is an account that brings to light little-known facts and illuminates tactical lessons learned that may be applied now and into the future.

Vietnam left an indelible mark on the American psyche. For some, this has been a highly personal imprint of emotional wounds and unfinished business. Yet, to revisit this period with the soldiers and their dogs is to bear witness to a vast and expansive portion of the human and canine heart. It is a place of great courage and compassion. Michael Lemish skillfully guides us through this special and unique history, and like the men who walked point with the dogs, we can only feel grateful for the privilege.

Nancy West
2009

INTRODUCTION

"Above all, Vietnam was a war that asked everything of a few and nothing of the most in America."

Myra MacPherson

"Dog. A kind of additional or subsidiary Deity designed to catch the overflow and surplus of the world's worship."

Ambrose Bierce

Many books have attempted to convey the history of the Vietnam War from a variety of perspectives and in many respects this one is no different. Yet the story to be told is not just of the war itself, but of a unique group of individuals and their trusted companions who, through a power beyond their control, had thrust upon them an arena of combat far away from home. This is a story of the bond between humans and animals that just happens to occur on a battlefield. For most of us, our bond with our four-legged friends will take place everyday when we say "Good morning" or take them for a walk around the neighborhood. The big difference is that our environs do not possess booby traps or punji stakes, and seldom is anyone shooting at you.

During the Vietnam War the relationship between a man and his dog was unique; it was a combination of the physical, intellectual, and emotional attachment. The handler hug, fed, groomed, worked with him, and helped in the dog's medical well-being. The dog in turn became his best friend, confidant, and protector. They both had a strong will to survive, although for entirely different reasons.

This special association between man and dog lasted a few days, weeks, or months. But in Vietnam this involvement seldom lasted for more than one year. Separation of the team could be caused by the man or dog or both of them being wounded or killed. For many handlers it was simply that their tour of duty was up and it was time to rotate home. With few exceptions, the dogs were in for the duration of the conflict and their handlers for just a year. Yet for most handlers this special bond transcends a lifetime even though the dog is just a memory and perhaps an image on a faded photograph.

The account of dogs in warfare can be traced back in time to before the written word. Be assured that it probably began soon after the domestication of *canis lupus* and when one man started tossing a rock at his neighbor's head over the possession of a piece of meat. For the United States military, the employment of dogs in battle is a relatively new adventure that formally began soon after the start of World War II. It was at this time that canines were officially recognized as part of the military establishment—a situation for better or worse for the animals often characterized as "man's best friend."

When Japan dropped bombs on Pearl Harbor on that fateful Sunday morning of 7 December 1941, the entire United States military possessed just fifty sled dogs. Many of these dogs were old survivors and offspring from the second Antarctic expedition of Richard E. Byrd that took place between 1933-35. In the spring of 1942, as America geared up for global warfare, a woman (and civilian) by the name of Arlene Earlanger helped launch a non-profit organization called Dogs for Defense. This association was comprised mostly of dog fanciers, trainers, and breeders from across the country who pooled their resources to persuade the Army to inaugurate an ambitious working dog program.

Many casual observers considered the project too challenging when the War Department stated that perhaps 125,000 dogs would be required for the war effort. Volunteers from Dogs for Defense began soliciting donations from civilians for dogs that would be trained by all the service branches for scouting, sentry, and mine detection, along with search and rescue. Some of the canine programs launched during the war years flopped, while others were quite successful. From 1942 to 1945 civilians donated over 40,000 dogs in a patriotic response to the military's request for four-legged recruits. For many people, their dog was akin to a beloved family member and their contribution was often a public-spirited gesture that is worthy of recognition. Stringent criteria weeded out many of the potential canine soldiers and more than 18,000 dogs were accepted by the military from this group, with 10,425 of them receiving advanced training. Many of the dogs at this time (approximately 3,600) served with the Coast Guard as they kept their eyes on the shorelines of the United States against possible enemy incursions. Others saw service worldwide with particular distinction as scout dogs in battles that took place on islands in the Pacific Ocean and in Burma against seasoned Japanese fighters. By the end of 1943, the term "K-9 Corps" became the unofficial phrase coined by Americans for any military activity involving the use of dogs and a term that continues to this day.

Large-scale demilitarization and the embracing of atomic weapons at the end of the war forced a cut-back in the inventory of American military dogs to just several hundred. Future development of finely skilled dog teams was at a standstill. Consequently, when war erupted in Korea and a need for military canines arose again, the Army had to scramble to deliver a sufficient number of handlers and dogs for operations overseas. The military never attained a measured response in such a limited time. And when hostilities eventually ceased, the K-9 program once again lay dormant for about a decade, until the United States acquired a monkey on its back that would take years to shake off – Vietnam. It was a name few Americans at the time knew much about but it would ultimately define an entire generation.

In South Vietnam there was no clear-cut order to bring all possible K-9 forces to bear down upon the enemy. The engagement of dog teams in warfare mirrored the overall military response against the Viet Cong and North Vietnamese Army: support our allies, build up the American presence, and then withdraw. The employment of dogs and handlers came in spurts and surges of critical action, often in direct response to a specific enemy encounter and with the expansion of involvement by the United States military machine. Military dogs would be trained to handle a variety of jobs that can be separated into several distinct categories:

Sentry and patrol dogs

These were trained to provide tactical and non-tactical security around a fixed installation and offer a powerful psychological deterrence against intruders or attacks. Sentry dogs were vicious and demanded a lot of respect. Patrol dogs were also trained to attack, were better socialized, and worked well around other dogs and people.

Scout dogs

Typically German shepherds, they alerted to airborne scents and silently signalled the handler to enemy personnel or dangerous objects. They could be trained to be worked either on or off leash. Like four-legged radar, their job was to illuminate the environment in front of a patrol to potential danger.

Tracker dogs

This is a Labrador retriever that works on-leash to follow a ground scent over terrain. Five-member teams were utilized as part of a reconnaissance element to follow enemy movements. They were used effectively to locate fleeing Viet Cong through a dangerous landscape.

Detector dogs

With outstanding olfactory ability, these dogs could be trained to locate buried mines, booby-traps, tunnels, and narcotics. Special jobs surfaced during the war, such as locating enemy divers and swimmers. They would become the forbearers of our modern explosive, detection, narcotic, and search and rescue dogs.

Like many endeavors, the local combat situation dictated and in some cases demanded the use of dogs. Even then it often turned out to be a slow process over the long haul. It should be acknowledged that American troops first entering the fray in Southeast Asia were trained originally to fight Soviet troops in Europe in a conventional warfare setting with the backdrop of nuclear weapons. There was no doctrine by the United States set forth for the warring of a guerrilla campaign in a jungle environment with no clear-cut battle lines. Unlike the previous major conflicts of the twentieth century that involved Americans, seldom did uniforms provide evidence of who was a civilian and who was the enemy. For some Vietnamese, their occupation changed as the sun went down—farmer by day and guerrilla fighter at night. Most civilians just wanted to eke out a living from the land. Many of the Vietnamese people could care less about who was in control;

just don't kill our ducks, chickens, or water buffalo and give us a chance to live and work in peace.

To better understand the men who kept company with dogs, you have to also look at the combat in Vietnam as a whole. The Vietnam War will always be remembered as the war we lost, but with every major battle won. This is an overly simplistic statement and does not truly reflect upon the reason of why we were in Vietnam, who was fighting, what the ultimate goal of the United States was, and if there indeed was an aspiration.

When I say we, I mean that in the collective sense: the American conscience and the thoughts and memories of everyone who was there or who shared the tragedy of that long-ago conflict. Unfortunately many of the men and women who served in South Vietnam still carry the burden of the war along with those wounded physically in battle and many others scarred mentally by what they have seen and done. Others, participants in the background, still suffer with the loss of a son, husband, father, or brother cut down in the prime of life.

Some men enlisted and went willingly off to fight. Others were drafted and served, while a few abdicated their responsibility and fled to Canada. The reasons for taking each path are varied and can often be justified. In some cases there was simply no choice. You might have been of the appropriate age and were drafted. Perhaps you enlisted believing in duty to God and country along with an inner urge to be a part of the action, even though you never realized just how deadly that action could be. For most people on the sidelines, you were either too young or too old. Unlike wars of the past, Vietnam became an armchair curiosity as visions of the conflict flashed across television screens in the nightly news.

Dog handlers were not much different from anyone else in uniform that landed in Vietnam within the ranks of the military. Some volunteered and had a background of working with dogs or at least had a dog as a member of the family. Others already walking point (the lead position on a patrol) in South Vietnam found an opportunity to learn the dog handler trade with on-the-job-training (OJT). Yes you'd be still at the head of the line, but this time with a dog that could sense danger, sniff out a booby-trap, or alert on Charlie. For the most part, dog handlers cut across racial lines, came from blue-collar families, and were comprised of men who never had a legitimate chance for a deferment. They also would have been several years younger than their World War II counterparts. This was typical of most of the fighting men in-country regardless of whether they were with a scout or tracker dog platoon or pulling nighttime sentry duty at an airbase. The primary distinction that separated these men from the thousands of others serving in Vietnam would be their dog.

The struggle to examine and understand the Vietnam War and how you relate to a dog handler can come in many forms. It all depends upon how the war touched you. A combatant in-country will see the war in an entirely different light than a parent who lost a son in the jungles of Southeast Asia. A World War II veteran will take an entirely divergent outlook from that of a conscientious objector. Those too young to participate will eye the conflict from an historical perspective and perhaps compare it with more recent struggles, tempered with the education and half-truths that always seem to bubble to the surface decades after such a confrontation.

If you think about it, the Vietnam War can be analyzed and observed from so many different angles as to become mind boggling. Take one example and look at the Vietnam War as a timeline. Extend that thought even further and consider the war only from before or after the Communist Tet Offensive of 1968. Strategically, Tet was a disastrous course of events for the Viet Cong, as over 85,000 enemy troops launched simultaneous attacks all over South Vietnam. Their tremendous losses effectively neutralized their ability to fight on the same caliber for the balance of the war. The Viet Cong would never regain the strength they possessed in the earlier years and their actions forced regular North Vietnamese troops into the war in ever-increasing numbers to keep the Americans in check.

The North Vietnam communist government had two goals in mind when the Tet offensive was launched. It might have been wishful thinking, but the communists believed it was possible to evoke a popular uprising in the South that would take the South Vietnam government by surprise. The other goal was pure propaganda, the bloodiest kind, as Americans back home witnessed attacks on U.S. bases throughout the country and even within the walls of the American embassy in Saigon. Tet had the desired effect, as six weeks later in his nightly dialogue with Middle America the well respected newscaster Walter Cronkite stated in part, "It seems now more than certain than ever that the bloody experience of Vietnam is to end in a stalemate… To say that we are mired in a stalemate seems the only realistic, yet unsatisfactory, conclusion."

Prior to the enemy offensive, many Americans believed we had the upper hand in the war and were told time and again by the clean-shaven talking heads of the United States military that indeed we were winning. Yet the actions surrounding the offensive and the firm fatherly voice of Walter Cronkite painted a different picture. After Tet, what was really happening and what the American public perceived were two different things. The ranks of the Viet Cong were decimated, American forces had acceptable losses, civilians in the south did not revolt, and the Army of South Vietnam remained relatively intact. Yet an increasing number of Americans perceived the war as lost, or at least one that could not be won in the foreseeable future.

So the first few months of 1968 can be considered a turning point in the conflict as the will to fight by Americans waned. As you read along, you will discover that this view will also be seen by the dog handler, how their job is examined, and a benchmark to gauge their success or failure. Supposedly the war was to be turned over to the South Vietnamese in a short period of time. Yet more American men perished after the Tet offensive than before. Drug use skyrocketed and the ability for the military to retain a coherent and professional fighting machine would be strained to its limits. And toward the end of the war, even dogs would be used to sniff out narcotics and contraband among our own troops.

As the currents of the war shifted and eddied like a swollen river after a torrential rain, so too did the deployment of dogs and their handlers. As new problems surfaced, the military, often in a knee-jerk reaction, tried to accommodate the situation at hand as quickly as possible. Euphemistically speaking, it was often a case of the tail wagging the dog. Like many other strategies, the information about what dog teams could accomplish in a war environment was often compartmentalized, politicized, and not spread properly throughout the various service branches. The use of dog teams also yielded to the overall military doctrine that superior firepower would provide the answer for nearly every situation faced in South Vietnam. As history has clearly shown, this was not always a sound strategy.

Another problem (or as some would contest an asset) is the very use of dogs in the first place. Every other member of the military depended on equipment and machinery to get their job done. It didn't matter if this was an M-16 rifle, an F-111 Starfighter jet, a Remington typewriter, or a Ford truck. They all came with operator manuals and basically worked as they were designed. But a handler relied on a living and thinking creature—an animal that felt pain and hunger and often shared the same happiness as his master. On the whole, the military establishment relegated working dogs simply as equipment; handlers did not. Because of the difference in perception of what military working dogs truly are, the employment of canines in combat would never really achieve their full potential.

Even without accomplishing the best possible results, dog teams, although small in number, would make a major and significant contribution to the war effort and in doing so avert thousands of casualties. The following pages will explain how this came about, the results achieved along with the failures enroute, and, ultimately, the legacy left by this pairing of living souls in a modern, often mechanical, and devastating war.

This book will also challenge the military establishment, raising beyond any doubt that a dog is more than a utilitarian piece of equipment. The bond forged by the handlers with their dogs decades ago is a testament to this. And as the years pass, many men might have forgotten the names of the buddies with whom they served, but none has ever forgotten their canine companion.

Although the war dogs of Vietnam are long dead, their accomplishments remain part of our military history and heritage. Many dogs carried the same name, even looked the same, but each was an individual in their own right. Whether it was a particular bark or the wagging of their tail, their eyes would always carry the same message to their masters—one of honesty and supreme trust. This is just one of the many reasons why the war dogs of Vietnam will live on in the hearts and minds of those who served with them.

1

The Seeds of a 10,000 Day War

"We are going to win in Vietnam
We will remain here until we do win."

Robert F. Kennedy
Attorney General
February 18, 1962

Vietnam is a word that not only describes a country but for many people it also defines a troubled period of American history. It is a single word and one utterance that can evoke a whole host of feelings depending on the person it is submitted to. In explaining the involvement of the United States with Vietnam, perhaps it is best to begin at the top of the ladder with the United States foreign policy makers. As noted in 1962, Attorney General Robert Kennedy would begin to see America's entry into the war first-hand, even though most Americans went about their daily chores and had little concern for the events that were unfolding there.

For the younger Kennedy, Vietnam meant an opportunity of victory for our country, and indeed his brother's administration, which certainly needed an achievement of some type at the time. In just a few short months after being in office, his older brother would be on the receiving end of three 6.5mm rounds shot from a thirty-dollar Mannlichea-Carano rifle fired from the sixth floor of the Texas School Book Depository. Six years after making his terse statement about America's commitment in Vietnam, Robert Kennedy would disappear from the stage as well, cut down in the kitchen of the Ambassador Hotel in Los Angeles. Like an unattended train running at full throttle, the fighting in Vietnam continued with both brothers gone and with the rest of the country in tow for the wild ride. [1]

Scout dog handlers from the 49th IPSD take a break with their dogs, prior to searching a village during Operation Fairfax in 1967. *(National Archives)*

Of course the Vietnam saga did not start nor end with the Kennedy brothers. To begin the story about K-9 operations during the Vietnam War with the first handler, dog, or even the concept of using canines in warfare would be a mistake. Some background needs to be entered into the equation and the scheme of events to take place—just enough for those readers who are not familiar with the history of that Southeast Asia country, the geography, or our involvement there only several decades distant. A multitude of fascinating books are available that detail the Vietnam War and this small introduction is by no means complete. It is intended to provide just a few baby steps for a simple and basic foundation for the readers, before setting out on the path followed by military men and their dogs. Even for those who have served their time in hell there, a few words of the history that landed you in that tortured country need to be brought forward.

Could the War Have Been Avoided?

Perhaps the most popular question that has resounded for years, since America's withdrawal from the war and the proverbial "peace with honor," is Who do we blame? For every name on that stark black-walled monument now situated near the reflecting pool between the Lincoln and Washington memorials in Washington D.C. or every life destroyed, who do you reproach? Do we examine President Nixon for expanding the war into Cambodia and Laos and not getting us out of the fight fast enough? Possibly the focus should be on LBJ for upping the ante with an increase of troops sent overseas and more money spent on the war effort. Perhaps we can go back even further and look at President John F. Kennedy and the role he played, or Eisenhower before him. That brings us back to the 1950s, when the French ruled Vietnam as a far-flung colony.

For the United States during the twentieth century, it appears our first inkling that Vietnam was a country that begged to be noticed took place during the administration of President Franklin Delano Roosevelt, amidst the turmoil of World War II. Scant attention was paid at the time to Vietnam and this is understandable. With the Axis powers of Germany, Italy, and Japan wielding a global war that would sap the will and resources of the United States for four long years, there was little reason to dwell on the future of what was then considered an insignificant nation.

As early as 1944, President Roosevelt considered that France should not rule Vietnam once the Japanese were vanquished, and even wrote to Secretary of State Cordell Hull annunciating that fact. France couldn't even handle their own affairs when Germany launched a blitzkrieg on their homeland. America watched as the French government capitulated in just several weeks as the Nazis marched into Paris uncontested. Roosevelt must have wondered how this same country would be able to support colonies around the globe, even if they did have the exile Charles DeGaulle at the helm of a defeated French military.

In the ensuing years and with the end of World War II in sight, Roosevelt argued with both DeGaulle and British Prime Minister Winston Churchill over several various colonial possessions that included Vietnam. Defense planners

As a signatory of the Atlantic Charter, President Roosevelt believed all people had a right to self determination. France elected to keep Vietnam as a colony after the conclusion of World War II. *(National Archives)*

within our own government reminded the President that the United States would probably need to provide "trusteeship" over several Japanese islands, effectively creating our own colonies. Although Roosevelt ultimately ceded possession of Indo-China to France, he still favored independence for the Vietnamese.

Unfortunately, Roosevelt died in office during his fourth term and an unprepared Harry S. Truman assumed control of the most powerful country in the world. Truman's administration was marked by signing the order to drop two atomic bombs (a weapon he was not even aware of until after he took the oath of office for the Presidency) on Japan, forcing the Japanese to unconditional surrender and ending the world war.

The very action that took place when a mushroom cloud of radioactive gas, smoke, and debris blossomed over Hiroshima and Nagasaki set in motion a host of events that could not be conceived of, even as they unfolded. These events can, however, be viewed with the critical eye of the historian and hopefully with enough information and logic to preclude the old adage that "hindsight is twenty-twenty." It also means bringing forth the natural truth and not a revisionist view from someone who was not involved at the time and a distortion of the recorded facts.

The advent of the nuclear age shifted the entire focus of the United States onto the Soviet Union and cast it into bronze when Josef Stalin's military scientists exploded a nuclear weapon in 1947. If there is any doubt here, a basic check on the affairs of South America, Africa, and even England as the Cold War began to materialize showed that American foreign policy was principally shaped on how we dealt with the Soviet Union, its satellite countries, and other communist governments world-wide. Everything else, including much of our domestic policy, became subordinate to the potential aggression that communists seeded around the globe.

It was during this time that Truman reinforced France's position in Vietnam, in July 1945, by collaborating with Great Britain as part of the Potsdam agreement. This effectively divided French Indo-China along the 16th parallel. It was stated at the time that it was done for "operational purposes," allowing the Japanese to surrender to the Chinese in the north and the British in the south. The British helped to rearm the French while the Chinese looted the northern part of the country. No mention or consideration was made during this period about independence for the Vietnamese people.

Aside from the nineteenth century belief of Manifest Destiny, the United States as a whole did not consider itself an imperialistic or colonialistic power during this period of time. This was quite evident during and immediately after World War II when America had the strongest military establishment in the world, and of course we were the only ones that did have the bomb. Ho Chi Minh (sometimes referred to as Uncle Ho by American soldiers) was undoubtedly the father figure of Vietnam politics during this era and a great influence among his people throughout much of the twentieth century. He had observed that the Philippines, a commonwealth of the United States, was about to be granted independence once the marauding Japanese had been overthrown. In many ways, he expected the same for his own country.

So why did Truman turn a deaf ear toward Uncle Ho when he asked for our President's support on several occasions during 1946? Ho himself was attached in many ways to American ideals and was even enamored of many philosophies presented by Abraham Lincoln, even though Ho was a middle-aged politician and a devout communist. Was it because, in the concept of world affairs for the United States, bigger games were to be played out? Or did Truman simply consider Vietnam, a country that only a handful of Americans had ever heard of at the time, as inconsequential? Perhaps it is more likely that Ho's embrace of communism drove an inseparable wedge between the two leaders.

The United States supported the Viet Minh during World War II in their fight against the Japanese and Vichy French forces with support from the Office of Strategic Services (OSS), the precursor to our CIA.[2] Trained in China, the Viet Minh forces began fighting the Japanese 21st Division in 1943. This would eventually help the Americans and British to drive out the Japanese from Vietnam in the early part of 1945.

Once the Japanese were ousted, the Viet Minh seized power, and on 2 September 1945 proclaimed the Democratic Republic of Vietnam with Ho Chi Minh as president. Ho's stance was that both the United States and the United Kingdom would support the Vietnamese people's determination for self-rule at the appropriate time, based in part on a meeting four years earlier between the two Anglo-Saxon powers. Ho's assessment would prove to be faulty, and thereafter the man would make few political mistakes.

It was on 14 August 1941, off the coast of Newfoundland, that a rendezvous took place between the battleships *Prince of Whales* from England and the *Augusta* from the United States. The two warships brought Churchill and Roosevelt together to sign a pact between the two countries that became known as the Atlantic Charter. In part, the document stated "…they [the United States and the United Kingdom] respect the right of all peoples to choose the form of government under which they live; and they wish to see sovereign rights and self-government restored to those who have been forcibly deprived of them." [3]

Replacing the French

Humiliated by the Germans during World War II, France was not about to award outright sovereignty to the Vietnamese or to a small oriental man, based on a document signed by two countries before the start of World War II. By the fall of 1946, war broke out between France and the Viet Minh. Two years later, as the fighting continued, Truman faced pressure from former ambassador to France William Bullitt and Secretary of State Dean Atchinson. They both persuaded the President to abandon any ties with the Vietnamese and continue to back the French for control of the country. At the same time, anti-Communist sentiments began to hit a fever pitch in our own country.

Around this same period, in 1946, and without fanfare or big press coverage, the Vietnamese-America Friendship Association held their last banquet in New York City. It is interesting to note that the affair was hosted by Major Robert Buckley, a former OSS agent who operated in Southeast Asia toward the end of World War II. Buckley, more than anyone else, appeared to understand how Vietnam should be handled and perhaps what was still to come. Yet he could muster no support from anyone with authority within the Truman administration.

Just two years later, thirty-five personnel, comprising the United States Military Assistance and Advisory Group (MAAG), arrived in Saigon on behalf of our old ally, France. [4] And in March of 1950, Truman set aside $15 million as the first installment in aid for the former European power. Supplies began flowing into Vietnam on eight C-47 cargo aircraft in June of that year, and by 1954 our figure of support topped $3 billion. With the United States picking up the tab for eighty percent of the war costs incurred by the French, there is no doubt who and what America would back in the upcoming years.

The American inspection teams that were sent there were strictly noncombatants who observed French Expeditionary Forces in the jungles, Hanoi, and also at the French outpost of Dien Bien Phu. In 1954 they also began instructing French and Vietnamese soldiers on the application of American weapons that were made available to them. Apparently the instructors saw much but comprehended very little about conventional French operations in a guerilla campaign. At the same time, the United States faced another distraction and needed to attend immediately to a larger problem with another ally, a bit farther to the north in another country called Korea.

If history is to be considered a chain, then the story of the Vietnam War had its first link forged with Truman and it extended and was strengthened by each succeeding United States president until the final link was stamped by Richard Nixon as the last American combat personnel came home. This makes 1946 a key year, and the indifference by our country to the plight of a strange foreign land meant that a lot of blood would be spilled before peace was at hand.

A Historical Perspective of the War

The Vietnam conflict is often referred to as a war of attrition, where one side, through continuous military pressure, would wear down an opponent until they were ready to quit the fight—not a quick, decisive victory from the battlefield, but still a conquest. Unfortunately, the Vietnam War is often compared to the events of World War I. Known at one time as the Great War, World War I escalated bloodletting to a grand scale. It was indeed a stalemate that both sides refused to recognize, and each felt that victory was in their grasp if just one more major offensive could be the deciding factor resulting in total victory. It was much the same in Vietnam. Ronald H. Spector noted in his excellent and authoritative account, *After Tet: The Bloodiest Year in Vietnam,* when he states:

> As in World War I, each side grossly underestimated the determination and staying power of the other. Both sides believed that if they persevered, the opponent would finally capitulate. Both sides always convinced themselves to be on the offensive, always on the brink of winning against an opponent who was near the breaking point. Thus Westmoreland calling for "maximum pressure on the enemy" following the Tet attacks; Abrams describing the "moment of supreme opportunity" in the autumn of 1968; Lyndon Johnson repeating the call for "maximum pressure" in the last weeks of his presidency; and the Hanoi strategists calling for further reprises of the costly Tet

> attacks in May, August, and February [of 1968] are psychologically closely akin to the generals of World War I, Haig in 1916, Nivelle in 1917, and Ludendorf in 1918. [5]

Spector's statements are all true, but there are several significant differences that are not considered. In World War I (and the same holds true for World War II), the participants fighting the battles were in for the duration. For the forces of North and South Vietnam, along with the Viet Cong, this is strikingly the same case—but not so for the Americans at the time, who could count on just one year of being in-country before rotating home with the option to re-enlist. [6] Of course for the South Vietnamese forces, they were already on home turf.

On a global scale and in the grand scheme of the United States administration, it was a war of attrition, although few people and definitely no one in the military would ever publicly say so. Dog handlers and soldiers alike viewed it as one year in hell, and so far-removed from everyone and everything they knew that just about any place back home was known simply as "the world."

Although World War I and Vietnam shared the bond of a stalemate in the battlefield, with each side waiting for the other to submit, the wars held little else in common. During World War I, the biggest killer was disease and pestilence, and that far outstripped the soldiers killed in the trenches during combat. And although deadlocked in battle, when President Woodrow Wilson thrust the United States into the conflict, obstinately to "save democracy," it tipped the scales of power in war-weary Europe. Thus America, with its vast resources and possessed with a land not scarred by the ravages of hostilities, became the turning point and the defeat of German forces.

It is wiser to step back just a little farther in time and look for an event that can closely parallel the years of fighting in Vietnam and our involvement there. The idea is to bring down the scale of the war from a global epic and political affair to the perspective of the foot soldier, and for the purposes of this book to the dog handler. This would mean looking at our first Asian war, a little-known event for most Americans today, known as the Philippine-American War of 1898-1902, sometimes referred to as the "Bolo War."

This unfortunate piece of history begins with the insurrection by Filipinos against the rule of Spain in 1895. The stage was set for this deadly drama for the United States when the American battleship *Maine* exploded in a cloud of smoke and an ensuing fog of mystery in Havana harbor, on 15 February 1898. Americans had at the time offered limited support for Cuban rebels, but with the loss of 260 naval officers and enlisted men aboard the battle wagon, hatred against Spain escalated to a fierce intensity. Public opinion fueled by sensational stories in the newspapers (dubbed "yellow journalism") persuaded President William McKinley to ask Congress to recognize the independence of Cuba and move to end the civil war there. The United States thus declared war against Spain on 25 April 1898.

In the Pacific, the Filipino population viewed this as an opportunity to achieve independence and with what was considered excellent timing, revolted against the Spanish troops. However, their independence did not come to fruition. Closer to home, in the Caribbean, Spain easily succumbed to American forces on the land and sea, and the Spanish promptly ceded Puerto Rico to the United States in an effort to end hostilities. This was followed by actions in the Pacific that saw the eventual surrender of Guam. Eight months later, the Spanish saw the writing on the wall and turned over the Philippines to the United States for the tidy sum of $20 million. Such a bargain!

That does not mean that we were about to grant independence to the Philippines at the time. The United States, after spending money and spilling American blood, did not see fit to grant freedom to the local population. At this time, Filipino patriots, under the command of General Emilio Aguinaldo, picked up the fallen flag of independence and battled American troops in Manila. Badly beaten by superior American forces, Aguinaldo swiftly changed tactics and abandoned conventional warfare against a strong world power and took up a guerilla campaign in the island jungles. With this change in strategy, the rebels became known as the "*insurrectos*."

For three years the conflict continued, with the United States sending in more than 126,000 troops in an effort to suppress the rebels. When it first began, civilian support back home was enthusiastic as the gung-ho troops waved goodbye to relatives after boarding transport ships from the West Coast. This support waned as the war dragged on and as the body count grew, with few positive results. American commanders set up free-fire zones, search and destroy missions, and

American soldiers stay on a narrow path somewhere in the Philippines. The American military fighting in the Philippines would mirror many of the activities that would take eighty years later in Vietnam. Even the weather and terrain evoked many similarities. *(National Archives)*

the establishment of strategic hamlets. These were all terms and strategies that would be used sixty-five years later in Vietnam. Soldiers suffered in the jungles, ill-equipped to fight under searing temperatures and humidity in their wool uniforms and afflicted with a variety of diseases, pounding monsoon rains, and slogging through mud on long marches. Weighted down with a ten-pound Krag-Jorgenson rifle, 200 rounds of ammo, and one-day's ration, the only thing that kept the infantryman going was the thought of being butchered by guerillas if he was left behind by himself on a march through the jungles.

After two years of struggle, with little to show for their efforts and things going badly, the American commanders sought the favor of Philippine civilians and began a program of benevolent pacification. It might be considered a turn-of-the-century program to "win the hearts and minds of Filipinos." Still, on a day-to-day basis, soldiers had no idea who they could trust. Atrocities became common on both sides as each antagonist tried to coerce the civilian population against the other or as a retaliatory gesture. With a bit of irony, this was also the same time that the introduction of "gook" surfaced as a derogatory term describing the Filipino people. [7] As in most wars, the noncombatants took the heaviest toll as nearly 200,000 Filipino civilians, mostly peasants, died during their struggle for independence.

Finally, on 23 March 1901, General Aquinaldo was captured and resistance began to collapse against the American occupation forces. Either by coincidence or as a well-established plan, the insurrection ended (officially at least) on 4 July 1902. [8]

Ultimately what defeated the Filipino patriots was not the United States Army, with losses on record of more than 4,000 troops, but simply logistics. The Philippines is a group of islands, Luzon and Mindanao being the largest. Unlike Vietnam, which bordered a main supplier to the north (China), the Filipino guerillas had no real benefactor for arms, equipment, or food. A naval blockade of the islands meant that nothing could be secured for the rebels by ship. Had the North Vietnamese been forced to operate in a restricted area like this, and not been so readily supported by China and the Soviet Union, the war of attrition may have had a decidedly different outcome in a much shorter period of time.

The United States to the Rescue

South Vietnam was created in part by the capitulation of the French garrison at Dien Bien Phu (which translates as "big frontier administrative center") on 7 May 1954, after a 57-day siege. It began back in November 1953, when the French commander-in-chief, General Henri Navarre, attempted to set up Viet Minh forces in a pitched battle against French heavy weaponry, in an eleven-mile valley northwest of Hanoi along the Laotian border. Called "Operation Castor," Navarre emplaced 15,000 men under the command of Colonel Christian de la Croix de Castries in ten separate French strongholds, each named after a girl, in an attempt to lure guerilla forces into a trap.

The Viet Minh saw through Navarres's plan and set up their own ambush. Diversionary attacks pulled French support away from Dien Bien Phu, and at the opportune time Vietnamese General Vo Nguyen Giap encircled the French forces with 200 artillery pieces and 70,000 men. On 13 March 1954, Giap launched his assault with heavy artillery fire and quickly knocked out both French airstrips. Thereafter, the French garrison could only be supplied by intermittent airdrops.

So desperate were the French at this time that some officials had even approached President Dwight D. Eisenhower, implying that only a couple of atomic bombs could save the beleaguered garrison. Fortunately, Ike declined to participate at this time. After 56 days of constant battle with 2,293 dead Legionnaires, the French surrendered. More than 10,000 French soldiers were captured and at least half of them were wounded. Giap's losses were far greater, but for the Viet Minh the end always justified the means.

The stunning defeat of DeGaulles's forces orchestrated by General Vo Nguyen Giap and his Viet Minh troops left little for the French to work with on the ground in Vietnam, and more importantly at the Geneva conference table. Two months later, world powers partitioned Vietnam along the 17th parallel. In the north was the communist-controlled Democratic Republic of Vietnam; to the south of this imaginary line was the Republic of Vietnam. A shaky, quasi-democracy in the south was under the control of Ngo Dinh Diem· a member of the Catholic minority who was little-known among his people and not trusted by those intimately acquainted with him. Yet, on 1 October 1954, President Eisenhower sent a letter to Diem effectively supporting the Catholic Saigon government to preside over six million Buddhists.

Around this same time, in the north, Ho Chi Minh marshaled his followers and began sending cadres southward to prepare for future infiltration. His organization became known as Dac Cong, or Viet Cong. The heart of his group was the 10,000 former members of the Viet Minh who remained in the south after division of the country. Although a brilliant move on the part of Ho, it proved to be the first of many violations of the Geneva agreement. For all intents and purposes, the agreement was trash as Ho Chi Minh was only interested in a unified Vietnam. As communist activity in the south grew, so did American involvement. After ninety-four years of tragic association and nothing to show for their effort, the last of the French forces quietly departed South Vietnam on 28 April 1956, thus opening the door for a new custodian to help maintain control: the United States of America.

In 1961, President Kennedy strengthened our partnership with Diem and increased the number of U.S. advisors to 16,000 soldiers. The advisors developed plans against counterinsurgency and began selective defoliation of jungle area and the development of strategic hamlets throughout the south. This also leads us to the starting point for the entry of dog teams into Southeast Asia. Numerically speaking, handlers and their dogs comprised just a tiny fraction of the resources that poured into Vietnam in the upcoming years. This is understandable given their duty and what was expected from them. Volumes have been written on the aerial bombardments, artillery, helicopter support, and overall firepower that were utilized during the war. Often just a scant line of reference is attributed to dog teams and even then they are often referred incorrectly as police dogs. Vietnam is not the exception of this historical oversight, but the rule and has been since

World War II. Although the United States has used dogs in combat for decades, their efforts have often become overshadowed or entirely erased by the sheer size of the engagements they participated in.

Military historians tend to overlook the accomplishments of dog teams for several reasons. First and foremost, military records tend to obscure the use of canines, further diluting any contribution they might have made. On a deeper level, there is a subconscious tendency to distance ourselves from the very use of animals in warfare. This has manifested itself not just with dogs, but also with mules, horses, dolphins, and pigeons. As Americans, we can bow and honor great man-made weapons of destruction, but there is something holding many of us back from giving credit to other living creatures in times of warfare beside ourselves.

To support this premise, simply look at the museums and displays we have that reflect the weapons of warfare. Then count among them the number of animals. The answer is that few, if any, museums recognize animals in combat. If they do, it is more as a curiosity than with an honest historical perspective. In truth, we will use animals as deemed necessary, but not truly identify with them. Either it is a callous oversight or a reaffirmation that man, willing to accept the abilities of animals for his reward, will not bestow upon them the same dividends that we reap upon ourselves.

A Short History of the American K-9 Corps

The German shepherd was popular with several artists during WWI. This print by Alexander Pope depicts a WWI Red Cross dog. The helmet indicates that the dog has located a wounded soldier in "No man's Land." *(Red Cross Museum)*

Although the story of dogs in warfare is as old as history itself, the United States did not begin using dogs for military purposes on an official basis until shortly after the start of our involvement in World War II. The duties that dogs performed at war were developed as the requirement surfaced in times of battle. In ancient history, before gunpowder and mechanization, dogs were trained as combatants, where they actu-

American artist Henry (Hy) Hystermeister's rendition of a Red Cross service dog has appeared on numerous post cards and even a puzzle during the same period. *(Author's Collection)*

ally became part of the fighting force to attack an enemy. As sophistication in weaponry developed, the dog was relegated to other tasks, most notably as a draft animal for carrying goods or transportation by pulling a sled. Their keen sense of sight, sound, and in particular smell would always render them useful in a variety of duties.

Even during World War I, with the advent of massive weapons of destruction delivered from artillery, machine guns, tanks, and planes, over 75,000 dogs saw service. These numbers only reflected the European countries involved, since the United States had no military dog program at the time. Numerous dogs were still employed as draft animals hauling ammunition, but many more would be trained as casualty locators. These dogs would be taught to locate wounded men left in "no man's land." Known as Red Cross dogs, they would skirt barbed wire and lethal gases to locate injured soldiers and then gather their handlers and lead them to the fallen men. Both the British and German armies even developed a mask for the war dogs to protect them from the deadly mustard and phosgene gases often employed in trench warfare. When America entered the war, dogs were borrowed from the British and French. Although a bill was sent to Congress to establish a military dog program for the United States, it faded away when peace was finally established in 1918.

When the United States entered the war against Japan and Germany after the attack on Pearl Harbor, the entire canine muster in our military inventory included just a handful of sled dogs. Even then, most of these dogs were not involved in direct military operations but were acquired when Admiral Byrd's expedition returned from Antarctica early in 1941. A few other sled dogs engaged in search and rescue operations could be found in Alaska, Newfoundland, and Greenland. By comparison, the Germans reportedly had 200,000 dogs in service and Japan had 75,000 at the outbreak of hostilities.

Charged with the procurement of animals, such as horses and mules, for the military, the Quartermaster Corps did not initiate the idea of dogs entering the combat arena. That distinction would come from the civilian sector. A woman by the name of Alene Erlanger, who was both a fancier and breeder of canines, approached the Army in January 1942 with the idea of using dogs in combat. Erlanger was a member of the stratified American upper class, far removed from the necessities of military engagement. Yet she understood the capabilities of dogs and how they could render

At the start of WWII most military dogs were trained to pull sleds. The government appealed to civilians to donate their dogs for the war effort. *(National Archives)*

assistance to the United States Army. Referring to the gung-ho attitude prevalent in America after the Japanese attack on Pearl Harbor, Erlanger stated, "Dogs must play a part in this thing [world war] too! Other countries have used dogs in their Armies for years and ours has not. We've got to do it." [9]

Surprisingly, the Army listened to a sound idea from a civilian woman. Erlanger enlisted support from the Professional Handlers Association, a nation-wide organization of professional dog trainers and not limited to any particular breed of dog. This formed the nucleus for a civilian group called Dogs For Defense that would have the resources to locate and procure prospective dogs across the country for the military. The organization also pooled instructional experience that they shared with the Army and helped to write the first canine military training manuals.

During the summer months of 1942, sentry dogs were tried at various military establishments around the country. They proved successful and also demonstrated that a single dog team could replace at least ten men standing guard. Word also began to spread that the other capabilities of dogs (i.e., scouting, detection, tracking, and so forth) should not be ignored. By the end of the year, the War Department figured they would require 125,000 canines for a military, working-dog program. This figure would be trimmed down substantially within the next few months.

At first, the military envisioned using dogs only as sentries, guarding the important facilities on the home front within the United States. So at the beginning of the war the initial groups of dog teams were confined to guarding factories and munitions dumps located in CONUS (a military acronym defining the Continental United States), around the strategically important Panama Canal, and at several small bases in the Caribbean region. Toward the end of 1942 the Coast Guard, in charge of securing our shoreline against potential enemy threats, began operating sentry dog teams along the vast seashore. The dogs augmented patrols by men in boats, on horseback, jeeps, and of course on foot. The Coast Guard had thus become the largest employer of dogs during the war, amassing more than 3,100 canines and more than 2,600 "coasties" were trained as handlers.

Once established as sentries, other uses soon arose within the military ranks and the training expanded. The Army began to employ canines as scouts, messengers, and mine detectors. Thirty-two different breeds were acceptable at the start of the war, but by the fall of 1944 just seven were deemed most suitable for military work. Heading the list were the German shepherd and the Doberman pinscher. Collies and Belgian Sheep dogs were found ideal for messenger work. Sled dogs such as the Siberian husky, Malamute, and Eskimo dog, retained their traditional job of pulling sleds.

Scout dogs were used by both Army and Marine units in both the European and Pacific theatres of war. It would be in the Pacific operations against the Japanese that the dogs performed admirably and beyond expectations. As the lead element for small patrols, scout dogs provided a silent alert to locating the enemy and became known, years later, as "four-footed radar." Over 450 scout dogs were sent out in the field during World War II and they proved their worth in assisting both Marine and Army units in the capture of many Pacific Islands.

Not knowing all the capabilities that dogs possessed, the Army still considered dogs useful if only for carrying ammunition. *(National Archives)*

At the beginning of WWII, just about any breed was deemed suitable for military service. In time, the military tightened their requirements and focused principally on the German shepherd. Specific breeds would also be employed in particular jobs that best suited their abilities. *(National Archives)*

The success of scout-dog teams can be measured by what was planned for in the future. With the invasion of the Japanese homeland on the drawing board, the Army had anticipated that 1,600 dogs would participate in the massive attack. The surrender of the Japanese after the firebombing of Tokyo and the atomic blasts over Hiroshima and Nagasaki shelved any possible immediate expansion of the military dog program. The attention of the Army and Marines changed and became a situation of what to do with the hundreds of dogs they had on hand at the end of the war.

The World War II military dog program was quite unique in the fact that civilians were involved in many aspects of the recruitment and initial training. This joint venture also ensured to a certain degree for the disposition of the surplus dogs at the end of the war. Quartermaster General Major General Edmund B. Gregory stated that, "...although the government [had] full title to the dogs in question, there was a moral obligation to return the dogs to their owners because of the agreement with Dogs for Defense." [10] It was decided that the military would "retrain" all medically fit dogs and return them to civilian homes. The program was so successful that thousands of military dogs wound up in the homes of average

Americans. Years after the war people still wrote to the Army and Marines asking for one of the K-9 veterans. By October of 1945, the Office of Surplus Property received over 17,000 applications for the 500 dogs still available for adoption.

The military still required dogs, even in peacetime. With their job accomplished, Dogs for Defense disbanded in 1946 and the Army Quartermaster Corps took over procurement of new dogs. A half-hearted attempt to launch a breeding program in 1945 languished for five years before the program was terminated. Called the Army Dog Association, Inc. (ADAI) it was intended to be a cooperative venture between the military and commercial breeders. It didn't really pan out since there was no need for having a large K-9 inventory or anticipating any future requirements for many dogs.

The War Department still planned the continued use of scout dogs during peacetime and had a big proponent in Brigadier Fredrick McCabe, who at the time was the Commandant of Infantry Replacement Training Center at Camp Robinson. During the war Camp Robinson (then called Fort Robinson) in Nebraska was a major reception and training center for military dogs. McCabe chaired a committee responsible for future infantry requirements for war dogs that gathered at Fort Benning, Georgia, in June 1946.

The first group of war dogs at the beginning of WWII were relegated for sentry duty and served alongside coastal gunners. *(National Archives)*

After reviewing the military dog contributions made during the war, the committee unequivocally stated, "(1) [That] Infantry War Dog Platoons be retained and attached to Infantry units for training and operations and (2) Experimentation be continued with dog units along all lines, especially breeding, improving technique of training, and extending the scope of usefulness of the dogs."

It looked good on paper, except fiscal and manpower cuts kicked in along with a common lack of interest. McCabe retired the following year and no one in a powerful command position assumed his role as staunch supporter for military working dogs. So it came as no surprise (except for the Army) that at the beginning of the Korean conflict only one scout dog platoon (26th Infantry Platoon (Scout Dog)) was available for action.

Korea was split on the 38th parallel shortly after the end of World War II. On 25 June 1950, the 127,000 man army of North Korea crashed across the border and soon overwhelmed the smaller South Korean forces supported by just 500 American advisors. Truman sent in General Douglas MacArthur and the United Nations jumped in with military aid.

The 26th IPSD did not arrive in Korea until June of 1951. The Communists were pushed backed to the 38th parallel and the war virtually stalemated. The Army realized the acute need for scout dogs and began to mount a crash program at Fort Carson, Colorado, to have a trained scout dog platoon for each infantry division.

Thousands of dogs were retrained and returned to civilians at the conclusion of World War II. It would be another fifty-five years before K-9 veterans would be available to the public for adoption. *(National Archives)*

USMC PFC Edward Fowler and Rolf take a break while patrolling on Okinawa. In every war, early, silent detection of the enemy can be a huge advantage. With their olfactory ability, keen eyesight, and hearing, scout dogs proved to be the infantryman's four footed radar *(National Archives)*

Handlers pose with their dogs after the fight for the city of Myitkyina, Burma in September 1944. The scout dog teams often worked with the legendary Merrill's Marauders. *(Author's collection)*

But the war would be over before another scout dog team could be deployed. The 26th was on their own.

For the scout dog teams, Korea was entirely different from anything that was done in the past or for what would be accomplished in the future. With few exceptions most of the scout dogs were employed at night on patrols searching for the enemy. A stunning highlight is that one dog named York (012X) led 152 patrols between 12 June 1951 and 26 June 1953, without the single loss of a man.

Over 1,100 combat patrols were led by scout dogs during the course of the war. How these patrols and their effectiveness can be judged is best supplied by the enemy. With the front line often stagnant, the Americans would dig in with the Chinese just a short distance away. On many nights the communists would set up huge speakers and broadcast a potpourri of propaganda to the young soldiers that did little to convince them to quit but often kept them awake throughout the night. On at least one occasion the speakers blared forth a distinct Chinese accented voice speaking in English, "Yankee, take your dog and go home!" [11]

After hostilities with North Korea and China ceased, the United States army again felt little appreciation for military dogs, either as sentries or as scouts, even though it was found that scout dogs that accompanied patrols reduced casualties by 60 percent in Korea. [12] The 26th with its excellent service, was awarded the Korean Presidential Citation, Meritorious Unit Citation, 3 Silver Stars, 6 Bronze Stars for valor, and 35 Bronze stars—all testaments to the capabilities of men and their dogs in modern warfare.

It seemed practical and worthwhile for the military to try to consolidate the training and procurement of dogs. The shift in military resources continued with the Air Force as the cold war with the Soviet Union heated up. Our response to the perceived nuclear threat included the establishment of Nike missile (anti-aircraft) sites across the country. The missile locations popped up in such a short time, and in so many different parts of the country, that security fencing could not be erected around each site fast enough.

To provide a secure environment, the Air Force immediately began the use of sentry dogs along the boundaries of each missile site. Sentry dog teams, once charged with protecting the perimeter of Strategic Air Command (SAC)

York distinguished himself by conducting more than 1,100 combat patrols. Returned stateside after the war, he spent his remaining years at Fort Benning and was interred at the animal cemetery located on the base. The marker was presumably stolen and where he actually resides remains a mystery. *(Author's collection)*

bases now needed to move to many different locations around the country. At the same time, there was an increase in bases outside CONUS and dogs sent overseas needed to deal with a wide diversity of climatic conditions and tactical situations.

Still, it remained easy duty for the handlers, especially back home in the states, since saboteurs were few and far between and the only challenges often made would be for drunks with a navigation problem or juveniles out at night on a dare to enter one of these sites.

The United States Air Force (USAF) thus became the major trainer of military dogs for all service branches in 1952. The Army even turned over most of its sentry dog and handler training to the Air Force in the process. The primary site for most dog training in the United States took place at Lackland AFB, just a stone's throw from San Antonio, Texas. The Army retained training responsibility in Okinawa (USARPAC Sentry Dog School, Okinawa) and Korea (Eighth Army Sentry Dog School, Seoul) where Air Force support was not available. [13]

In 1960, the Department of Defense (DoD) issued an urgent appeal to breeders and dog owners to sell their German shepherds to the military. A shortage had developed as police organizations and private security firms saw the advantages of this versatile animal. Several months earlier a requirement was set for 1,000 dogs, with 110 to be purchased each month. Prices varied, but upwards of $150 would be paid out for an outstanding dog. The average was more like $110. Good money for

Scout dog teams gave patrol members a distinct advantage against the enemy in Korea. This Bell H-13 Sioux helicopter was modified to quickly deliver a scout dog team to where they were needed. *(National Archives)*

Sentry dogs were deployed to Nike missile sites throughout the United States. During this period of time the Air Force became the largest employer of military working dogs and established themselves as the sole procurement agency for all military branches. *(National Archives)*

the time, but a savvy owner or breeder could usually get a bit more from a police department or a private security firm. [14] Although the Army Quartermaster Corps still obtained some dogs at this time, effective 12 October 1964, the responsibility for obtaining all "live animals not raised for food" went to the Air Force. This was to be expected, since they had become the largest user of dogs in the military.

Obtaining dogs in this method is in stark contrast to the efforts embarked on during World War II with the help of Dogs for Defense. In the early 1960s, the United States was not at war, although the need for military dogs was genuine and a similar program at this time probably would have flopped. Times had changed and, after all, there was no major conflict and none was on the horizon. The cold war with the Soviet Union was just that, and if push came to shove it would be played out against a backdrop of nuclear mushroom clouds, not a small confrontation in some Third World country.

The widespread procurement of German shepherds would have had a tangible effect within a few short years if military planners had access to a crystal ball. There was absolutely no long-range vision in building up a large military dog population. The procurement rate for acquiring dogs was in place to meet the current needs of the period. And that was for the protection of air bases at home and abroad, along with the numerous Nike missile sites that dotted the landscape. What no one realized was that a strong and effective military dog program takes time and discipline. That lesson would be learned the hard way in South Vietnam.

Touchdown in Southeast Asia

One of the first priorities for Americans helping the South Vietnamese was to establish proper security for airbases, ammunition depots, and key installations. Developing a sentry dog response in South Vietnam would not move as swiftly or with the same results as the inherent need to protect nuclear arsenals back home. The Air Force never really had any experience in placing sentry dog teams in hostile territory, or better to say a territory where the probability of an enemy attack was extremely high.

In the past, sentry dog teams provided both a physical and psychological deterrent against thieves and saboteurs in a relatively peaceful environment outside of a war zone. Handlers would have to adjust in Vietnam where perimeter security is a tactical situation and where the threat originates from guerillas, both well armed and trained, and in some cases both fanatical and suicidal in their efforts. This means a change from the standard Air Force definition in place for a sentry dog, that is "...to detect intruders, alert his handler, and when necessary, pursue, attack, and hold any intruder who tries to escape." A simple change for the handler would be: "Alert any intruder. If my dog doesn't kill him, I sure will." But another troubling question remained unanswered. What can a single dog and one man do against a large group of attackers?

Beginning in the spring of 1960, the Air Force, under direction of the Defense Research and Development Command, dabbled in developing a dog that would be suitable for both scout and sentry duty. This would be a precursor to another, similar, Air Force program several years off in the future. Even at this time it was generally understood among knowledgeable dog people within the military that multi-task dogs were not desirable. Although dogs could be trained to work several different jobs, their corresponding effectiveness would diminish as they attempted to take on a greater variety of chores. It would also involve taking a relatively vicious sentry dog and have him double as a scout dog that could silently alert his handler while on patrol. Although the Air Force has a fine history of training sentry dogs, they were never in the scout dog business and had to refer to the Army FM 20-20 manual for proper training.

In the first couple of months of 1961, MAAGV launched their military dog program, dubbed "Project No. 19." This new enterprise had two goals in mind. The first was to provide the South Vietnamese Air Force with trained dogs capable of both scouting and sentry, along with "other duties" during daylight or night-time conditions. Air Force personnel reviewed combat operations records from the previous year and discovered that South Vietnamese patrols and sentry positions were being ambushed by the Viet Cong in ever-increasing numbers. Under the management of Lt. Colonel Julius Langley, the requirements of Project No. 19 would have the dogs trained and deployed to ARVN Ranger and Infantry Companies along with Paratroop Units to help stem ambush attacks by enemy elements. The Air Force would also establish a training program for the ARVN handlers.

The second part of the project was perhaps a bit more ambitious and definitely long-term. This involved having the Air Force help the South Vietnamese start a dog breeding program. Procuring and delivering German shepherds for delivery to Vietnam turned out to be a very costly procedure. If dogs could be bred in-country, it would alleviate the Air Force from tapping their limited inventory of military working dogs and also prove to be a cost-saving measure. It was also believed by those involved with the program that a dog born and bred in Vietnam would be much more resistant to indigenous diseases and be able to acclimatize much better than imported dogs, regardless of what breed they were.

In March 1961, eight dogs (six U.S. and two Vietnamese) arrived at the Tan Son Nhut Air Base, the large airfield on the outskirts of Saigon. Two canine instructors were dispatched to handle training of the prospective handlers and newly acquired dogs.[15] An Air Force Veterinary Officer, Captain Carlton Lose, along with a veterinary technician, Sergeant Hague, all on six-month temporary duty (TDY), provided veterinary support for the dogs. The American team moved to a small dog training facility at Go Vap, which is a little village located at the southern end of the sprawling Tan Son Nhut air base. Years earlier, France had established a dog center at this location and now, long after the departure of French troops, there could still be found a pair of bloodhounds that were left over, three Doberman pinchers, and several German shepherds.[16] An informal group of Air Force personnel was supposed to begin development of a military dog program to help the South Vietnamese Air Force (VNAF) to establish better base security. The Americans would make their commitment, yet the South Vietnamese obligation would be a matter of conjecture.

By October 1961, the Air Force had delivered 46 trained dogs and Air Force personnel attempted to train the ARVN handlers. Several months earlier, two dogs (Monty and Rinty) were trained with new handlers and entered service with the Capital Military District that was to provide security in sensitive parts of Saigon and the Presidential compound. Yet, in a period of five months, the dog teams worked just a total of eight days.

The Chief of Research and Development for Project No. 19, Colonel Virgal R. Chilson, was fed up with the entire situation as he tried to get the Vietnamese to deploy their dogs and use them in

Although bloodhounds are regarded as the ultimate tracker dog, they were not suited to the environment of Vietnam. Noisy on the trail, they labored under the extreme heat and humidity. For the ARVN, the German shepherd would become the dog of choice. *(National Archives)*

a combat environment. He also wanted to make sure all the handlers were both volunteers and trained combat personnel adept at scouting and patrolling. Not only should they like dogs, they [handlers] should possess sufficient intelligence to grasp the many facets of the training process. Chilson stated, "This point can be sharply proven by observation of the eight dog handlers recently assigned to work with the six U.S. and two VN dogs in the R&D program. With but few exceptions the dogs appear to be more intelligent than the recently recalled reservists assigned this duty." [17] Chilson obviously saw little success in the future months with the Vietnamese personnel provided as prospective handlers.

The project had little support at the very beginning from the higher echelon, and the program was not directly associated with MAAG, but with the Advanced Research Projects Agency (ARPA). In a nutshell, there was little or no funding for the undertaking from the very beginning. The Air Force pushed for additional help for the endeavor from the Army, but they showed little interest in breeding dogs. In retrospect, MAAG was really just a group of competing entities with limited co-operation and each service branch trying to get their share of the monetary pie. With little or no supervision from a superior authority and apparently with no established program goals, the entire exercise fell apart in just a short period of time. After Captain Lose left, a Captain Thayer filled in for veterinary service, followed by Captain William J. Welch. Welch recalled his experience:

> "I arrived at Tan Son Nhut from Beale AFB [California] in early 1961. We had been ordered to travel in civilian clothes, but when we arrived everyone was wearing uniforms. The bus that picked us up had chicken wire over the windows. Some of the bars [in Saigon] had recently been bombed and the wire was to keep out the grenades, so we were glad to see it. I was met by Captain Tom Smith, the second veterinarian in charge of the project, which had been ongoing for a year to eighteen months. They had a male and female bloodhound, a male and two female Dobermans, and the rest were German shepherds. We thought we could use the best of the male patrol dogs as breeding animals. They had twenty kennels, twenty breeding animals, and twenty Vietnamese servicemen as handlers and one Vietnamese veterinarian. There was some talk about the program being discontinued when I arrived but no decision had been made, so we continued to breed. There were six pups when I arrived, forty-six when I left, and more were on the way." [18]

GoVap was getting crowded by the beginning of November, with about fifty-seven American dogs held in the kennels. Chilson was ticked off about the two dogs (Monty and Rinty) that arrived five months earlier. Both dogs had been assigned to the Capital Military District but had only worked about four days over five months. Meanwhile both RVNAF and U.S. officers were making moves to get their own personal sentry dog to protect their homes.

Several of the men involved with Project 19 gave little attention or thought to any established regimen for training either the dogs or potential handlers. The Air Force also wanted to get out of the dog breeding business and the Army, operating independently, wanted to import German shepherds to South Vietnam. As the initial dog program fostered by the Air Force and ARPA in South Vietnam floundered, the United States military launched an aggressive campaign back home to obtain dogs for a variety of jobs at hand. In 1961, 173 dogs had been purchased by the Air Force, but this number jumped to 585 just a year later and the following year another 524 had been acquired. Apparently there was no urgent appeal made directly to Americans to donate their dogs compared to the effort made during World War II and in 1961 there were no donations of dogs by civilians at all. A year later only twelve civilian contributions were made and the year after that, American citizens offered just ninety-two dogs to the military.

The Air Force found it increasingly difficult to obtain quality dogs due to a couple of factors. The competition for a good German shepherd increased as more civilian police departments and law enforcement agencies scrambled for the few dogs available. Private security firms also stayed in the hunt for a good dog. Many organizations and people across the country saw a bright future for working dogs. Couple the demand with the stringent criteria set forth by the Air Force and the number of suitable dogs available was quickly whittled down.

To meet the challenge of its assigned quotas, the Air Force sent out recruiting teams all over the country to purchase dogs. A typical working party involved twelve men (procurement officer, a veterinarian and assistants, trainer, handlers, and a transportation officer). Usually the recruitment team dropped anchor at a military installation for a few weeks and then tapped the local media for news coverage and waited for the prospective donors or sellers to come forward.

This program seemed to be fairly effective. The recruitment teams could give exams on the spot and immediately accept or reject a dog. Top dollar was usually paid (about $150 at the time) so little haggling ensued. This meant the red tape was eliminated and owners could get a quick reply rather than wait several weeks to find out if their dog was accepted or not.

As the Air Force scrambled to procure more dogs at home, during this same period they were also able to disperse fifty-one dogs across Vietnam once the handlers completed their training. Considering the lack of veterinary care available, it is doubtful that these dogs could survive for a long period of time. The buildup of South Vietnamese veterinary services lagged well behind the speed at which dogs could be deployed to the field. Working independently, the United States Army began gearing up a military dog program they could call there own. Had there been more coordination between the services, this might have resulted in an entirely different outcome.

"Where Are All These Dogs Going?"

The idea of supporting the Army of the Republic of South Vietnam (ARVN) forces by importing scout and sentry dogs began in late 1961 with the Operations and Training Branch of the Army Section of MAAG. The officers organizing this effort either dismissed the previous attempts by the Air Force or did not know there was already an operation in place to field military working dogs in Southeast

Asia. During the fall of 1961, MAAG had set ARVN requirements for 468 sentry and 538 scout dogs. [19] The talk that went around at the time was that they would be earmarked for twenty sentry and twenty scout dog platoons. This seemed to be an aggressive proposition and may have been wishful thinking and something that would never actually occur. The United States military possessed about 1,200 dogs worldwide in their inventory at this time. They did not have enough dogs for the South Vietnamese nor were they in the recruitment pipeline. Even with the Air Force canine conscription program, the Army needed to go beyond our own borders and purchase additional dogs from foreign private sources to meet their own growing demand. It may have been an issue of asking for an incredible number of dogs to be secured in a short period of time and settling for less.

With Project No. 19, the Air Force had placed dog teams in South Vietnam with ARVN forces (Ranger, Infantry, and Paratroop) scattered around the country, and this turned out to be a logistical and medical support nightmare. The Army stepped in and decided it was best to keep the sentry and scout dog handlers housed and commanded as platoons—not a solution but a much more sensible plan. This would mean staging the dog teams in groups attached to other units, and dispersing them to the field as required. It would be the same model used by both the United States Army and the Marine Corps in the future.

The largest concentration of German shepherds to be found in the world at the time was in Germany. Here the dogs could be purchased by the American military using funds siphoned from the Military Aid Program (MAP). The plan was to have United States personnel inspect, purchase, and deliver dogs to South Vietnam and then provide instructors to teach ARVN handlers how to train and deploy the dogs. This is a basic concept and a very simple plan on paper, but it turned out to be much more difficult to implement in reality. MAAG still had little knowledge about military working dogs and even less on how they would cope and operate in an environment like that of South Vietnam. From the very early stages of this endeavor a glaring mistake would enfold—veterinarians, either at home or abroad, would not be involved in a constructive capacity that would help make the program a total success. As with soldiers in the field, a strong medical commitment is absolutely essential on the modern battlefield.

Army Major Robert C. Miller directed the proposal to acquire dogs and deliver them to Vietnam. The project appeared sound on the drawing board, but purchasing the dogs and getting them sent to South Vietnam was the easiest part of the assignment. Few people understood the nature of the war that was unfolding in Southeast Asia. Keeping the dogs alive once they arrived in South Vietnam and having the Vietnamese accept them would be a continuous headache for the MAAG advisors. MAAG personnel did very little when planning veterinary support, feeding the dogs, and the development of adequate kenneling. Most of this was done in-country "on the fly" as the problems appeared and were noted by the American advisors or by the few overworked veterinarians. It was a haphazard approach at best and did not bode well for the dog teams that would be deployed in the field.

The Department of Defense (DOD) figured that an initial allotment of 300 dogs could be purchased in Europe through the USAEVR Dog Training School located on Prince Hienddrick Kassern in Lenggries, West Germany. One of the most beautiful areas in Europe, Lenggries is nestled in the Bavarian Alps between Garmish and Munich. The kennels could house 100 to 150 dogs with little problem and the training school boasted a well-stocked veterinary clinic with about 10,000 square-feet of floor space.

The commanding officer of the school at this time was Capt. Barton "Pat" H. Patterson, who received the orders for acquiring the dogs in the latter part of 1961. "Who are we going to ship the dogs to? Are there American units that need that many dogs?" Patterson asked. [20] Only a little while later did he find out that they would be going to Vietnam.

Patterson, along with the veterinarian officer, Capt. William E. Callahan, V.C., the commanding officer of the 51st Medical Detachment (Vet Svc), formulated plans on how they would fill the requirements of the order. The pair traveled throughout the country along with two instructors and a veterinary technician and began purchasing German shepherds for about $40 each. These sales were brisk in design and were usually set up with the help of a local German shepherd dog club so that 20 to 50 dogs could be purchased at a time.

The instructors started by field-testing the dogs for gun shyness and temperament. Callahan and the vet tech gave each dog a brief physical and would accept or reject the animal on the spot. After passing all the field examinations they were then delivered to the Dog Training Detachment aboard a thirty-two foot-long tractor-trailer packed with shipping crates. Arriving back at Lenggries, the dogs were further checked with X-rays for hip displaysia and with additional laboratory blood work for worms and filliaris. All of this took place during the middle of winter and often during a snowstorm, which only compounded the work at hand for the veterinarians and technicians.

Another problem was that the school in Lenggries quickly filled all the available kennel spots and there wasn't much of a choice of what to do with the quick jump in the dog population. "As it turned out we had to tie them to trees, bushes, fences, or any other place we could find," said Patterson. "We had dogs breaking loose, getting into dogfights, and all the other usual problems, only magnified three-fold because of the extra dogs." [21] Meanwhile, Captain Callahan spent an enormous amount of time patching up the dogs and trying to keep them healthy and in one piece for their long journey to Vietnam.

On 1 February 1962, the first fifty dogs departed Rhine Mein AFB in Germany, for what would turn out to be a smelly, messy, and exhausting nine-day trip to Vietnam aboard a C-130 cargo plane. Little consideration was paid to the dogs that had to move from a cold European environment to the tropical climate of Vietnam. Both Patterson and Callahan accompanied the dogs on the flight. American military aircraft could not pass over neutral countries, so a circuitous air route from Germany to the United States and then across the Pacific Ocean was required.

Leaving Germany, the planeload of dogs went to the Azores, on to Newfoundland, Maguire AFB, Offut AFB, Travis AFB, Hawaii, Wake Island, Guam, and then

The biggest group of German shepherds were located in Germany and many of these dogs would present unique challenges for their future Vietnamese handlers. *(National Archives)*

Manila for the final leg to Tan Son Nhut. "You can only imagine what the inside of the plane looked and smelled like. The flight crew was real happy to get rid of us," said Patterson. The C-130 pilots only tolerated one more flight with their plane smelling like dog crap. The remaining four flights would be charted civilian jets contracted through the Military Air Transportation Service (MATS).

Another problem, among a host that would soon arise, was acclimatizing the dogs to the tropical environment and the diseases associated with the area. Even before their arrival in South Vietnam one dog would die of heat exhaustion. Some steps were taken beforehand to help them cope with the new environment and some of these actions seem to have misfired.

Each dog received 60cc of Pittman Moore's highly concentrated globulin in conjunction with a distemper vaccine. Canine distemper is a transmittable viral infection that manifests itself with the dog as a loss of appetite or partial paralysis, discharge from the eyes or nose, lethargy, or even death. A couple of weeks later they received a vaccine for hepatitis and leptospirosis. In retrospect, the large dose of globulin may have interfered with the effectiveness of the distemper vaccine. In essence, when the dogs finally arrived at Tan Son Nhut, their immunity against this disease was greatly diminished. With all the problems that were to be encountered in the future, the dogs from Germany already had one strike against them.

Problems arose immediately as the dogs arrived in-country before MAAG realized there were few competent ARVN veterinarians to care for them. Although there were about twenty veterinarians in South Vietnam, only four were army officers at the time and two of them shuffled papers in Saigon. Another veterinarian could be found in Ban Me Tuet as Commander of the 4th Veterinary Detachment. He was quite busy taking care of 200 ponies, several elephants, some local cattle, and a signal pigeon detachment located at Pleiku and Nha Trang. Add in the pack mules cared for at Contun in the Highlands and this animal doctor had his hands full. The fourth candidate had no experience with dogs and was relegated to food inspection services in Saigon.

The Air Force was already encountering problems with the dogs they placed in the field. Colonel William P. Brooks, Jr. who acquired responsibility for Project 19 stated in a memo, "It is understood that there are plans to assign Vet [veterinary] personnel to each of the Corps areas to care for the assigned dogs, but this action is not expected for some time. There appears to be no plan for medical care of

Few qualified South Vietnamese veterinarians were available to care for the military dogs. Technicians could help out, but most of the medical care in the upcoming years would be from American veterinarians assigned to Vietnam. *(Carlisle Barracks)*

the dogs in the interim."[21a] Brooks went on to suggest that American veterinary personnel be assigned to RVN on a temporary basis and recommended that dogs be evacuated that could not be properly treated in the field. It was quite obvious to Brooks that the dogs were deployed without adequate military support and it was a situation of closing the gate after the horses had left the barn.

SCHOOLING THE ARVN

By May of 1962, 74 dogs were available for service. Go Vap, located just outside of Saigon, was still being used by the Air Force at this time for dog breeding and would need to be expanded to accommodate more dogs. This slowed the importation of dogs until construction of new kennel facilities could be completed.

Even though the facility at Go Vap was in good shape, the dogs advisors soon realized there would not be enough room for future development. A decision was made to clear twenty acres of forest at Thanh Tuy Ha, about twenty-five miles south of Saigon. This would serve as the centerpiece of the ARVN Dog Training Center under the command of ARVN Major Le Thanh Do, who would have 400 men under his authority. Three hundred "bird house" type kennels were built. The kennels were aluminum boxes that stood on a pole about two feet high off the ground. About half of them had a base pad of concrete. The large volume of concrete being poured and the rising costs of the project scared the MAAG advisors to the point to where the remaining kennels simply had pea stone laid as a base. The pea stone turned out to be a poor substitute as it was difficult to completely remove feces during the dry season when there was little rain. As a consequence, hookworm infestation plagued the facility for the duration of the war. [22]

This photo shows the ARVN Dog Training Center at Thanh Tuy Ha under construction. The bird cage style dog houses had concrete pads, but military advisors eventually switched to gravel pads to lower the overall construction costs. *(Otis Archives)*

Although everything was of new construction, only the veterinary hospital could be considered a permanent structure. The remaining fourteen buildings, nine of which were considered sleeping quarters, were built of mud, thatch, and palm branches with sand floors. Things were quite crowded with 40 men housed in each of the sleeping quarters and sanitary conditions were marginal at best.

By July of 1962, 235 dogs arrived in South Vietnam and another 102 arrived by the end of September. During this same time period, ARVN soldiers began to show up as prospective dog handlers and veterinarian technicians. Project 19 limped along as a separate entity with the Air Force now playing second fiddle to the Army war dog project. Air Force veterinarian Capt. Alvin W. Smith indicated in a memo that the Air Force should look into getting out of the dog breeding business and noted that; "The United States military does not operate a dog breeding project anywhere in the world." Smith was less than enthusiastic about the dogs already deployed to the South Vietnamese and stated, "In the last six months, not one piece of information has been received in the R&D section to indicate that a single Viet Cong has been detected or apprehended as a result of the dog program." [23]

As seen by the results to date, starting a military dog program from scratch for the South Vietnamese would be a frustrating experience for American personnel involved in the program. There simply was no background in Vietnamese culture to the true nature of dogs and what they could accomplish as a military asset. As SFC Jesse Mendez, one of the first American advisors assigned to the South Vietnamese recalls: "There were many difficulties encountered in getting the ARVN handlers to

A close up of the bird cage dog house. Replacing the concrete with gravel caused a problem with hookworm and screw worm infestation with the dogs. *(National Archives)*

accept their dogs. Of course many of the Vietnamese were Buddhist, who believed in reincarnation and none of them wanted to come back as a dog. Many of them wanted to return as a tree or a blade of grass, or a flower, anything but a dog. It was very difficult to show how valuable the dogs were for security and scouting purposes."

Another problem, not addressed at the time, was the fear of the dogs that many handlers possessed. Mendez and the other advisors knew that to be successful, the

An ARVN sentry dog handler undergoes a training exercise at the Thanh Tuy Ha compound. Note the size of the dog and handler. Many Vietnamese had a tough time working with the large imported German shepherds. *(National Archives)*

ARVN handlers engage in obedience training with their dogs. Instructing the handlers was a frustrating experience for the American advisors and was compounded with the language barrier and how the South Vietnamese treated their dogs. *(Carlisle Barracks)*

handler needed to be the master and the dog subservient. Although generally known among dog trainers, it never really became well explained until decades later. It would also make clear the greater success of American handlers over their South Vietnamese counterparts. In his book, *Cesar's Way*, dog behaviorist Cesar Millan clearly states over and over again that the "energy" projected by humans is read, interpreted, and acted upon by a dog. Millan says, "I can be sure of this [fear in humans] from decades of close observation: you cannot "bluff" a dog the way you might be able to bluff a drunken poker buddy. Once you shift into the emotion of fear, the dog instantly knows he has the advantage over you. You are projecting weak energy." [24]

Once that projection of fear or weak energy is made, the dog became the dominant force and the handler submissive. In other words, the dogs would be running the show. The best dogs, whether scout, sentry, tracker, mine, or tunnel, would be most effective when the handler was the boss and the calm assertive strength displayed by them would envelope the dog. Once the dog recognized who was in charge, it would make for the best working friendship.

Yet that was only one of a litany of problems facing the American advisors. Although the best attempt was made to match the handler and a dog, if things didn't happen as expected, the handler often sought out another dog and then swapped with a comrade. If this occurred during the early training phase, it was a minor inconvenience and worked out for all involved. When a handler gave up half-way through the course, it presented just one more obstacle to getting a well-trained dog team deployed.

The Vietnamese students who graduated from the eleven-week handler program often over-protected their dog in the field. Many feared that their dog might be killed in the line of duty, although a slow death by malnutrition and disease seemed to matter little to them. The Saigon government reinforced this perspective by often stating that a German shepherd was more valuable than a soldier. In one incident a Doberman pinscher turned on its handler and was about to separate his arm from the torso. An American veterinarian hit the dog so hard that he broke its femur. The Vietnamese handler, rather than being thankful for averting a serious injury, chastised the vet for injuring the dog.

For the advisors, the eleven weeks of training for scout dogs (eight weeks for sentry dogs) was really not enough. All instruction needed to be carried out through interpreters, which slowed the entire process. Military manuals needed to be translated and copied, which took additional time. Even then, many of the English words didn't exist in the Vietnamese language, and a creative method had to be employed in order to get the point across to the students.

Many of the first graduates worked with the Vietnamese Ranger battalions and were successful. The ARVN officers, with some left-handed logic, figured more is better and if they shorten the training period they could get dogs out to the field even quicker. The American advisors wanted a longer time frame for training to deliver the best possible dog team to the field, but eventually caved-in to the request.

Sure enough, the first batch of dog teams that trained for just eight weeks had many problems in the field. Casualties escalated with the patrols, and within a couple of months the ARVN backed off on their demands. The advisors returned to their original schedule. As the better-trained teams hit the field, the casualty rates dropped dramatically.

THE ARVN TRIES TO GET THEIR ACT TOGETHER

A host of other troubles remained. A local Vietnamese national at Tan Tuy Ha was found to be selling dog food on the black market. After his apprehension by authorities, no court date was set and the man simply "disappeared." Vietnamese handlers with a fondness for opium would kick their dog out of their kennel box in the morning, climb inside, and light up a joint. The MAAG advisors on hand quickly found out that it was best to "let them do their thing" and then go on with the day's activities.

Another difficulty not considered by the Americans was how the civilian Vietnamese population viewed the arrival of these dogs. As one newspaper report stated:

> **Saigon, Vietnam, Sep 3.**
>
> A U.S. military spokesman today denied press reports that 200 war dogs bought and trained at a cost of $100,000 to protect Vietnamese villages have been eaten by the villagers. That would work out a cost to the American taxpayer of about $6.50 a pound, compared to 20 cents a pound which is the going price for dog meat in the Saigon market. However, the American spokesman said the report was unfounded, "As far as we can determine." The English language Saigon Post said 200 dogs had been flown to Saigon from Germany on commercial airliners, put through six weeks of training, and airlifted

> to tribal villages for sentry duty. When dog handlers returned to the villages a few weeks later, they found most of the animals that had ended up in family cooking pots, the Post claimed. The Post headlined its story "Costly Counter-Insurgency Brainstorm Goes To Pot." While denying the story, the American spokesman did reveal that the U.S. has so far supplied 330 war dogs for the Civil War against the communist's Viet Cong guerilla. He said 100 were on duty with scout platoons, 170 worked with sentries at military installations and 60 were still in training. He said it cost $560 to put a war dog in action, not counting the cost of his training. The dog alone cost $235, his equipment cost $100, his vaccinations and medical care $45 and airfreight charges $180. [25]

Turning scout dogs into a family meal turned out to be an unfounded rumor and might have prompted Lieutenant General Paul D. Harkins, Commander of the Military Assistance Command, Vietnam (MACV), [26] to investigate the ARVN dog program and determine how the dogs were being treated and what results they were getting in the field with them. Harkins had acquired the appointment six months earlier and was described by Secretary of Defense Robert McNamara as "an imaginative officer, fully qualified to fill what I consider to be the most difficult job in the United States Army." It is well understood that McNamara never walked point as an advisor with an ARVN patrol out in the boonies, so his definition of a "difficult job" will always be suspect.

Meanwhile, Captain Welch began looking into the possibility that the local populace was truly eating some of the military dogs. The only problem he found was that up north, along the coast in Da Nang, three military dogs were missing. The commanding officer of the veterinary hospital stated that the dogs died from natural causes and were buried. When an ARVN general ordered that the dogs be exhumed, the bodies could not be located.

If you look at many Asian cultures you will find that dog meat is considered a good source of protein. The American experience with dogs is entirely different from the people in Southeast Asia. Military dogs are tracked, recorded, and leave a paper trail. Welch knew that a variety of records followed every military dog and the handler would be held accountable if the dog disappeared. Of course, all that changed years later in 1975, when South Vietnam fell and the fate that befell the more than 700 German shepherds that the ARVN had at the time.

Yet during this critical period of time Harkins, who was a deputy chief of staff under General George S. Patton during World War II, vacillated on what to do. A directive stopped the purchase of further dogs but stated that MACV would continue to support the ongoing program. No one wanted to give up on the program, and still it appears no one had the fortitude to provide the necessary support to make it successful. As a result, veterinary officer replacements would be available on temporary duty (TDY) and the Air Force would shut down its research activities at Go Vap. Under general orders, U.S. advisors were still not able to accompany scout dog teams out into the field (although many did).

While the Army continued with their program, the Air Force kept the breeding program alive—although it could be considered on life-support by this time.

Another big difference from the Army program is that the Air Force followed a different route. Although they had German shepherds within their program, they would focus on breeding bloodhounds and Dobermans for the field. By October 1962, they managed to have eleven bloodhounds and seven German shepherds ready for training and expected ten Dobermans available the following month. If the plan could be followed there would be seventeen trainable pups every three months. The biggest obstacle would be that this project was taking place in Vietnam surrounded by a growing war environment.

Project No. 19 began to fall apart over the next few months. Some of the events that took place highlight many of the differences on how the Americans and Vietnamese viewed the situation, and also what needed to be done to make the dog program successful. USAF Capt. John H. Kothman arrived to replace Dr. Welch and immediately went head-to-head with Captain (Doctor) Do Thoung Tan, the commander of the breeding center at Tan Tuy Ha. Kothman wanted to know why the chemicals supplied were not being used to chlorinate the water. Tan said that the water was okay and didn't require chlorination. Kothman then filled a glass and offered it to Tan and asked him to drink it. Tan refused and only then promised the water would be chlorinated by his personnel in the future. [27]

The following day during a meeting, the new MAAG advisor for the breeding center, Capt. Kotouc, an infantry officer, stated that the training for the bloodhounds should be discontinued. Apparently there was some dissension among the trainers who considered the bloodhounds a liability in the field. Colonel Brooks couldn't argue the point and said if that were the case, he would ship them to the R&D Field Unit in Bangkok for field testing. This would also mean discontinuing their future as potential breeding stock.

A couple of weeks later, Dr. Tan pulled Dr. Kothman aside for a little talk. The head of the Vietnam Veterinary Corps, Major Du, wanted to open up the breeding center to the public for the purpose of breeding private dogs with a stud fee attached. It would appear the Vietnam doctors were looking for a little monetary kick back. Kothman told Tan that this had "unhealthy" political and financial implications. In an internal memo Kothman stated, " I'll send the dogs back to the United States before I'll let private people in Vietnam line their pockets from profits on dogs brought here by the U.S. Government." [28]

MACV still continued with its evaluation of the ARVN war dog program until March 1963. General Harkins sent over Lt.Col. Rawlins to the breeding center to snoop around and find out what the Air Force had been up to. The perception seemed to persist that if MACV ignored the problems at hand they would go away.

Perhaps Harkins truly believed his own words when McNamara asked him how long it would take to pacify Vietnam. He replied, "Mr. Secretary, I believe we can do it in six months. If I am given command of the Vietnamese we can reverse this thing immediately." That mindset, a World War II mentality carried over from fighting the Germans, would haunt not only the ARVN military dog program but also the American dog teams that would be arriving in-country in just a few short years. A few months later, Harkins reconsidered what he had said and determined that one year would be required to end hostilities. Ho Chi Minh, a bit more realistic, was working on a victory schedule of fifteen to twenty years down the road. [29]

The report to Harkins recommended (but not implemented until 11 June 1963) that the thirteen under-strength ARVN scout dog platoons be reduced to five full-strength units. For military purposes, South Vietnam was divided into five separate areas of responsibility, called Corps areas, with a special area of designation for Saigon proper, called the Capital Military District (CMD). One platoon would be assigned to each Corps area and the CMD. Excess dogs in the military population would be shifted to sentry duty and any remaining dogs would be retrained for both sentry and scout dog teams. And there would be yet another evaluation, to be concluded by the end of the year once these changes were implemented.

In this training exercise this scout dog correctly located a VC booby trap. Note the leather working harness on the dog. *(National Archives)*

An American advisor was assigned to each platoon to keep things moving forward and to spot potential problems. The five United States Army advisors at this time included S/SGT John W. Hood, Jr., SGT. Jesse Mendez (I Corps), SGT Alfonse E. Pizzarelli, SGT George Schwietzer, and MSGT Robert Woolverton.

Among the biggest problems to be faced was the total lack of understanding, by Vietnamese officers and American infantry advisors alike, of the role of the scout dog team in a combat situation. Crazy as it sounds, many ARVN officers felt threatened by the dogs, as if they were in some type of competition about who could do the best job. This problem would resurface later with American scout dog teams and constituted a difficulty that would never truly be resolved during the course of the war.

In actual combat one of two scenarios would take place. Officers (both American and Vietnamese), with absolutely no inkling as to the capability or limitations of a scout dog team, would place them in situations where they were not effective. Little instruction was given to officers about how and when a scout dog team should be deployed and what their function was. Another problem, and one that came with dire consequences, was to have the patrol leaders dismiss the alerts that a scout dog may provide. When a handler called an alert, for the most part, it was legitimate.

With all the troubles associated with the program, scout dog teams still managed to post impressive results. Between 1963 and 1964 each scout dog platoon averaged about 70 operations a month. Operations consisted of combat and reconnaissance patrols, ambushes, outposts, and search and destroy missions. Sentry dogs, scattered throughout the country at sensitive and critical sites, were well received. Once the Army decided that the ARVN dog program was up and running, little thought was given to continued support over the long haul. This philosophy encouraged the ARVN to take responsibility across the board for the training, deployment, and healthcare of the dogs they were given.

As the Army program grew and expanded, Project 19 completely fell apart. In May of 1963, USAF Colonel Vito S. Pedone met with Colonel Jacobsen, Chief O&T (Operations and Training) at MAAG, and both agreed the idea of breeding dogs be terminated as soon as possible. [30] Phelps concurred and recommended the program be terminated on 1 July 1963, and that all trainable dogs be turned over to Tan Tuy Ha and any puppies be given to "select" personnel. This action formally ended the experimental breeding program for South Vietnam. The dogs already committed to the field would continue to work, but eventually they were replaced by formal sentry and scout dog platoons.

It is hard to grade the success or failure of the ARVN dog program. Based on canine mortality rates it was a complete disaster. By 1966, the ARVN dog population dropped to just 52 scout dogs and 80 sentry dogs. Ninety percent of the canine deaths could be attributed to malnutrition. Another 210 dogs were

American advisors often accompanied ARVN scout dog handlers out in the field. This was crucial to find out how well the scout dog teams were working. *(National Archives).*

procured at this time, followed by an additional 102 in 1968. This brought the population of viable working dogs back up to about 444 (166 scout, 186 sentry, and 92 in training). Any further acquisitions came from the American draw-down and turnover of dogs that began in the latter part of 1969.

There were many accomplishments in the field to be sure, but little information is available except anecdotal reports. Based on the accounts in newspapers and military magazines during this time, and interviews with advisors like SGT Jesse Mendez, it would seem that the 3rd ARVN scout dog platoon was the best of the lot. Other information would also filter in as the Vietnamese dog teams began to support American infantry and Marine elements as they arrived and began operations. Over a period of time the ARVN successes were encouraging enough for the United States to awaken its long-dormant scout dog program at Fort Benning.

The war was evolving, as do all conflicts over time. President Diem, who had visited Tan Tuy Hay and seen the military dog program in April 1963, was dead by October of that same year, killed in a coup by his generals and with a wink and a nod by the United States administration. No viable leader for South Vietnam who could challenge Ho Chi Minh ever emerged after this time. This caused the United States to be drawn into the civil war even more, and not just militarily, but politically as well.

Local ARVN troops guard Vietnamese villagers while searching for Viet Cong suspects. *(National Archives)*

This map shows the deployment of the ARVN scout and sentry dog platoons. The 5th Sentry Dog Platoon (not shown) was stationed at the Presidential palace in Saigon. *(Author's Collection)*

With a weak and ineffective government, South Vietnam relied more and more on American military intervention. The United States, of all the countries in the world, did not realize at this time that a sovereign state can only successfully be led by its people, not a military entity— no matter how benevolent or with the best of intentions.

Thus began the involvement of military working dogs in Vietnam. It was not long before the Americans arrive. The ARVN continued with the program even as American dog teams came on the scene and several years later when the last one left. However, the focus of United States military planners shifted away from the South Vietnamese to support and advance our own dog program.

Unfortunately, this is also where history, or specifically recorded military history, steers in an entirely different direction. As American forces were drawn more deeply into the war, a shift was also made in how the war was reported, both by the press and by military historians. The focus was now on the American component and this also included the use of dogs in the military conflict.

On paper, the ARVN military dog program was not an experiment; in retrospect it was a good idea gone bad. It was based on the premise that foreign fighters would learn, accept, and utilize the same skills that were successful with an American soldier. It is one thing to show someone how to use a weapon—such as a knife, rifle, or grenade; just about anyone could acquire the basic proficiency to make them effective in their use. Using the same techniques with a living creature does not always work as easily.

American and Vietnamese culture and history clashed over the use of dogs. Both sides viewed the dog in entirely different perspectives and with little common ground. Since the United States financed and propped-up the ARVN dog program, it would be our government's responsibility to dictate how best to use the dogs and how they would be treated. The Army held ultimate responsibility and could have pulled the plug on the program at any time. The dogs deserved at least that much. It is difficult or even impossible to improve on a military working dog program if the bulk of the time and resources is spent on keeping the dogs alive on a day-to-day basis. The American advisors

Looking mighty sharp, dogs and ARVN handlers march in the Armed Force Day parade in Saigon in 1971. *(National Archives)*

ARVN veterinarians visit the 936th Veterinary Detachment in Long Binh in 1969. *(Otis Archives)*

and veterinarians performed extraordinarily well considering the cards that were dealt to them.

Even though dogs employed in the armed forces are classified as "equipment," the military still needs to be held accountable to a higher authority. During World War II that upper power turned out to be the civilian men and women from Dogs For Defense. During the Vietnam War, the civilian component did not exist. The dogs brought into the conflict had no advocate for their rights. It would not be until American handlers appeared on the scene and a handful of people back home began to speak up that the military wheels would slowly begin to turn and help define what privileges, if any, should be accorded to military working dogs. But in such a tumultuous time, the appropriate measures that our dogs should be accorded would be swept away like grains of sand in a hurricane. In the hierarchy of action during the Vietnam War, the disposition of military dogs hardly registered as a blip on a radar screen for the American people. It was more than two decades after the conflict ended before canine veterans would attain some respect in regards to their final disposition.

Once the United States began to take control of the war the American-inspired military dog program established for the South Vietnamese took a back seat in both major operations and how it was characterized by history. The ARVN K-9 activities remained in place until the end of the war, but were overshadowed in day-to-day operations of the American dog teams. It would continue this way until the very end of the war when those dogs, not destined to return home or medically unfit and euthanized, would eventually be turned over to the South Vietnamese. [31]

2

American Boots and Paws on the Ground

"No sane person in the country likes the war in Vietnam and neither does President Johnson."

Vice-President Hubert H. Humphrey [1]

Marines Come Ashore

A light veil of drizzle in the predawn twilight did not blot-out the Vietnam coastline for the men who waited to come ashore as they stood aboard the four ships that comprised Amphibious Task Force 76: the USS *Mount McKinley, Union, Vancouver,* and *Henrico*. More than 3,500 Marines on board the four ships stared at the beach they would soon assault. It was 8 March 1965, and the United States Marines were about to launch a full frontal assault on Da Nang, a port city near the imaginary line separating North and South Vietnam called the demilitarized zone, better known as the DMZ. In the past and before the arrival of the Americans, Da Nang was controlled by the French before WWII, the Japanese during the war, and then the French again after that war was over.

Most of this operation was headed by General Frederick J. Karch, the Commanding General of the 9th Marine Expeditionary Brigade. The Navy SEAL (sea, air, and land) teams went in first and emerged from the heavy surf along the shore in small inflatable boats. The Marines then packed 34 men each into eleven LVTPs (amphibious tractors) and 200 each into the huge 61-ton LCM-8s. The first group ashore crashed through eight-foot breakers and landed at 0903. Within an hour, 1400 young men, armed to the teeth and not knowing what to expect, stepped onto dry land in South Vietnam.

Yet when the Marines stormed onto the beaches they were not greeted with a hail of machinegun fire, like their predecessors endured at such places as Guadalcanal, Tarawa, Peliliu, and Okinawa during World War II. Colorful banners proclaimed

"WELCOME" and a few of them were even spelled out in French. Vietnamese girls festooned the saviors of democracy with garlands of flowers and hugs. The mayor of Da Nang smiled, shook hands, and took Polaroid photos of the event. This greeting for the Marines quickly signaled that this was not going to be an ordinary fight. [2]

Da Nang is the second largest city in South Vietnam. It teemed with people as refugees swarmed in from the countryside to avoid the fighting that took place well inland, away from the coast. The migration of villagers boosted the local population to well over 200,000 people. The defense of Da Nang for the time being was to be the responsibility of the ARVN, that is until the Marines could settle in. The Marines would be in charge with added security of the Air Force base, which at this time consisted of a single 10,000-foot runway surrounded by a perimeter fence. As one Marine noted, it was not truly a continuous barrier, "[just] holes, with sections of fence at various intervals." The only dog teams to be found in the immediate area at the time consisted of the South Vietnamese 1st Sentry Dog Platoon along with the 1st Scout Dog Platoon.

The pattern of the war was beginning to change dramatically for all the participants involved. A week before the Marines landed on the beach, jet bombers took off from Da Nang to strike at targets in North Vietnam. Once the surge of Marines was established, President Johnson authorized the use of napalm as part of the bomb-

A Marine and his scout dog take a break on Okinawa during World War II. The Marines that landed on the beaches of Da Nang had a much easier time than their predecessors at Okinawa. *(National Archives)*

ing campaign. All of this was clearly an effort to slow the replenishment of enemy materials and men from the north. This large-scale bombing campaign north of the DMZ became a long-term action known as "Operation Rolling Thunder."

At this phase of the war over 20,000 American soldiers were already in Vietnam by invitation of the South Vietnamese government. Technically speaking, the soldiers were not to engage in firefights with the enemy. In fact many of the Marines that landed in Da Nang were told not to chamber a round in their rifle until fired upon. That was all to change quite rapidly and it would still be a few days before an American soldier who landed in the recent deployment was killed in a combat situation. Even then, the first two Marine casualties would be from friendly fire, signaling an ominous start. It happened when a three-man patrol lost their bearings at night and came upon friendlies in the dark. Jittery with anticipation when every sound or a shifting shadow might be a VC guerilla, it is little wonder why a quick trigger on an automatic rifle fired by a young soldier would quickly cut down two of his comrades.

If Da Nang was considered part of the war zone, then the Marines really didn't see much of the conflict. The ARVN had an occasional firefight with the enemy and even then no assistance from the Americans was asked for or offered. Within a few short weeks, boredom set in among the young soldiers. No American dogs were in place around the air base at this time to support the security forces. Beer cans, of which many empty ones could be found, were tied to strings staked out along the air base perimeter. Other wires were attached to trip flares and provided

An aerial view of Da Nang circa 1968. *(Author's Collection)*

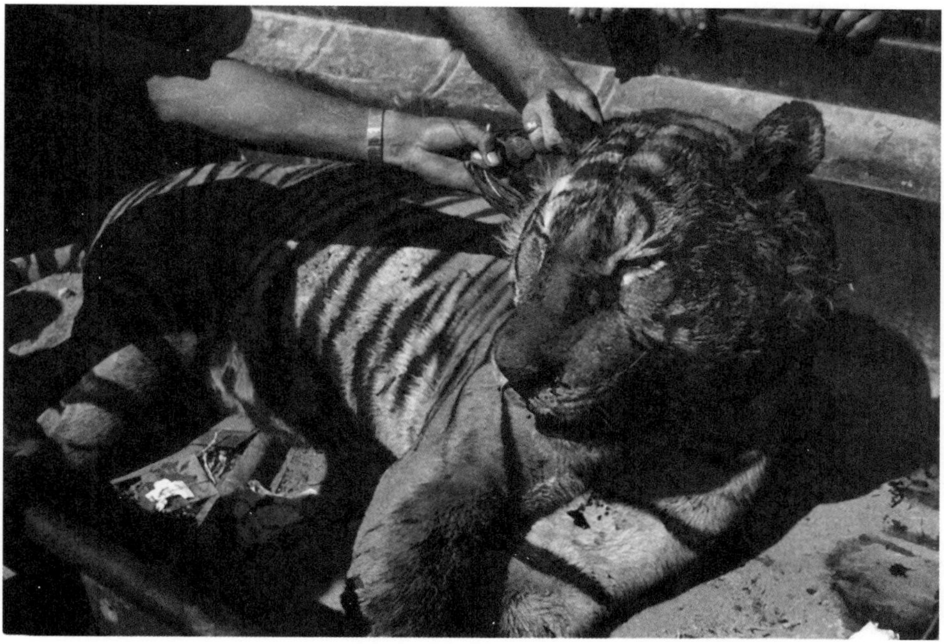

Not all casualties of war are human. This tiger happened to be in the wrong place at the wrong time. *(Courtesy of Joseph Ertel)*

the only early warning system of the approaching enemy. Every couple of days a monkey or some other creature would set off a flare, gunfire would erupt for a few brief seconds, and then everything would go quiet again.

For a brief time the American forces stayed within their fences until commanding General Frederick J. Karch finally cut them loose. A seasoned veteran from many Pacific battles in World War II, Karch really wondered what they were doing here and in short order began to get his soldiers more involved in a battle - that is if one could be found somewhere. Karch didn't have to wait long as an escalation of hostilities would soon bring the Marines away from the beaches and out into the countryside to the west of Da Nang in VC held areas soon to be known by Americans as "Indian country." Karch's policy and one never publicly stated, is that the Americans were there, very simply, to kill the Viet Cong. Although the Joint Chiefs back in Washington and even many commanders in I Corps failed to comprehend at this early stage of the game that was to be the ultimate purpose for the Marines. No one really knew what to do or where to go. The Marines defended six square miles of the surrounding airfield and Charlie was not about to go toe-to-toe with them. The first real engagement of any substantive nature would take place six months later with Operation Starlite, which coincidentally occurred about the same time the 1st Marine Provisional Dog Platoon arrived in-country. [3]

If a legitimate reason was needed for the deployment of sentry dog teams in Vietnam, then Col. James M. McBraver, chief of security and law enforcement for the 7th Air Force (the organization responsible for conducting the air war over

Vietnam), found it on July 1, 1965. It was at this time that the Dac Cong, an elite group of VC combat engineers also known as sappers, made their first major raid on an air base during the war. [4] The Communists had learned very quickly it was a lot easier to knock out an aircraft on the ground rather than in the sky.

As more and more Marines headed out into the countryside in search of the Cong, this naturally resulted in fewer personnel left behind to provide base security. The VC knew of these activities and decided it would be an opportune time to strike. The assault engineers for this operation were composed of about 100 men from both the Viet Cong and North Vietnamese Army (NVA). They easily overran the South Vietnamese guards on that cloudy night and then deftly skirted three perimeter fences with their compliment of empty beer cans and the occasional trip flare. Racing along the ramp area among the parked aircraft they tossed satchel charges and grenades. In just a few minutes the sappers were able to destroy three Lockheed C-130s transports, three Convair F-102s fighters, and damaged several other aircraft before withdrawing away into the night. In less than thirty minutes it was all over. The material damage overall was quite minimal, even though one USAF Sergeant was killed and three other men wounded. The small attack produced worldwide publicity and brought forth the question of just how much security there was around the American bases in South Vietnam.

Arrival of the American Dogs

Colonel McBraver may have reasoned that if security could easily be compromised at Da Nang, then what about the other bases in-country with far fewer perimeter defenses and the newer air bases under development or expansion? Many commanders considered Phu Bai a defense nightmare, and talk of Pleiuku air base out in the Central Highlands always seemed to be mingled with the events of Dien Bien Phu and the humiliating defeat of the French there just eleven years earlier. Just two days after the attack on Da Nang, Air Force Project Top Dog 45 was implemented. [5]

This four-month plan called for the deployment of forty handlers on a 120-day temporary duty (TDY) along with their dogs to Vietnam, as part of the 6250th Support Squadron. This was a classic knee-jerk action, and once again little consideration was given to medical and logistical support for the dogs.

The call went out to SAC, TAC, Headquarters Command (HQ COMD), and the Aerospace Defense Command (ADC) to provide dogs and have them assembled at Lackland AFB in San Antonio, Texas, as soon as possible. A scant three days of additional training were added stateside for the benefit of the dog teams, and it was expected that the men would need to be resourceful and think on their feet once they landed in Vietnam. Few, if any, handlers had any comprehension about what Vietnam was like and the situation they would face there. No matter how many training exercises were carried out stateside, you always knew it to be just that—training. In a very short time, the dog teams would encounter the real thing.

Those handlers and their dogs were expected to follow the doctrine of the Air Force Field Manual as stated: "The mission of the sentry dog is to detect intruders, alert his handler, and, when necessary, pursue, attack, and hold any intruder who tries to escape. Normally, the dog has done his job by detecting the intruder and then alerting his handler who is then responsible for taking appropriate action."[6]

The decision to have the handlers assigned to Vietnam for just four months was predicated by three reasons. Air Force commanders were still unsure whether or not the dogs would be useful as a deterrent against potential sapper attacks. This was based on the history of air base defense by the United States in previous conflicts. In the past, all air bases remained behind enemy lines and were not typically subjected to a ground attack. Secondly, those in a command position also questioned the dogs' ability to tolerate the tropical climate. This reasoning is incredibly shortsighted, considering that sentry and scout dog teams were already in place with the ARVN and the history of American dogs in the Pacific theatre during World War II. If sufficient time were given and the dogs were not overworked, most of them would acclimatize okay. The third and final rationalism that might have been pondered is that the war would be over in short order once the United States began to flex its military muscle.

The forty handlers and their dogs boarded a C-130 transport carrier and took the three-day trip to Vietnam, arriving on July 17, 1965 at Tan Son Nhut air base outside of Saigon. In Vietnam, the organization of the Air Force sentry dog teams fell under the command umbrella of McBraver's deputy, Lt. Col. Jim Black. Some of the sentry dog teams stayed at Tan Son Nhut, which was a main staging area for many troops arriving in-country, while others dispersed to Bien Hoa in

The first twenty USAF handlers to be deployed to Vietnam load up at Lackland AFB. *(Courtesy of Vance McCrumb)*

As the sentry dog teams board, note the movie camera positioned to record the event. *(Courtesy of Vance McCrumb)*

Dogs were housed in their shipping crates until permanent kennels were finished. *(Courtesy of Vance McCrumb)*

Top Dog 45 handlers lived in Tent City located on the opposite side of the active runway from the kennel area. *(Courtesy of Vance McCrumb)*

II Corps just north of Saigon, and Da Nang, much farther north on the coast in I Corps and butting up against the DMZ.

As with just about everyone else who landed in Vietnam, the handlers found the heat and humidity stifling when they arrived, even for the boys from the deep south. No kennel facilities were available, just the handler's tents and the dog's shipping crates. On the very first day at Tan Son Nhut, Mac, a three-year old male German shepherd couldn't adapt quickly enough as his body temperature ratcheted up in a very short time. In a vain attempt to bring his core temperature down, men placed the dog in a tub and packed ice around the dog's body – but it was too late. Just a few hours later the dog's internal organs began to shut down and then his heart stopped. Mac had been assigned to a United States handler and became the first truly American dog to lose his life in Vietnam. This would happen too often, and would occur throughout the duration of the war when the dogs were not allowed to get accustomed to the heat and humidity of Vietnam. [7]

Heat stroke needed to be diagnosed and dealt with swiftly, although it eventually would afflict many of the dogs that landed in Vietnam and often with fatal consequences. If the newly arrived dogs could hang tough for a few weeks and lose their inside coat of fine fur, they usually made out okay. After the initial break-in period for the dogs, only light training would be conducted during the day and the patrols for the sentry posts would be carried out only during the cooler nights when they were really needed.

For the first week or so the Air Force handlers were armed with only a .38-caliber revolver and six rounds of ammo. Then some handlers were also issued World War II vintage M-1 Garand carbines or later model M-14s. The M-1 was a fine

A night shot show Dick Bachmann shouldering an M-14. Alongside him is his dog Toby. Note the white t-shirt peeking out. *(Courtesy Dick Bachmann)*

rifle, but was a semi-automatic that carried just eight rounds and could not stack up against the automatic weapons often carried by the enemy. [8]

At this early stage of the war, many of the handlers also made their patrols in a soft Australian style bush hat, since none of them had been issued a steel helmet. Water needed to be trucked out to the so-called "kennel facilities" on a daily basis. According to Dick Bachmann, one of the original Top Dog 45 handlers, "I think most of the time was spent rounding up loose dogs. All we had for kennels was a tent and our dog's shipping crates. This made for close quarters and we had a lot of dogfights. Even now and then I look back at some of the photos [of myself] and say geez, is that really me going out on duty [at night] with my white T-shirt showing?" [9]

As with the American scout dogs that would soon enter the country, the Viet Cong misunderstood the capability of the sentry dog teams. It would take a while for the enemy to develop some type of countermeasure (if one could indeed be found) and this would be by trial and error. Meanwhile, Charlie smartly spread the word to avoid the animals at all costs. Many handlers at the time found their

A sentry dog could be your worst enemy or your best friend as demonstrated by Rick Marty and Rinny (969F) at Cam Rahn Bay Air Base. *(Courtesy of Rick Marty)*

(Courtesy of Rick Marty)

sentry dogs throwing amazing alerts at great distances on the Vietnamese. This is probably due to the fact that Vietnamese, like the majority of Asian people, based their diet on rice, while Americans quartered theirs on wheat. The body odor thus generated varied widely between the two races (as far as the scent that a dog can discriminate), and consequently the local population gave the dogs an entirely different scent. (This same situation was first noticed during World War II when Army and Marine scout dog teams initially encountered Japanese soldiers on Pacific islands.) Although this attribute was tempered over the course of time, the dogs usually had little trouble distinguishing friend from foe. Of course, in Vietnam there was no way to determine an ARVN soldier from VC or a VC from a civilian, and this poised a few problems in the field throughout the course of the war.

This sense of smell, called the olfactory ability, is clearly the number-one capability that canines possess. Depending on the breed, a dog may have 200 million scent receptors or more in the nose compared to 5 million that humans have. A much greater portion of a dog's brain is geared for interpreting scent images compared to humans. Dogs live in a world of odors, and to a lesser degree sight and sound. They are unique in the animal world by the fact that dogs can be trained to take commands and taught to distinguish between different scents (i.e. a land mine or a human for instance).

The old adage "the smell of fear" may have had its roots in the canine world. Dr. Bruce Fogle is a veterinarian and authored a book titled *The Dog's Mind*, where he relates studies that determined that dogs can identify butyric acid (a component of human perspiration) in a dose one-million times smaller than humans can detect. [10]

The German shepherd has a long nose with membranes arranged in folds to help filter smells. The dog's wet nose also helps to dissolve odor molecules and filter scents. By sniffing rapidly the dog creates turbulence within their nasal cavity that helps to distinguish different scents. Over the course of the war, the Viet Cong would use different chemicals and materials as a "scent disguise" to confuse the dogs. But a well trained dog could still differentiate between them and determine the original source. [11]

It appeared that the war was ramping up on a daily basis. On 5 August 1965, the VC attacked the Esso gasoline storage facility near Da Nang destroying two million gallons of fuel that represented about 30 percent of the country's inventory. China started rattling her own saber and warned that it may enter the fight. Meanwhile, back at home, draft evasion could land you in prison and President Johnson stated we would not continue to fight if our help was not wanted or requested. There had already been half a dozen regime changes in the south and no one was able to strongly hold the South Vietnam government together.

The worldwide affairs changed little for the boots on the ground. Each service branch demanded their own opportunity for protection, and as such the Marines were not about to pass the buck to the Air Force for either perimeter defense or for scouting purposes. For the Marines venturing out into the countryside, it was deemed necessary to reconstitute the scout dog team.

It had been quite some time since the Marines had used dogs in combat—a good twenty years. Although seven Marine War Dog Platoons saw service against the Japanese during World War II in the Pacific, they opted to discontinue training and demobilize the platoons shortly after the war was over, just as the Army did. The majority of the dogs that survived that war was split fairly evenly between Doberman pinchers and German shepherds; they were retrained and returned to their original owners or their wartime handlers during the winter of 1945-46. [12]

The haphazard approach the Marines undertook of introducing dogs into I Corps in 1965 is quite evident in the selection process for the first group of handlers. It came down to and simply involved finding out which guys liked dogs. Twelve volunteers left Da Nang in July 1965 for Japan to form the 1st Marine Provisional Dog Platoon

The superior senses of a German shepherd all come into use, whether it is on a patrol in the jungle or perimeter sentry in the dead of night. *(Courtesy of Joseph Ertel)*

Throughout the war, galvanized culverts were often cut in half to provide temporary shelter for dogs. *(Courtesy of Joseph Ertel)*

under the command of 1Lt. Bruce Davis. For the men it was an exciting time and a relief just to be out of Vietnam for a couple of weeks. One man went the full route off-duty and contracted VD, was soon kicked out of the unit, and was replaced. Although they were all volunteers and had dogs as kids, none of the men had any inkling about conducting scout dog operations or working with dogs in a combat environment. Then again there wasn't anyone around the local area who did, since scout dog training remained the sole venue of Army operations at Fort Benning, Georgia. According to one of the Marine handlers, Gary Cates, "Once we got to Japan we found out that the dogs had already been trained as sentry dogs at Lackland AFB and we were supposed to retrain them. In actuality, our time there was spent training us, not the dogs."

Of the eleven dogs, nine were purebred German shepherds, one a Shepherd-Husky mix, and the largest of the lot was a Shepherd-Great Dane mix. There was little question that Hershel Holt, a big guy who weighed in at 280 pounds, would be assigned the largest dog in the group. [13]

The men who completed the course received certificates of graduation on 20 August 1965, from the Air Force, and a week later they returned to Da Nang. Few if any of them had any idea what they were supposed to do when they returned to Nam. Little or no consideration at all was given to medical technicians, veterinarians, kennels, or the support needed to maintain healthy dogs in a combat environment. Essentially the men had sentry/attack dogs, perhaps toned down a bit in temperament, and were expected to carry out search and destroy missions, along with scouting and reconnaissance patrols, and to provide sentry duty as well. It was indeed a classic case of trying to be too many things, for too many people, in too short a period of time.

Around the same time, Marines who were going out on patrol procured scout dog teams on a case-by-case basis from the ARVN. This meant getting a South

Vietnamese handler who might understand a little English and a dog that didn't understand any. The operations typically lasted for two to four days, and were most effective when the ARVN handler could communicate easily with his American counterpart. Even then, the Marines were anxious to get their own handlers and teams. This might have been one of the reasons why the 1st Provisional Dog Platoon was being pushed into a more aggressive scouting role as soon as possible, rather than keeping the team in a defensive sentry posture.

Even adding the 1st Provisional Dog Platoon appeared to be a stopgap measure. The Marines clearly wanted scout dogs trained at Fort Benning. An urgent teletype communication on 11 July 1965, to the Pacific Command, MACV, stated:

> THE MAF WAS USING TO ADVANTAGE ARVN SCOUT DOG TEAMS ASSIGNED TO I CORPS COMMANDER, BUT THAT SINCE THESE DOG TEAM RESOURCES WERE INSUFFIECIENT TO MEET ITS REQUIREMENTS, THE MAF REQUESTED THE SUPPORT OF TWO ADDITIONAL PLATOONS OF APPROXIMATELY 25 SCOUT DOGS TOTAL FOR BOTH PLATOONS. AS AN INTERIM MEASURE MACV HAS REQUESTED RVNAF TO ASSIGN TEMPORARILY, AN ADDITIONAL SCOUT DOG PLATOON TO I Corps TO FURTHER SUPPORT MAF. [14]

Marine Sgt.Tim Hiller and his scout dog Rip take a short break on a sweep about ten miles south of Da Nang. *(National Archives)*

Based on this teletype message, the Marines wanted more scout dogs as soon as possible and believed them to be a positive resource. It marks the first time since World War II that a request of this type was made.

While the Marines looked to the future for formally trained scout dog teams, they relied on the 1st Provisional Dog Platoon to help with both scouting and sentry obligations. Sentry duty posts in I Corps could be found at the ammunition supply points, LAAMS Battery sites, 2nd ARVN division compound, and the Marble Mountain Air Facility. With so little experience to draw upon, the whole process became a hit-or-miss operation. On Monkey Mountain, where few personnel were present, the dogs worked great. However, the dogs often alerted to the monkeys that were indigenous to the area and this turned out to be a headache for the handlers. The men had to quickly determine if the dog was alerting to the enemy or something else. Neither the men nor the dogs truly had adequate training to accomplish all the tasks at hand—at least in the beginning. Experience in the field would prove to be the best teacher, assuming you or your dog didn't get killed in the process.

Handlers coming down the pipeline in the future would hone their skills at Ft. Benning, undertaking twelve weeks of training with dogs destined to become scouts early in their lives. For the present time, orders are orders and the handlers and dogs were expected to complete any task assigned to them. After a few days of arriving in Da Nang, Cliff Alderman and his dog, Rex (A061),[15] went out on their first patrol.

"We didn't take the point," Alderman says, "We didn't know what we should be [doing]. We just went out with the group and felt our way through it. Sometimes we would be out front of the platoon and sometime we'd be in the middle. There was no set procedure. We were on our own."

As a first patrol, it turned out quite successful. Oftentimes, the VC would stash their supplies in a secluded area and Rex alerted to an ammunition cache hidden in a cave. Attributes of the American military dogs during this time began to spread in-country, and this obviously reinforced the notion that the dogs could do anything asked of them. Heat stroke, missed alerts, disease, booby-traps, and snipers would shake that attitude quite a bit in the weeks, months, and years to come. As the days passed, little distinction was given to the jobs handed out to the dog teams, whether it was scout, sentry, or participation in search and destroy missions. According to Cates, "We did whatever was needed at the time and were expected to be successful in everything we did…and for the most part we were."

A few months later a decision was made to retrain four more sentry dogs for scouting. This was done for two reasons. One was to get some field experience that could be passed on to the green scout dog handlers that would be arriving from Benning. Secondly, it would help determine the capability and length of time to retrain sentry dogs into a scouting role should a future need arise. At the time, there also seemed to be some confusion at the command level of the III Marine Amphibious Force as they discussed a requirement that every dog coming overseas have two handlers. The basic reason was that if a handler was wounded or killed another handler could quickly step in. Dog trainers at both Benning and

Lackland looked at each other, chuckled, and quickly squashed this inane idea and kept to the traditional doctrine of one man with one dog.

Army sentry dogs began arriving in RVN toward the end of August 1965 and came under the command of the military police. Within a week the first of these dogs teams became operational at Pleiku. The dogs and handlers were from loosely knit, military police detachments and nothing formal was enacted at the time. As was often the case in Vietnam, it was a quick response to a particular need in a short amount of time.

According to Rick Young's book, *Combat Police: U.S. Army Military Police in Vietnam*, the official formation of an Army sentry dog unit originated on 6 Oc-

German shepherds often picked up leeches and other parasites as they crossed rice paddies and fields with stagnant water present. *(National Archives)*

tober 1965, when the 89th Military Police Group (at the time the highest military police command in Vietnam) requested the formation of a sentry dog company. This new company would be part of the 148th Military Police Detachment and comprise 48 enlisted handlers and a corresponding amount of dogs. The plan was to have the 148th replace the 72nd Military Police Detachment, a dismounted platoon not structured for sentry dog work.

This platoon maintained more typical police operations involving discipline and law, not the deployment of tactical dog teams until formally established as the 212th Military Police Company (Sentry Dog) in January 1966. This action formed three companies under the direct command of the 18th Military Police Brigade. Besides the 212th, the 981st Military Police Company (Sentry Dog) would be activated at Fort Carson, Colorado, in February 1967 (deployed to Vietnam in November 1967), and the 595th Military Police Company (Sentry Dog) was activated in Da Nang, Vietnam in January 1970.

The Army provided sentry services to at least fifteen different locations that consisted mainly of ammunition depots, airfields, signal sites, and supply depots. The locations were scattered across South Vietnam from Qui Nhon in the north to Vung Tau in the south. The security staff consisted of 250 officers and enlisted men and approximately 200 dogs.

On paper the 212th existed, but in reality it remained an empty detachment with no handlers and no dogs. So a call went out to military police units in Vietnam for volunteers to become dog handlers. The caveat, and a mighty big one, would require these volunteers to shuttle off to Okinawa on a 30-day TDY basis for training under the auspices of the United States Army Pacific Command (USARPAC) and conducted by Air Force personnel. Of course that one-month of training with your dog would work against your one-year tour of duty. It would be hard to resist, unless of course you didn't like dogs or had some inkling to what the end job would entail. And no one who considered volunteering considered it such a dangerous duty; hence there was no shortage of volunteers.

Veterinary Service Gets A Jump Start

With an open check book and no need to balance it, the United States poured more men, materials, and dogs into Vietnam. The personnel that comprised the Army Veterinary Corps and to a lesser extent the USAF Veterinary Corps also increased dramatically. Command and responsibility for veterinary activities in South Vietnam was confusing and haphazard for the entire war. If there was one blanket statement that could be made, it is that the veterinarians did their very best with what they had to work with—and that often was not very much.

The veterinary service in Vietnam was responsible for the care and medical well-being of all the military working dogs, and this was well known to everyone. Yet that was only part of their overall job and not the largest one. Every soldier that served there owes at least some measure of thanks to the veterinary officers who were responsible for food inspection. Veterinarians ensured that both locally procured food and that which originated in CONUS and shipped to Vietnam was safe and wholesome. Sanitary inspection of food processing plants and local establishments, condition of storage facilities, and safe transportation was a tedious and thankless job, with little reward. Little consideration was given by those soldiers that averted hepatitis, severe diarrhea, or food poisoning.

Sanitation in Vietnam was an anachronism. Water was seldom chlorinated and contained an unknown number of nasty organisms that could wreck havoc with your stomach and digestive tract. Many fruits and vegetables were locally grown in earth enhanced with a fertilizer dubbed "night soil," which had a high content of human excrement. Perishable foods shipped from the United States were often found spoiled by the time they arrived.

Napoleon Bonaparte has been quoted as saying, "That an army marches on its stomach." It was true then and is accurate today. This is one of the areas seldom if ever discussed in the history books of modern warfare. Food and how it got to the battlefield and the condition it arrives in is given little or no consideration. This type of information is published in obscure histories or monograms passed over by many people who believe war is a matter of combat in the field and the weapons employed in battle. Information is seldom conveyed in the history of warfare about the infrastructure of the support given to the men on the front lines. Few people recognize that the majority of people involved in a conflict (upwards of ninety percent) were relegated to support positions. When a kid asks, "Daddy, what did you do during the war?" seldom is the response, "Oh, I was a cook."

Dogs wait their turn for a monthly check up. The tests varied but usually included blood work and a check for worm infestation. Veterinarians serving in Vietnam often did whatever was necessary to ensure the best possible care for all the working dogs in-country. *(Carlisle Barracks)*

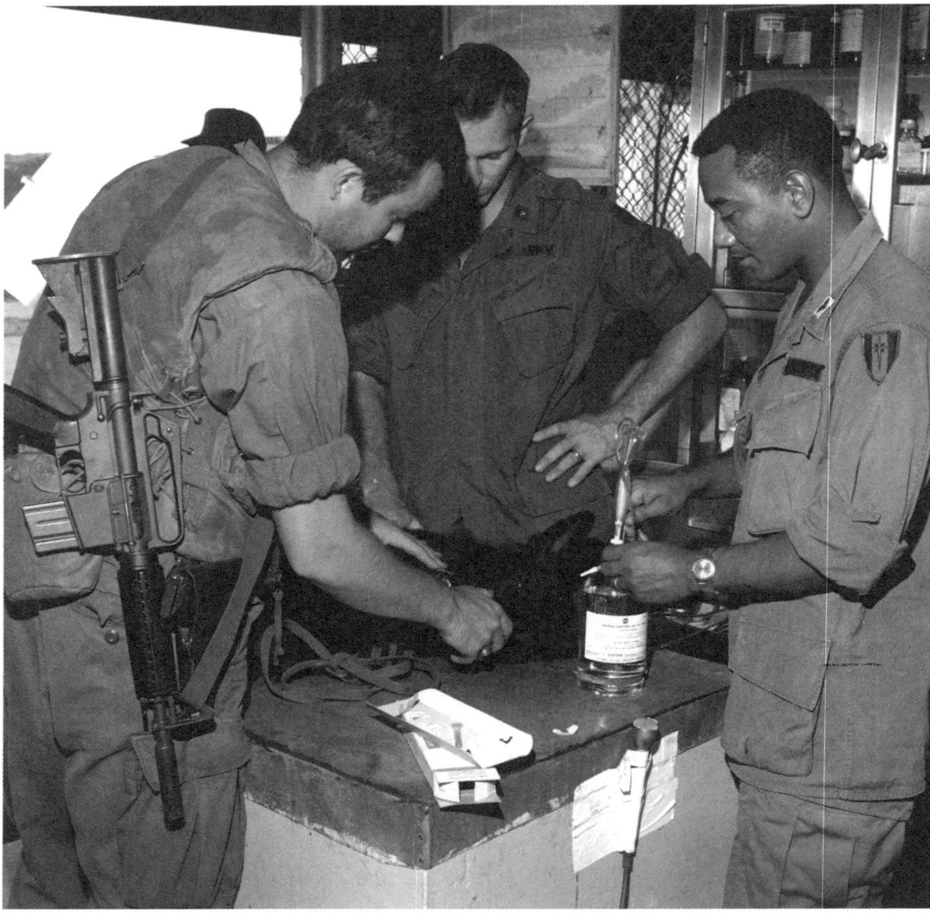

With the handler holding his muzzle, an infusion drip of Dextran is given to a scout dog wounded in action. Dextran was occasionally used to replace lost blood in emergency situations or when a blood donor dog is not available. *(National Archives)*

By the middle of 1965, the veterinary services in Vietnam were finally beginning to expand at a rapid clip, but would never fully met the needs of both men and dogs. The command and control of veterinary services changed as well. MACV was still in overall command of military operations, but on 20 July 1965, the U.S. Army Support Command was re-designated U.S. Army, Vietnam (USARV). This change shifted logistical support responsibilities for the Army away from the Navy component to USARV in October. This was a huge change, considering that the Navy brought the materials from the west coast of the United States, half-way across the world to Vietnam. It was the first of many attempts to centralize responsibilities of logistical support, the backbone of any fighting force. It also meant changes for the Veterinary Corps.

The 4th Medical Detachment assumed all operational veterinary operations in-country. By the end of the year, the 68th Medical Detachment (JA), located at Fort

Sam Houston, Texas, was brought to Vietnam. Within days of that deployment, the 949th Medical Detachment (IE) Veterinary Dispensary, originally assembled at Walter Reed Army Hospital, deployed to Okinawa to help care for the dogs that resided there. These personnel movements may sound like a lot of people were involved, but consider that the 68th comprised just two officers and fifteen enlisted men at this time. In 1965, over a billion pounds of food was inspected in RVN and care was provided for 350 Army and Marine dogs by the Army Veterinary Corps; this was accomplished with a force that had an authorized strength of just four officers and twenty-two enlisted men.

Not Your Typical Battleground

By October 1965, all service branches had their initial sentry dog teams in place. During that same month, Operation Top Dog 45 expired and those handlers that did not extend their visit abroad went home. The dogs of course remained and were taken over by handlers already in-country on a one-year tour of duty. Lackland continued to supply dogs for the American buildup and slowly began to transfer much of this responsibility to locations closer to the action. The PACAF Sentry Dog Training Center at Showa, Japan, and Kadena Air Base on Okinawa began to assume the duty of replacing dog losses, retraining, and providing some of the handlers. This positioning of resources helped to cut costs associated with the military working dogs and greatly sped up the response to a war that was just starting to heat up in grand fashion.

Helicopters like this Bell UH-1H Iroquois, known as a Huey, was the primary air vehicle for all Allied forces from 1962 until the end of the war. The Huey was often referred to as a "slick." *(Courtesy of Bill Bodnar (42nd IPSD) '69-'70)*

High temperatures and humidity, dense jungle, and just being in the enemy's backyard, can wear out even men in the best of shape and dogs too. *(Courtesy of Joseph Ertel)*

During this hectic time, the face of the ground war really changed as a full division, the first Air Calvary Division (Airmobile), arrived at Qui Nhon. Search and destroy would take on a whole new meaning with the added mobility of helicopters that could quickly dispatch troops to suspected VC locales or hotspots as they cropped up. Success of the 1st Air Cav also positioned General William Westmoreland to send men into the jungles of Ia Drang Valley and into the heaviest fighting to be seen in the war to date.

The impact of the war affected every handler in different ways, although at this time only a small number had seen action, not in Vietnam but back home, sometimes by skirting around protestors picketing an induction center or anti-war activists holding up troop trains in California. As the pace of war picked up in the latter months of 1965, so did protests against it here in the states, pitting one American against another.

On the nightly news, the landscape of the Vietnam War could be seen in practically every household. Many Americans now saw the bright orange flame and black smoke of burning napalm set against the backdrop of lush green jungles, as viewed on their newly acquired color television sets. The war in Vietnam only contrasted with the burning of Watts in August and college kids yelling "Hey, hey, LBJ! How many kids did you kill today?"

In October of 1965, David Millar, a Jesuit charity worker in a Bowery, New York soup kitchen, became the first person indicted under a new federal law that made burning your draft card a felony. As he held a match to his card Millar yelled, "I believe the napalming of villages is an immoral act." Millar apparently didn't believe the same about the spilling of blood from a generation of our youth destined for immortality—the names now on a black-faced granite wall in Washington, D.C. The events stateside did not go unnoticed by the handlers in Vietnam nor by those who had yet to be drafted or who chose to enlist. Even during the early days of the war, there appeared to be little support back home for the troops on the ground. Perhaps it was part of the counter-culture that permeated the American landscape at the time. [16]

Acts of protests are part of our national heritage. What few people realized at the time was that they were beginning to tear the country apart and in the process rip the moral support from the very souls that needed it the most—the young men who went to Vietnam. Anti-war protestors spit their venom at everyone instead of directing it where it counted the most and where it would make a difference: to those who held reign on the war. [17]

Words from Washington, like those of Senator Robert Kennedy talking about people donating blood to North Vietnam, [is] "…in the oldest tradition of this country" did not help. For the men in Vietnam, and those yet destined to go there, their fate was often in those around them; and for the handlers, it usually meant their dog. Yet the problems and rhetoric back home and skyrocketing use of drugs stateside would have a profound effect on how soldiers conducted themselves. This would truly be seen, as the war eventually wound down and Americans headed home, turning control of the war back to the South Vietnamese.

The end of 1965 also brought a change in how the war was to be conducted by all the parties involved. Ho Chi Minh became convinced that a quick victory could not be achieved over a South Vietnam bolstered by the influx of American men, material, and money. And this sounded a bit like our entry into the First World War. Ho could not envision a situation like Dien Bien Phu, that had sealed the fate of the French a few years ago, happening to the 'imperialistic' and powerful United States. America was not involved long enough and had not yet suffered enough losses of their young men. Ho knew where victory could be secured and clearly saw "the light at the end of the tunnel" before any American president ever did. His counterpart, President Lyndon Baines Johnson never stated that victory lay with the defeat of North Vietnam. Which only meant if victory did not mean the defeat of the enemy, then what was it?

President Johnson's non-declaration of war only meant a defensive battle, so similar to a good portion of our own Civil War. During that time in the nineteenth century, when our country was torn apart, the south could not possibly defeat the north and was destined to lose. The south wanted a war of attrition, but Lincoln was not going to provide them with the means to do it. A hundred years later, a similar battle would be played out in Southeast Asia, with another drawn-out battle and one of attrition. Ho Chi Minh's philosophy is well stated when he said:

> "If the tiger ever stands still, the elephant will crush him with his mighty tusks. But the tiger will not stand still. He will leap upon the back of the elephant, tearing huge chunks from his side, and then he will leap back into the dark jungle. And slowly the elephant will bleed to death. Such will be the war in Indochina." [18]

If Ho's assessment of the United States military was that of the powerful slow-moving elephant, then surely the air bases within South Vietnam represented a modern-day version of Old West cavalry outposts on a larger scale. These bases were entirely different from those of World War II and Korea, where they were situated well behind the front lines. In Vietnam there were no front lines and the war could potentially be found anywhere. It could be in a bar or hotel in Saigon as a grenade is tossed into a window or to the inside perimeter of an American air base.

With their concertina wire, bunkers, and diverse set of devices designed to thwart any potential intruder, American air bases were an oasis of power surrounded by a fast-moving, vigilant, and often undetected enemy. As the war expanded, so too did the role of the sentry dog teams in protecting these bastions of airpower. Although the sentry dog teams supported fixed installations, they were mobile to a certain extent, covering a set distance along the air base perimeter during the night. Just after the dogs arrived in South Vietnam, the Viet Cong found sentry dogs to be more than just a minor nuisance. Sentry dogs had two primary assets: being an excellent detector of enemy personnel and as a psychological deterrent. As an early warning system, the alerts made upon an enemy probing or attempting to infiltrate an air base are well documented. When a sapper was captured and interrogated at Phu Cat air base, he revealed how his company commander told him, "...that they [sentry dogs] were very intelligent and were to be respected. If any man heard or saw a dog he was to lie down immediately, hold his breath, and remain motionless until the dog left." [19]

Battalion-size standoff attacks would take place regardless of who or what was on the perimeter. The dog teams excelled in deterring sapper raids comprised of just a handful of intruders. As a combat engineer with great discipline, the sapper relied on stealth to penetrate an air base, avoid the defenders, complete his

A1C Richard Morley (35th SPS) and Satan alongside the concertina wire perimeter at Phan Rang Air Base. Sentry dogs proved to be both a physical and psychological deterrent for the enemy. *(National Archives)*

mission, and then get out (typically within thirty minutes) without being detected. His biggest asset was the knowledge gained beforehand, prior to launching any type of probe or infiltration. And the men and women who built the air bases for the Americans gained this information quite easily.

Originally it was suggested for simple security purposes to hire only Korean and Thai laborers. However, the upper echelon felt this is not how to "win the hearts and minds" of the Vietnamese people. You do that by providing jobs for the widows and kin of ARVN servicemen. Of course, no loyalty oath was given and consequently every sapper attack or mortar barrage that took place during the war was either led or carried out by someone who had intimate knowledge of the base. Although the fixed emplacements, mines, and trip flares might be well known and avoided, the same did not hold true for the dogs whose scent detection could range for many hundreds of yards.

Many Vietnamese did not identify with dogs nor did they like them, especially large ones. As the air force handlers trained the dogs during the day or late afternoons, many Vietnamese workers on base had the opportunity to see these vicious sentinels in action. If a German shepherd can haul down a big American in a padded "bite suit," it didn't take a rocket scientist to know what they could do to a smaller Vietnamese man with no protection.

John Risse (633rd SPS) and his dog, Duke (645F), arrived at Tan Son Nhut on 17 October, 1965. A week later they packed up and boarded a C-130 for Pleiku, where he was surprised when told that they were not expected. Too often the dog teams were deployed so fast that no one spread the word about their impending arrival. Risse had assumed kennel master duties one day and related the following experience:

> "I told the Vietnamese workers to stay away from the staked out dogs, but of course with our language barrier I could only hope they understood me. As I was sitting in my tent watching them work I noticed a man attempting to walk between the staked out dogs. The dogs were watching him as well. I yelled for him to stop, but it was too late. One of the dogs jumped out at him and as the worker tried to get away, he jumped closer to another dog on the other side. The dog bit him on the arm throwing him to the ground. I ran out to the kennel area and tried to separate the dog from the man. The man was hitting the dog with a handsaw, trying to free himself from the dog's jaws. I grabbed both the dog and the man and pulled them apart. The dog was none too happy about it either. The bite only left some small puncture wounds on his arm. He was a very lucky man and knew it. But the villager made it out OK. The dog was quite satisfied with himself…I saw him smiling and saying to me, "See, I can do what you taught me!" [20]

With expiration of operation Top Dog 45 in November 1965, many of the dogs were turned over to qualified handlers already serving a one-year duty tour. Project Limelight was then implemented to bring in more dogs and handlers to be placed at air bases throughout South Vietnam and to provide security at the newer ones being built and expanded. This ascension of dog teams mirrored the overall growth of the American military presence in Vietnam at the time.

Often equipment and materials seldom moved fast enough through the military supply chain to keep up with the ever-increasing number of dog teams entering the country. It was like this in World War II and Korea, and why should Vietnam be any different? This included such essentials as veterinary medicine, kennels, and dog food. Don Poss, a handler with the 366th SPS at Da Nang recalls that toward the end of 1965 kennels were being constructed for the fifty dogs the air force now had on the base, but there was no office building to house the unit staff. This simply meant that personnel would need to appropriate a suitable structure from someone who had one. In this case, an Air Force Colonel went outside channels and grabbed a prefabricated building from the Marines when they weren't looking and quickly had it freshly painted. Poss recalls:

> "Some very irate Marine officers sniffed around the compound scratching their chins and heads while eyeing the newly painted structure, which seemingly resembled one missing from their facility. "Someone absconded with an entire screened structure? Those thieving ARVN bastards...and what you brave Marines have done for their country!...That building? No, no...we've had that building forever..."

Of course the relieving of material goods went on every week, and not just buildings but steaks, beer, and prime rib. Any guilty thoughts were soon cast aside as dictated by the Robin Hood syndrome: "take from the rich and give to the poor" took precedent. The newly painted Air Force K-9 office immediately became known as the "Da Nang Growl Pad."

While the men in Vietnam attacked their immediate day-to-day problems, back in Washington, D.C., the Joint Chiefs of Staff huddled together in their air-conditioned confines to decide what type of men and material were to be sent to Vietnam. Many of their decisions were based upon Westmoreland's recommendations along with his subordinates. This was to be expected, since the chiefs had little acute knowledge about Vietnam and even less on what was to be accomplished there. One suggestion brought forth was to support the infantry troops with professionally trained scout dog teams. This was something that should have been considered and implemented months earlier as American troops entered a more active phase in the defense of South Vietnam.

The official military definition of a scout dog is, "A German shepherd trained to work silently either on or off leash, day or night, to "signal" the handler when it has picked up the presence of nearby dangerous objects or personnel, and to support maneuvering infantry elements in a wide variety of tasks." Quite a job given the official description for a man, but the Army was talking about a dog. Based on this interpretation of scout dog teams by the military, and considering the situation of the ground troops in Vietnam, the conflict not only warranted their employment but in fact demanded it. Vietnam was shaping up to be an entirely different fight than World War II or Korea. If anything, it was more akin to the banana wars that the U.S. participated in during the 1920s and 1930s in Central America or, as previously discussed, the Philippine-American War of 1898. (See pages 25)

Ken Scharnberg (39th IPSD) and his dog Alp cross a shallow stream. Terrain and temperatures varied throughout South Vietnam. A one-year tour of duty gave ample time to sample all weather conditions. *(National Archives)*

As American involvement escalated, so too did the casualties rise and at a very alarming rate. The Viet Cong had changed their tactics very little and, based on their results, had no reason to do so. Since the Americans intervened, Charlie always attacked when everything was to their advantage. More American troops meant an increased opportunity for quick strikes before disappearing into the countryside or blending in with the local populace in a nearby village. Trip wires attached to mines, bamboo whips, and punji pits took their tolls both physically and psychologically on the average American grunt pounding the ground each day.

In Vietnam, small arms fire would be the biggest contributor of fatalities among Army troops. In comparison, booby traps (including mines) accounted for eleven percent of the deaths and fifteen percent of all wounds received. Combat casualties from fragments (grenades and shells) caused thirty-six percent of the deaths and sixty-five percent of the wounds. By contrast, the casualties induced from mines and booby traps during WWII were only three percent and grenades just two percent, while artillery caused the highest amount of casualties against ground troops in both Europe and in the Pacific. These statistics are among the main incentives for the introduction of scout dogs to the Vietnam landscape. [21]

During the summer of 1965, the Joint Chiefs of Staff decided to reactivate the Army scout dog program, using the 26th Infantry Platoon (Scout Dog) under the command of the 197th Light Infantry Brigade at Fort Benning, Georgia. The 197th would be responsible for training four Army scout dog platoons and one for the Marines. USCONARC assumed responsibility and it began as a one-time training requirement assigned to the 1st Battalion, 29th Infantry. As a crash program, a multitude of problems soon arose. Originally planned as a one-shot operation, it appears that the Joint Chiefs still considered Vietnam top be a short-term affair. The training requirements would soon extend beyond the five planned platoons and swelled to twenty-three, and that did not include replacing personnel already in-country along with a newly developed mine-and-tunnel dog program.

Within a couple of years, it would soon play out that the 197th could not accomplish the tasks at hand. More and more experienced officers and NCOs (non-

USMC SGT J.M. Jones and his dog watch a tree line for possible VC movement. *(National Archives)*

commissioned officers) would travel to Vietnam depleting the instructor rank back home. It would be tough to scrape together enough personnel to fill the void and in the upcoming years the 197th earned the nickname "the one-ninety-worst." [22]

The entire program was assigned to Captain Arthur H. Bair, Jr., who had recently returned from assignment in Vietnam. Bair would be immediately assisted by 1st Lieutenant Jack Clark, who was then CO of the 26th IPSD. Bair knew there would be numerous problems right from the start and that the Army never gave the scout dog program serious consideration. Bair stated, "Another indication of the low priority given to this project was the selection of me to head the program. My only qualification for working with dogs was my totally undisciplined Dachshund." [23] Realizing their shortcomings, the brigade asked for a fill of forty-four personnel for the 26th IPSD along with expansion of the veterinary and kennel facilities. This request was cutback to thirty enlisted men and one officer. The 26th at this time comprised just three squads of just six scout dogs each, plus an additional three dogs in case of injury, along with a headquarters element.

This was a confusing arrangement in itself, as the squads had no business within the platoon. A handler and dog, the two beings comprising a scout dog team, is deployed separately to a maneuvering infantry platoon or a company (sometimes battalion)-size unit within the brigade. It was purely administrative on paper, but squad was soon changed to section, and yes, don't forget the dog handler, who at this time, officially at least , was designated a Scout Observer. This was corrected with the new title "Dog Handler." The MOS (Military Occupation Specialty) was also changed from 11 F (Intelligence) to 11 B (Infantry), and the suffix letter "D" to denote dog handler.[24] The new designations appeared appropriate since most scout dog teams would be deployed with active line units and not from intelligence units stationed in the rear. All that can be said is that it's the Army's way of doing things and you can almost say it was a heritage of why keep things simple?

In Vietnam the plan was to have one scout dog platoon assigned to one brigade, or two platoons delegated to a single division and then further assigned to one of the brigades. Ultimate control of the platoons would be at the brigade level and the scout dog platoon headquarter element would also be established at the brigade level. From there, each scout dog team (handler and dog) would be sent out on an "as-needed" basis.

Trained in Just Twelve Weeks

Once again, there is a great disparity between what the Army lays out on paper and the actual implementation of the perceived plan. Starting with the handler, the men were officially considered "volunteers or selected individuals," although in reality this was seldom the case. If someone did not bring motivation to the job and did not understand or like dogs, they would never fully appreciate the limitations and capabilities of the scout dog. You could have the best dog in

A scout dog team during their twelve week training at Fort Benning. The quality of the training varied widely over the years and depended on the knowledge and experience of the instructor. *(National Archives)*

the world on the front end of the leash, but with a misfit at the other end it could easily be a recipe for disaster in the bush.

The other fault was with the training course itself. You have to recognize that it was not a continuous block of instruction involving the dog and handler. There would be in-processing and out-processing of personnel, sick leave for a man or animal, and additional training for the individual who was going overseas. But twelve weeks (compared to eleven weeks for the ARVN program) was never a time period cast in stone. Some dog teams would advance quite quickly while others would need to obtain additional training upon arrival in Vietnam. As learned later in the war, many dog handlers that OJT'd in-country in a much shorter period of time faired quite nicely. In the future, training would be standardized based upon feedback from deployed teams and lessons learned in the field. As platoons spent more time in-country, information about what worked andwhat didn't work would eventually filter back to the instructors at Fort Benning.

The first two weeks of training were spent on basic obedience. The following weeks would be a slow introduction into the scouting role, as defined by the Army's FM 20-20 manual. By the seventh week, night training would commence, with longer patrols carried out and the integrated teams working with helicopters. Specialized training, such as river crossings, rappelling, and ambush techniques, were implemented during the final weeks of the course. Although there was an acute shortage, seasoned instructors were required to

Bunkers such as this one are often difficult to see even in broad daylight from a short distance away. Scout dogs would often alert to these structures even if they were not inhabited at the time. *(Courtesy of Joseph Ertel)*

Rappelling from a helicopter sometimes became a necessity in Vietnam when inserting a scout dog team. If no landing zone was established, a dog was often extricated via this method. *(National Archives)*

pull off this type of training. One of the first things Captain Bair did was to locate and acquire the right personnel for the job. The most prominent among this group was SFC Jesse Mendez.

Mendez would become a legendary figure to those handlers who would pass through the gates at Fort Benning in the upcoming years. Born in 1928, Mendez found his home in the Army, and in particular with military working dogs. Having pulled three tours with the ARVN as a scout dog advisor, Bair managed to acquire perhaps the best possible person to become Chief Instructor for the scout dog school at Benning.

While working as an ARVN advisor, Mendez would routinely accompany the teams he trained out in the field. This practice was never advocated by higher officials, yet the experience gained could never be duplicated in the classroom. Mendez also kept meticulous records and was responsible for writing the bulk of the training manuals and establishing how best to train the dogs and men.

It was decided that the Marines would be the first to obtain scouts dogs on an official basis for use in Vietnam. Being out of the scout dog business since the end of WWII, the Marines would have to take their lessons from the Army, unlike their fathers before them who acquired their skills at Camp Lejune before engaging the Japanese in many Pacific battles during the WWII. Of course, once trained, these dog teams would be sent up north to I Corps near the DMZ. As the Army began to formulate plans for sending over their own scout dog teams, their deployment would depend on at least two factors: the geography of Vietnam and where Charlie was expected to be found.

The Landscape of Vietnam

Understanding the deployment of dog teams in Vietnam, how they could be used, and what obstacles they faced are irresistibly tied to the climate and the terrain to be encountered, as well as the routes taken by the Viet Cong and NVA who filtered into the south. The size of the country and its distance from the United States poised their own set of problems for transporting men and materials.

South Vietnam is considered tropical and lies between the equator and the Tropic of Cancer. It is often pounded by heavy rains during the summer monsoon season, that begins in May or June and ends in October, with an average annual rainfall in the lowland areas of about seventy-nine inches. During these months, an occasional typhoon could also be encountered. The heat can be oppressive and the high humidity debilitating from March to October, but temperatures did not fluctuate much for most of the country. November to January is considered the cool, dry season, and February to April or May the hot, dry season.

A chain of mountains known as the Central Highlands is north of Saigon. The plateau is a series of rugged mountain peaks ranging from 2,900 to 7,400 feet,

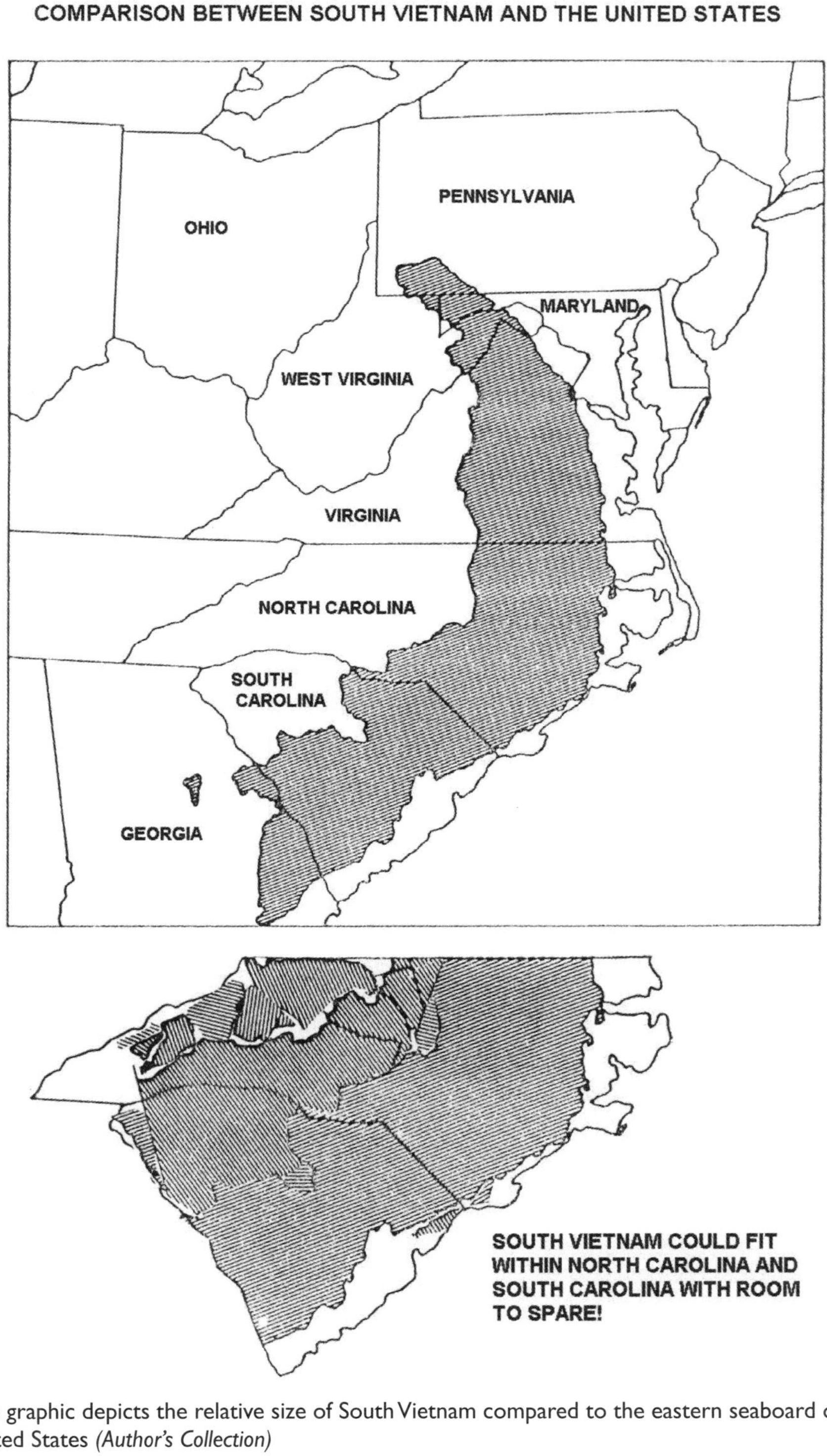

This graphic depicts the relative size of South Vietnam compared to the eastern seaboard of the United States *(Author's Collection)*

with extensive forests and rich soil ideal for growing vegetables. Temperatures remain fairly cool here, varying between sixty-three degrees in the winter and sixty-eight degrees in the summer. This area is sparsely populated and is principally inhabited by an indigenous people known as the Montagnards (mountain people or mountaineers) by the Americans, or "moi" or "savages" by the general Vietnamese population.

There were about a million Montagnards living in these remote regions during the wartime, and attempts to recruit them came from both the Americans and North Vietnamese. The vast majority sided with the Americans, under the direction of the CIA or the U.S. Fifth Special Forces Group. The Montagnards were instrumental at times in preventing Communist forces from infiltrating easily into the South via the Ho Chi Minh trail. [25]

The mountainous areas covered about the same amount of territory as the lowlands, which bordered the South China Sea and the Gulf of Tonkin. It was here where most of the population resided, primarily engaged in agriculture or fishing. Saigon was, and still remains, the primary urban center. South of the city is the Mekong Delta, a major rice-growing region, with extensive swamps, jungle, and forests. Some of the heaviest fighting could be found here and the Viet Cong controlled most of the northern half of this region for the duration of the war.

From the mountains to the lowlands, a common link for transportation, supplies, and economic support was the Ho Chi Minh trail. This was a network of roads, bridges, and footpaths that stretched from North Vietnam, through eastern Laos, and into the delta region of South Vietnam. As early as 1963, over 5,000 Communist troops were assigned to the trail, which was eventually lengthened to more than 800 miles.

The trail was a supply route that was constantly under attack by the American military, starting with infantry operations (like "Leaping Lena" in 1964) and Air Force bombing campaigns (that began with Rolling Thunder in 1965). Relay stations and splinter trails could be found as the road swung south, and it was at these junctions that infantry units and their accompanying scout and tracker dog platoons eventually positioned themselves. [26]

3

Joe, the Dog, and Charlie

"Our numbers have increased in Vietnam because the aggression of others has increased in Vietnam. There is not, and there will not be, a mindless escalation."

President Lyndon B. Johnson

1966 and the War Heats Up

In the early days of 1966, not much had changed in Vietnam since the previous year. The Army and Marines had no shortage of battles or bloody operations with names like Crimp, Van Buren, and Masher/White. The toll so far in American lives was 2,337. After the military launched these actions and with the temporary conclusion of hostilities, the glowing reports with their attached body counts were often spelled out during the Saigon daily news briefing. This exercise took place in front of reporters in an event dubbed the "five o'clock follies." [1] By the spring of 1966, Westmoreland was looking for 16,000 more troops, President Johnson was hoping for a little peace, and for the guys already in-country just a chance to come back to the states in one piece. There were already about 181,000 troops seeing action and by the end of the year another 194,000 would be added. Back home, Senator Strom Thurmond was in Washington, D.C. calling for the use of nuclear weapons in Vietnam if no other way was possible to win the war. Meanwhile, Montana Senator Mike Mansfield advised President Johnson that a military victory was just not in the cards.

It is incredible to witness how each end of the combat scale would be implemented to achieve a perceived American victory in this Southeast Asia guerilla conflict. On the one hand there was massive bombing north of the DMZ with thousands of pounds of explosives raining the countryside. Then at the same time on any given day you could find a scout dog and handler leading twenty-four men on a patrol through the jungle on a small search and destroy mission or perhaps a tunnel rat holding a 45-caliber pistol and crawling underground in a VC sanctuary. This pendulum swing of force that exerted itself daily in Vietnam would ultimately continue every day and every month for the entire course of the war.

While Thurmond looked for mushroom clouds on the horizon, stateside in Washington a Senate report estimated that the North Vietnamese could field just 59,000 "full time" guerillas. God only knows how many guys took up the job on a part time basis. What the well dressed within the Washington belt said had little if no impact on the day-to-day operations in Vietnam; the fighting still went on, men continued to bleed, and the body bags kept coming home occupied. Already 205,000 troops were in Vietnam and President Johnson was being pressured to commit more. Apparently some of these reinforcements would include sentry and scout dog teams, some American dog teams were working in RVN already and the first stateside-trained Marine scout dog platoon was finishing up their twelve-week course at Fort Benning and was about to join the fray.

In the earlier stages of the conflict, Marines on patrol worked with dogs from the Provisional Scout Dog Platoon and sometimes dogs attached to an ARVN scout dog unit. Many of these missions out in the field usually lasted from two to four days. There were plenty of successful operations but also ones that yielded poorer results. In Operation Orange, during March of 1966, scout dogs were employed in the Quang Nam Province as part of search and destroy operations conducted by Marines and it was specifically noted that they worked "...without notable success." According to the after-action report it was determined that the dogs'

These dogs are being worked around a smoke grenade so that they will be accustomed to the sight and smell. *(National Archives)*

performance was hampered by the extreme heat and large amounts of powder and WP (white phosphorus) residue in the area. [2]

At this juncture of K-9 operations in Vietnam, one of the immediate problems in the field stemmed from the language barrier between the ARVN handler and the Marine patrol leader. Hand signals and Pidgin English (simplified speech) didn't always cut it out in the bush. As reported in monthly combat reports, the results were considerably better when the ARVN handler understood some English, because few United States Marines acquired a working knowledge of the Vietnamese language. Even with the communication deficiencies the Marines on the whole valued any scout dog team, even if it was a South Vietnamese one. Seeing what the ARVN could do, a couple of Marine units attempted to retrain several of their own sentry dogs and transition them more into a patrol and scouting role. It was a haphazard approach to training. The men knew they wanted a better dog as a final product, they just didn't know how to accomplish the task.

The first formally trained Marine scout dog platoon arrived in DaNang on 1 March 1966 and came under the command of 1Lt. Robert Wilder. This is of historical importance, since it had been more than twenty years since the Marines deployed scout dogs overseas in a wartime environment. On the downside, they would be the first platoon to go through a scout dog training class at Fort Benning with instructors who had limited combat experience. Wilder kept to standard operating procedures and he made no deployments during the first month in-country, thus allowing time for the dogs to acclimatize to the heat and humidity that they soon would be laboring in. Construction work also began at the location for a new kennel area by clearing brush and installing a drainage ditch.

As the end of the first month approached, Wilder sent out word to his superiors that the scout dog teams would soon be ready for deployment. He also began to push commanders for night patrols as he found the dogs worked best with cooler temperatures. In fact he wanted to see them used almost exclusively at night, just like the scout dogs that worked patrols during the Korean War. However, the tactics of the enemy in Korea compared to those in Vietnam were entirely different. Although he was an officer, Wilder was just as green and inexperienced as the newly arrived handlers were. Scout dogs in general were more efficient in their jobs at night, but there were many other factors to take into account.

The young lieutenant may have based his idea of nocturnal maneuvers on the assessment of K-9 operations in Korea. But scout dog patrols in Korea and Vietnam were a world apart. A major reason was the terrain on which the fighting took place. Korea had a lot of open country and any reconnaissance patrol could easily be spotted during the day. There were also few booby traps or trip wires to contend with from Chinese communists as patrols scouted terrain during the night.

In Vietnam, few units were willing to go out at night since many areas were heavily booby-trapped; it was trouble enough during the day in a heavy jungle or dense brush, never mind at night with no visibility of the trail ahead of you. One exception was the use of dog teams employed after sundown on fixed LPs (listening posts). Here patrol members were not required to cast about in the dark looking for the enemy, but instead waited for the bad guys to come to them. In many parts of the country it was difficult enough to see just a few meters ahead during daylight hours in heavy triple-canopied jungle. Like every commanding officer (CO) new to the field, Wilder had to learn exactly what the dog teams needed to deal with and capitalize on their strengths while working around their many weaknesses.

And one of those vulnerabilities was the firearm carried by the handler. At this time many handlers carried a Colt .45 semi-automatic pistol and relied on their rifle-carrying coverman for protection. It would be a while before the majority of handlers were issued something more substantial, like an M-16 or CAR-15 rifle.

So during the month of April 1966, the results by Wilder's teams seemed very impressive as over fifty booby traps were found along with more than one hundred VC suspects who were hiding in tunnels. These facts were based on fifteen dog team commitments sent into the bush with most of the time spent searching villages and tunnels. Although the dog teams spent a maximum of just five days in the field, two dogs died of heatstroke out in the field. Wilder noted that, "...these dogs were easily excitable and would not remain calm during the heat of the day as most other dogs." Yet with just a month into operations Wilder was reporting a few other nagging problems. Some dogs were beginning to tire and get run down easily. Hookworm infestation increased dramatically along with a "weird" skin fungus that was appearing on several dogs. After a couple of months in-country the Marines were still waiting for permanent kennels to be built and better veterinary support. In what would be a prophetic statement for hundreds of dogs that participated in the war, Wilder wrote in a report, "The sooner the dogs are put in cement type kennels [pads] and off the ground, the greater chance they'll have in their everlasting battle with parasites that inhabit the dirt in the Republic of Vietnam." It was also noted in the same report that quite a few dogs seemed to be disinterested in their work after spending several days in the field. Wilder later stated, "The quality of food available is also a health hazzard (sic) for the dogs (C-Rations and Prime)." [3]

Parts of Vietnam featured heavy jungle vegetation. In many cases it was difficult to negotiate during the day and impossible at night. *(Courtesy of Joseph Ertel)*

In the beginning of June, the permanent kennels for the Marines were finally finished. Three dogs checked in with heartworm infestation and were sent down to Saigon for further treatment. Surgery was required for a dog that had tripped a booby trap. All four dogs were expected back on duty within a month. Basic supplies such as flea powder, rectal thermometers, and decent food had yet to be delivered. Even with the health problems encountered, fifteen commitments were made during the month involving 47 scout dog teams.

It was during July that the first Marine scout dog was killed in action. [4] Handler LCpl Alfredo Salazar and Kaiser had already worked about thirty combat patrols. During a search and destroy mission with "D" Co., First Marines, the VC hit the patrol with grenades and heavy automatic fire. Out in front on point, Kaiser was the first to drop. The platoon hit back hard as Salazar knelt next to the shepherd. "He tried to lick my hand," he later said, "and then he died." The Marine motto "leave no man behind" also applied to dogs. The men within the patrol helped carry Kaiser back to camp and buried him in what would become an ever-larger canine cemetery. From that time forward the dog compound became known as Camp Kaiser.

It was also starting to become evident just what a dog is capable of accomplishing and where their deficiencies resided. For instance, many patrols were encountering booby traps comprised of a grenade attached to a vine. Although the dog may alert on the grenade, it is doubtful that he would do the same to a vine or any natural vegetation unless it was an Asiatic odor from the person that

Whenever possible, dogs killed in action were brought back to be interred in local cemeteries. This is one of the USMC cemeteries located west of DaNang. *(National Archives)*

laid the trap or perhaps some sixth sense that many dogs possess within them that things were not quite right on the trail.

Marines also discovered another use for the dogs and one that would never be found in the Army's FM 20-20 manual of scout dog training: the intimidation and interrogation of VC suspects. The first recorded time this took place was during a squad action as part of Operation Coronado on 7 August 1966. A scout dog team worked a small village consisting of women, children, and old men who lived in one-room huts with hard dirt floors. As was typical during a large-scale operation, Charlie would have fled and perhaps leave behind a straggler or two. The villagers, scared both of the VC and the Americans, hid in their hootches, bomb shelters, or nearby caves. It often proved futile for the Americans to coax them out, even with an ARVN interpreter that came along and yelled at them in Vietnamese. Yet once the handler cajoled his dog to growl and bark at the entrance, each hiding spot seemed to empty in seconds. As it turned out (and it didn't take long for the Marines to discover) the Vietnamese were frightened not just of them but also of the big German shepherd dogs they brought with them.

The dogs also proved quite useful during interrogation of VC suspects, actually much more effective than other methods employed in the past. A typical scene would come together like this: if the Marines believed that the person was indeed VC but not cooperating, a handler and scout dog team would be called in. Held on a tight lead the dog would be induced to lunge at the suspect, barking and growling with a good show of teeth and spittle. Often this had a desirable effect for the interrogator and the suspect VC would turn in his own mother to get away from the dog. Many Vietnamese had an unnatural fear of large canines. The majority of dogs in-country that the people were familiar with were small mutts, not large intimidating German shepherds that could easily weigh as much as a local peasant. This type of tactic took place throughout the war as deemed necessary by the patrol leader. This was done at the local command level and was never formally accepted by military commanders nor was it ever listed as part of any training regimen.[5]

It was not just the Marine scout dog teams that were seeing action around this time. At a small Hawk missile site near Chu Lai, Anthony Giorgi and his sentry dog, Spade (3A43), began their post patrol slightly after midnight. [6] The pair had flown from Lackland AFB together in February and were in-country for just a few weeks. It was only the second time the pair had worked this post. Armed with a shotgun and .45 caliber pistol, Giorgi placed a leather working collar on Spade and started their nightly routine by whispering, "Watch'em boy. Let's get 'em." [7]

They had walked no more than thirty feet when Spade immediately alerted. The dog jumped to the left and pulled his handler another ten feet and face-to-face with a VC hiding in the bushes. Spade grabbed the enemy's leg and Giorgi leveled the shotgun firing point blank. The blast blew the VC backwards killing him instantly. Giorgi would later state, "All the training, love, and faith I had in Spade paid off that night. He saved my life…" [8]

During these first critical months of American involvement it became evident that even though all dogs appeared to acclimatize to the heat in a couple of weeks,

The HAWK was initially designed to destroy aircraft and later adapted to destroy other missiles in flight. The missile entered service in 1960, and a program of extensive upgrades has kept it from becoming obsolete, although it was never used in combat. *(Courtesy of Rick Schurette)*

some would never be able to cope with the extreme temperatures for a long period of time. Handlers also needed to quickly recognize the onset of heatstroke in the dogs that could occur after working just a few hours on patrol. A few problems arose simply because dogs were unfamiliar with certain situations, such as the use of shotguns and flares by patrol members. The last thing anyone needed to have happen was for a dog to start barking after a flare was popped up during a nighttime ambush. This information also needed to be passed on to future dog teams that would soon be arriving. In September, the Marines fielded the Second Sentry Dog Platoon in DaNang and were followed a month later by the Second Scout Dog Platoon.

For the Air Force sentry dog teams posted throughout Vietnam, a problem was encountered, not the enemy outside of the wire but friendly officers inside checking on the local situation. At Cam Ranh Bay Air Base in February of 1966, Airman 1C Bill Atwell patrolled nightly with Shadow (0A10). One night after immediately being posted, the pair swept the area to make sure it was clear of unfriendlies. After a few minutes a jeep approached and Atwell yelled "halt" and issued a challenge, knowing full well that it wasn't the enemy but still required to follow procedures. It turns out the occupants were an Australian officer and his driver.

Atwell and Shadow approached the jeep and the leftenant (U.S. equivalent of a Captain) asked, "Don't you salute an officer when reporting on post?" Atwell replied, "No, unless ordered to do so." The leftenant replied, "Airman I order you to salute me when reporting to your post." [9] Atwell saluted and the officer returned the compliment. So too did Shadow who saw the officer's hand go up.

The dog growled and leaped up grabbing his arm as Atwell immediately shouted out the release command. "Sir," Atwell said, "That is why dog handlers don't salute when reporting to their post." Atwell and probably every other handler at Cam Ranh Bay did not have the opportunity to meet another officer during their nightly patrol for at least the next three months.

Within a few weeks of his arrival Wilder was replaced by 1Lt. Ronald Neubauer. In one of his first reports, Neubauer stated that, "Everyone wants our scout dogs, although people have to be convinced that the dogs will be a positive use to them. Once a unit uses our dogs they always come back for more. At times, requests have to be turned down because of the limited number of dogs available."

What Neubauer soon learned, just like many platoon officers in World War II did, was that a lot of field commanders did not know the best tactical advantage for employing scout dogs. At first they were simply a curiosity or considered an unnecessary burden on the battlefield, but once they proved themselves they became a hot commodity in I Corps.

The Army quickly followed on the heels of the Marines and landed their first two scout dog platoons at the beginning of the monsoon season in June 1966. These were the 25th IPSD supporting the 1st Calvary Division and the 35th IPSD supporting the 1st Infantry Division. The 35th landed at Tan Son Nhut as planned. For some unexplained reason, the 25th went directly to Qui Nhon, bypassing a physical examination by the doctors at the 936th Veterinary Detachment. The following month the 38th IPSD attached to the 25th Infantry Brigade set up shop in Cu Chi, and a week later 39th IPSD arrived and was attached to the 173rd Airborne Brigade.

Hill 724, which hosted a HAWK missile site is a good example that shows Vietnam was not just one big jungle. *(Courtesy of Rick Schurette)*

USMC sentry dog handler Rick Schurette and his dog King (1A83) take a break at their base camp in DaNang. In the background is Hill 327 that hosted a HAWK missile battery where the dog team often patrolled. *(Courtesy of Rick Schurette)*

SSGT. Mike Konthawski (38th IPSD) indicates an alert from his scout dog Kelly. Every dog alerted differently and it was up to the handler to interpret the signal and pass the information onto the patrol. *(National Archives)*

The 38th IPSD established permanent kennels for their dogs. Housing for all military dogs varied widely throughout the course of the war. *(National Archives)*

Like many scout dog platoons to follow, the 25th IPSD Commanding Officer, Lt. Teddy Hampton, began to have his platoon acclimatize the dogs to the tropical heat and provide some refresher training before moving north to Phouc Vinh. There is little doubt the handlers also needed to adjust to the rain, heat, and oppressive humidity as much as the dogs did.

In the beginning of August, several dog teams from the 25th accompanied a 200-man company of the 1st Cav on a major search and destroy operation. As is so often typical in such endeavors, no enemy was to be found, or so it would appear. Things changed drastically on 9 August when SP4/C Jerry L. Brown saw his dog Tiger (3A17) pull up short on the trail and alerted. Brown shoved two accompanying riflemen down and

In many instances a dog's transport crate would be modified to serve as a kennel. This was not desirable, but often a necessity. *(Courtesy of Gary Zemel)*

Not all scout dogs teams were mobilized by helicopters. Many scout dog teams were transported by armored personnel carriers (APC) which was a variant of the M-113. Introduced in 1960, the APC carried 11 personnel and one driver. *(National Archives)*

then spun around to see Tiger take several VC rounds. Brown dove down himself and tried to pull Tiger by his leash toward him and received a bullet in his hip for the effort.

Tiger had alerted to a VC ambush just 1200 feet away. Lt. Hampton later stated, "After Tiger gave the alert, the company swung left and hit just the trailing edge of the ambush." Artillery and then helicopters were called in, effectively neutralizing the enemy and fortunately the infantrymen of the 1st Cav received only light casualties. Interrogation of a VC prisoner later revealed that Charlie assembled about 300 men for the botched ambush that was broken up by Brown and his scout dog, Tiger.

In just a couple of months, the 25th conducted over 300 patrols in Ia Drang Valley action and accounted for forty-one NVA soldiers captured along with seventy VC suspects. With the loss of Tiger, it appeared that the VC would attempt to make the first sniper hit on the scout dog or handler, a fact to be proved out on numerous occasions in the upcoming years. The VC understood by this time that the Americans had many men to engage in combat and just a limited number of dogs available in the field.

The 39th IPSD touched down at Tan Son Nhut on 26 July 1966 for a couple of days before moving out to Bien Hoa. Nothing was set up yet, but they were in an ideal position, as the platoon was inside the sprawling base perimeter. Army engineers quickly started to lay out the concrete footings that became a set of top-notch kennels. A hydrant was even provided so that a hose could be attached and the runs could be washed down efficiently.

Among the dogs that comprised that 39th was Budda (4A82), who had the typical temperament and about the same disposition as most of the German shepherds in Vietnam. Budda was handled by Sgt Robert (Brownie) Brown and within a few months the pair was entrenched in a host of operations, including Operation Sioux City, Attleboro, Cedar Falls, and Junction City. Budda was regarded as a top-notch scout dog, but his mark on history would be his longevity. Through skill, courage, luck, and having the right handler at the other end of the leash, Budda would dodge bullets and booby-traps, disease and accidents, and survive—even though he was wounded three times. He managed to do this with eight different handlers over a period of five years, longer than any other scout dog in Vietnam. As one handler later noted, "He bravely served his country for the "human equivalent" of over 40 years." Like so many other dogs, Budda was destined to never come home.

Operation Safeside

Coinciding with the introduction of Army and Marine scout dogs in Vietnam was the execution of a new test program by the Air Force dubbed "Safeside." Prior to the implementation of Safeside, the defense of air bases in RVN was two-fold; the USAF took care of everything within the perimeter, and beyond that security was to be maintained by either elements of the Army or in the case of DaNang, the Marines. Safeside was a crash program that bypassed many established staff procedures. It would change the current method of how to extend the security perimeter surrounding the area around the bases for which the Air Force would ultimately be responsible. It was designed to be a permanent, independent, mobile, and quick reaction force. Designated as the 1041st Security Strike Force, a small portion of the 226-man team roster would involve Air Force dog handlers but with one significant difference; they would be working scout dogs, not sentry dogs.

The test program called for fifteen handlers to be trained with fresh dogs. Recruitment for the new dog teams began in April of 1966. All handlers were honor graduate students from the Lackland AFB Sentry Dog School and were pulled from various locations within CONUS. For many handlers, like Mike Wenger who walked with King at Beale AFB in California, the initial call for volunteers in April 1966 came as a surprise. As Wenger recalls:

> "I got a call from an Air Force officer who told me that I had been selected to take part in a new operation and asked if I was interested. I really didn't think about

> it. I just said "sure." "Can I take King with me?" No was the reply. King was not the right type of dog for this new mission. At the time I didn't ask too many questions. I was just told that I'd get a new dog. I was pretty upset about that [since] King was a great dog and if I was going off to war I wanted him by my side. But I also wanted to get the best possible training before I went to Vietnam. So I volunteered." [10]

Wenger along with fourteen others received their TDY orders on 24 May 1966 to report to the 3279th School Squadron at Lackland AFB. Few of the guys knew what a scout dog was and for what they would be used. They soon found out as they arrived on 6 June to attend Scout Dog School at Camp Medina, a short distance from Lackland, under the tutelage of Army instructors.

The timing of Operation Safeside, and in particular the K-9 portion, seemed to have arisen at an appropriate moment in the war. Although various sentry dog teams at different bases were blunting probe attempts by the VC, many attacks came from outside the perimeter wire at a significant distance in the form of mortar rounds. As a healthy sign of respect for the sentry dog teams a number of these mortar rounds were specifically directed at kennel areas. Back on 13 April, at least thirteen rounds were received at Tan Son Nhut. The small thirty-man VC unit managed to destroy twelve helicopters and nine planes and inflicted at least

Sentry dogs usually alerted more aggressively to enemy personnel than a scout dog. A sentry dog would be released if deemed necessary by the handler. *(National Archives)*

140 American and South Vietnamese casualties. A week later a mortar barrage was launched at Pleiku. In neither case were handlers or dogs killed, although at Tan Son Nhut, handler A1C Gordon M. Poland took some minor shrapnel wounds. It was attempts exactly of this nature that the Air Force scout dog teams would hope to break up as they set up ambushes for the VC outside the perimeter wire.

The scout dog training was managed by Army instructors from Fort Benning, but conducted at Lackland AFB. After the training, orders were cut on 1 September as "Reassignment to 1041st USAF Security Strike Force Test Sq., Headquarters compound, APO San Francisco, 96321 (Schofield Barracks, Hawaii). Airmen will report TDY enroute to the sentry dog center, Lackland AFB, Texas, to pick up dogs and equipment." According to Wenger, "All of us arrived back at Lackland, got our dogs, put them in temporary shipping crates and left for Hawaii on a C-97. We had fifteen dogs and were told two new handlers [two dropped out during training] would join us in Hawaii."

The plan was to have all elements of the 1041st train as a team for fifteen weeks on the islands. "I felt real good after completing the training," Wenger said. "We were working as a team and I had confidence in myself, my dog [Muggs (4A58)], and the rest of the unit. We were as prepared as we could get. It was time to go on and we were looking forward to it."

An advance group that included the dog handlers landed in Vietnam on 17 December 1966. The balance of the 1041st arrived at Phu Cat Air Base on 25 January 1967. This was the beginning of a six-month test with the mission to "...actively engage the enemy at or beyond the 29 mile base perimeter, preventing enemy access." The squadron was broken into five fire teams denoted as mortar, observation, machine gun, APC, and scout dog sections. Each could work independently if necessary or as a cohesive team. It would only be a couple of days for the newly arrived unit to engage the enemy. Just two days later outpost Arizona was pinned down by small arms fire and the 1041st responded along with a dog team.

During this test period, the scout dog teams participated in fifty-four ambush positions, 430 outposts, and thirty-six patrols, totaling about 4,000 hours of service. This allows for fifty days lost because of handlers sick or injured and forty-one days because of the dogs that were ill. In addition, more than 150 camp security patrols were conducted. For those involved it seemed to be a successful program. Ernie Dewaters remembers going out on patrol one night with his dog and an Air Force enlisted man as backup and related:

> "Goldie (0H27), my shotgun [coverman], and I were heading out to a night LP. We had been in-country for a while and my shotgun was pretty casual. We weren't very far from the base camp and I guess he wasn't so worried. It was dusk and Goldie was out in front of us. He was working off leash and I was trying to keep my eye on him. The shotgun was supposed to back behind me, but he was up next to me talking about something. I saw Goldie stop and move to his right. He disappeared for a moment and then came back into view, but he had turned around and was facing us. I knew he had found something. I started to grab my shotgun and push him behind me, but it was too late.

> His leg hit a trip wire and he got wrapped up in the wire. I told him to stop moving and radioed for help. I walked slowly around to see what else might be about and got Goldie back next to me. When help arrived we traced the wire to a grenade. We were very lucky that night. The grenade pin was not crimped properly and it didn't pull all the way out, so the spoon could not release properly. I was pretty upset at my shotgun and myself. We almost blew ourselves away, even though Goldie had done his job." [11]

Exactly why the 1041st was disbanded remains a bit of a mystery. Dewaters thought it was political or service rivalry. K-9 teams had spent more time training than actually employed in the field. The eleven Air Force scout dogs were also brought home and did not get redeployed to Vietnam. Instead they were used as patrol dogs at Fairchild AFB in Washington. On 21 January 1968, the 1041st was placed under operational management of the Tactical Air Command (TAC) and faded away, eventually morphing into the 82nd Combat Security Wing. [12]

Hunting Down the Viet Cong

Since the beginning of the war, the ability of the Viet Cong to strike and disappear into the local landscape poised an ongoing and frustrating problem that yielded a variety of responses from American forces. This was a guerrilla war on a daunting scale. In the history of the United States military, this type of armed conflict surfaced on many occasions, but the lessons learned seemed to have been lost in a short period of time. Even during the large-scale wars and grand battlefields of World Wars I and II, and the earlier Revolutionary and Civil Wars, guerilla activities often took place. Of course it was more predominant in the Spanish-American War and the so-called *banana wars* that erupted in Central America. As in all these cases counter-measures were typically made on the fly, not entrenched within the standard military framework established. Nor were they ever incorporated into the structure of military operations in future wars.

Guerrilla is a name taken by Spanish civilians who battled the French Army during the 1810-1812 Peninsula campaign of the Napoleonic War. The basic premise was to wear down and harass the enemy allowing conventional forces to mount more effective combat operations. As related earlier, General Emilio Aguinaldo employed the tactic after the failure of his men to successfully engage the United States in conventional warfare. In the 20th century, French resistance members operated as guerrillas against the German Wermacht as part of the Allied offensive during World War II. This included the destruction of railroad lines, disrupting communications, and assassination of German officers. In Vietnam, as with the French earlier, it was the Viet Cong conducting guerilla operations, with the NVA forces assuming the role of the traditional antagonist during large-scale operations.

Scout dog teams only provided a partial response to the problem of locating the Viet Cong. The intent of a scout dog team was not to track and locate the enemy by following a ground scent. After all, the dogs relied mostly on airborne scent, and kept their noses in the air, as they were trained to do. Patrols of this nature did uncover Charlie, but had great difficulty in tracking and then establishing contact with the enemy through rough terrain or thick vegetation over a long distance. The dogs were just not proficient to function in this role.

If Charlie was known to be in a particular area, another response was to simply blanket a suspected enemy position with massive firepower. Air strikes with heavy ordnance and napalm were sometimes effective, much like going after a house fly with a shotgun. If the VC went underground and into one of their labyrinthine tunnel systems, as often found in III Corps area surrounding Saigon and Cu Chi, this method seldom worked. It also yielded no intelligence information on the enemy, found no cache of weapons that could be later used by them, and the effectiveness of these operations could not always be confirmed. Too often after an area was saturated with tremendous firepower, Army personnel simply assumed (often incorrectly) that everyone in the immediate target area was dead.

The concept of tracking the enemy was a new proposition for a modern American Army, but its roots can be traced backed through United States military history to the U.S. Calvary of the 1800s. The Calvary at that time used Indians and Indian-raised whites to function as both guides and forward scouts in hostile territory of the western United States. These scouts knew the local terrain and were usually savvy about the activities of the enemy and how they operated under a given set of circumstances.

The Indian trackers of the time were known as *trailers*. Their effectiveness can certainly be attested to in military lore. General George Crook (1828-1890) found the trailers to be of such potent use against the Apaches in Arizona that he even awarded them their own guidron that consisted of white crossed arrows and a company letter against a red background. [13]

To emulate the American Indian with the ability to follow and locate the enemy, the Army employed Vietnam locals, colloquially know as Kit Carson scouts. Although hostile territory in Vietnam was called Indian country, the Kit Carson scouts were ralliers or Hoi Chanhs—in other words former VC converted to the Allied cause. The men engaged for these operations came from an amnesty program that began in 1963 by the South Vietnamese called Chieu Hoi (Open Arms). Presumably the idea was to convert the rank and file Viet Cong to the RVN side and in the process lower the morale of the ones that remained. This was accomplished through both psychological and monetary means. The ralliers could be very effective and provided a valuable tactical aid to help boost propaganda against North Vietnam. But common sense dictated that the trust bestowed upon them only went so far. Chieu Hoi, no matter what you called it or in what language, promoted treason.

Kit Carson scouts provided just a small piece of the total answer that was deemed necessary. The converted VC scouts were not always available and lacked the basic skills of being able to follow the enemy in the bush. A visual tracker who could follow a physical trail left by a fleeing enemy would be essential. And when no physical evidence could be spotted, a trained dog that could acquire a scent track left behind by enemy personnel would be needed.

A few military personnel considered using tracker dogs early in our involvement in Vietnam. This was seen by the retention of several bloodhounds by the

ARVN at their compound in Tan Thuey Ha and earlier at Go Vap. In April of 1966, MACV discussed the use of bloodhounds but didn't know where they could be procured. A few suggestions came forth about contacting the Justice Department and various U.S. law enforcement agencies to obtain bloodhounds. It was also suggested that SFC Leonard Hardinger, one of the military dog advisors, be brought in for advice. While MACV blindly cast about for answers, little did they know that a civilian by the name of Robert L. Hughes was already working to address the potential use of tracker dogs in Vietnam.

As a representative for the Advanced Research Projects Agency (ARPA), Hughes was based in Singapore. ARPA was a quasi-government agency charged with keeping the United States ahead of its enemies in many technological fields. It is also an organization that probably posted a number of 'black' or covert operations during the Vietnam period. [14] In various confidential memorandums, Hughes was part of "G", the Operational Requirements & Analysis department for FARELF (Far East Land Forces). In 1966 this group would invariably be dealing with problems arising in Vietnam on a daily basis.

Hughes and his people began to collect information on equipment requirements for counterinsurgency operations beginning in November 1965 under the codename "Project Agile." This had involved a complicated trip to Malaysia in January 1966 where he met with British war dog program personnel and a representative from the Royal Malaysian Police. The APRA agent came away with valuable information about the recent counterinsurgency efforts in Borneo by the British and a history in the use of tracker dogs. [15]

On 2 May 1966, Hughes landed in Saigon and two days later met with General William Westmoreland and his staff. In the comfort of air-conditioning afforded those of higher rank, he wove a convincing story of how the British successfully used tracker dogs in many counterinsurgency operations since World War II. Hughes related that toward the end of the war, the British 4th Army needed to mop up pockets of Japanese soldiers. These men were often abandoned on many Pacific islands but still kept fighting on individually as best they could. The British began what was then called *wrecke* patrols to find these hidden pockets of the enemy in caves and tunnels. Small groups of specially trained men literally tracked and hunted down scattered Japanese soldiers through the jungle and dense growth. After following them to their various sanctuaries, they were routed out by machinegun fire, grenades, or flame-throwers. As was often the case with the Japanese during the war, few of the enemy chose to surrender.

The wrecke patrols were so effective that it was one reason the British established the Jungle Warfare School in Johore Bahru, Malaysia, based on the principles they learned during the war. Besides men skilled in the art of tracking in the bush, they also employed tracking dogs. The British favored black Labrador retrievers to follow ground scent trails that eventually led to the enemy. Their success can be noted against many insurgent groups they faced in Malaya, Borneo, Cyprus, and Kenya. Besides the use of tracking dogs, the British often employed their own version of the Kit Carson scout during many of these engagements and operations. [16]

The jungle could engulf and cover men in just a few feet and it was a challenge for both a fleeing enemy and someone trying to locate them. *(Courtesy of Joseph Ertel)*

Westmoreland pounced on the opportunity Hughes provided. He effectively reasoned it would involve a small number of personnel and, better yet, a limited amount of money. A week later, several of Westmoreland's staff members traveled to the Jungle Warfare School in Malaysia. This group included Brigadier General A.E. Cowan, Director of the Joint Research and Test Activity (JRATA); Colonel M.G. Hatch, Commanding Officer of the Army Concept Team in Vietnam (ACTIV); and Captain W.G. Campbell from the USARV. The trio spent three days observing the British methods and how they could help develop US Army tracker teams for Vietnam. To Westmoreland's representatives, Malaysia proved to be the ideal setting for a U.S. tracker school. The country closely resembled many portions of South Vietnam and was only 400 miles south from the fighting across the South China Sea. With the school only located about thirty miles from Singapore, transportation for American trainees could easily be provided.

Of course there would be some minor difficulties—petty problems always seem to abound in the Vietnam conflict. Great Britain, a signatory on the 1954 Geneva Convention declaration that divided Vietnam along the 17th parallel, held an officially neutral stance during the present conflict. Malaysia was also neutral regarding the ongoing war with its neighbor to the north. The neutrality issue was bypassed discreetly with a little diplomatic arm twisting with our allies, followed by the congratulatory pats on the back. An agreement was hammered out that was called the Joint US British Proposal to Train Combat Tracker Teams (CTT) for the US Army, in September 1966. It was then reviewed and approved by Major General H.A. Lacelle, Far East Land Forces (FARELF). This agreement allowed the first fourteen U.S. tracker teams to train in Malaysia. The British and Malayan governments set October 1967 as an initial cutoff date for U.S. forces to be schooled there, which would force the Army to establish a tracker program on its own turf and with their own instructors.

As a ground scenting animal, the Labrador retriever proved to be the best dog for the tracking job. With an easy going nature, great stamina, quiet on the trail, and very loyal, they established themselves as the premier tracking dog. *(National Archives)*

The joint agreement called for a three-phase plan to be developed. First steps involved having the initial teams trained in Malaysia and then deployed to Vietnam for evaluation. Phase two called for an instructional capability to be developed within the US Army. The last phase would be the establishment of a Combat Tracker Team Training Center in either Thailand or if the agreement could be extended in Malaysia. The USARV sought to extend the joint agreement with the British in June 1967, hoping to keep all fourteen tracker teams operational. Some consideration was given to establishing a training center in South Vietnam; but it soon became obvious that a large-enough area with adequate security could not be found. The joint agreement between the two countries was extended until November 1968. It was at this time that the best possible location for a tracking school would be in the United States.

Some of the decision-making personnel knew that the expertise to begin such a program could be found back home with Americans. Of course the Army would have to draw upon civilian personnel to accomplish this task. Even though bloodhounds are used extensively by many police departments throughout the country, the techniques of training and following a track could easily be adapted for the black Labrador retriever. Finding suitable trainers would have been an easy task. Proficient man hunters on the other hand—those with the ability to follow a track left by a human without the benefit of a dog—may be more difficult to locate. The biggest consideration would have been that the British had developed these tracker techniques in a military environment and were successful at it. Based on the future results, the Army got it right.

The USARV decided to go with the British program. This would work out fine for those involved, but the system would weaken in particular areas because of several different factors when training eventually commenced outside Malaysia. Although no one knew it at the time, it also set up a deadly scenario that had the potential to neutralize the entire American military working dog population in Vietnam.

Naturally, much of the organization of the US Army tracker teams developed from the way the British were structured. Their teams comprised ten men, separated into three distinct team elements; command, tracker, and protection. Command consisted of a senior NCO, junior NCO, and signaler. The tracking element consisted of two visual trackers, three cover men, two dog handlers, and two Labrador retrievers. If deemed necessary another cover man and a medic were added to the team.

The US Army followed the British organizational structure but separated the 10-man teams into two five-man teams to better fit the combat profile of activities in Vietnam. The smaller U.S. team size probably stems from the overwhelming use of helicopters for transportation and the limited space they afforded, whereas the British in previous engagements usually walked or picked up ground transportation for whatever distance was required rather than flying.

The training program began in October 1966. The first two tracker teams would also be the evaluation teams once they deployed to Vietnam. Twelve more teams would also be trained. Since the training at the time was classified, the organization structure still needed to be developed. The first fourteen teams trained thus made up Combat Tracker Teams (CTT) 1 to14. The formal organizational structure was approved on 15 February 1968 and this meant a combination of Tracker Platoons (IPCT) and Tracker Detachments (IPDT). The platoons consisted of four five-man teams for each division and detachments of two five-man teams for each separate brigade.

Steps were also taken at this time to constitute a CONUS program and establish an ambitious goal of 80 fully trained tracker dogs by July 1969. After evaluating potential sites, Fort Gordon was selected as the training center and the program designated the United States Military Police School (USAMPS) as the agency to

A group of trackers, their dogs, and instructors, pose for a graduation photograph prior to their deployment to Vietnam. *(Courtesy of SFC Robert Himrod, USA, ret.)*

Working together and silently was an integral part of the combat tracker. Hand signals were often used. *(National Archives)*

Once a Labrador retriever closed in on his quarry, the handler needed a good grip on the leash to keep him in check. *(National Archives)*

Tracker dogs were always be kept on leash in the field. *(National Archives)*

In training scenarios, American personnel often dressed in the same garb as worn by the enemy. *(National Archives)*

run the CTT program. It is unknown why Fort Benning, with a well-established scout dog school already in place, was bypassed in favor of a site that turned out MPs and sentry dog handlers. By 1968, 200 officers and men were authorized to begin training. A special request for British and New Zealand experts to begin the training program at Fort Gordon was also approved at this time.

The British also provided the first tracker dogs for the American teams. In contrast to the German shepherd scout dogs, black or yellow Labrador retrievers were the breed of choice. The retrievers typically had a gentle and docile temperament and they could withstand a reasonable amount of heat and humidity. They also excelled at ground sniffing dead scents, compared to the airborne-scenting German shepherd scout dogs. For this reason, scout dogs sometimes accompanied tracker teams, since they could detect a live scent at a further distance much faster than the retrievers. They kept many a tracker team from literally walking right into the enemy.

The Labrador retrievers are very bright and begin training at about two years of age. Their easy-going temperament also means a trouble-free transition period between handlers. Like any other loyal dog, the retriever might attack if there is an immediate danger to his handler. Although typically ground sniffers acquiring a human scent, they also alerted to trip wires, mines, booby-traps, and of course live scents. These dogs gained immediate respect from the men, since they often could make the difference between life and death for the entire combat tracker platoon. The first three dogs were supplied by the British, at a cost of about $1,800 each, were named Sambo (5A15), Lucky (1383) and Bruce (5201). [17]

Dog kennels were built at Fort Gordon, Georgia after the British disengaged themselves from the initial training period.*(National Archives)*

As a specialized team, these platoons had distinct missions. First and foremost was the re-establishment with an enemy after either friendly or enemy units broke an initial contact. Tracker teams not only hunted the VC, but also tried to determine their movements, number of personnel, and even their morale based on the clues left behind. The CT platoon would only engage the enemy for its own self-defense. Once enemy contact is made, a follow-up infantry unit usually took over from the CT platoon to engage the enemy. All operations were conducted during daylight hours. Obviously the dogs could scent just as well at night (if not better), but there would be no visual support clues the team would be able to follow. The probability of tripping a booby-trap was quite high for anyone traveling at night over unknown terrain. It was also imperative to deploy the team quickly to follow a fresh track.

Since a lot of territory needed to be covered by just a few teams, often it would be a long stretch of time before a tracker unit arrived. A good example of this took place on 23 June 1967, when CTT #6 was called in by an element of the 9th Division. Although the track was twelve hours old, the visual trackers were able to identify the enemy's pathway and the dog picked up the scent. The enemy even used evasive maneuvers by walking along a rocky stream bed. The team located the enemy base camp, at which time they withdrew and called in artillery. Although quite difficult, many teams did manage on occasion to follow an enemy track that was more than 24-hours old.

Dogs were only one part of the tracking component and were not always used out in the field during an operation. The tracker students would need to learn how to use the "bush arts" developed by the British over a period of many years. With diplomatic problems brushed aside, a net would be cast out to draw-in a suitable number of volunteers and then set them up for a rigorous training schedule that would soon take place in remote sections of Malaysia. To maintain the charade of British neutrality, Army volunteers could not simply board a military aircraft and fly directly to Malaysia. Steve Craddick was in-country and volunteered as a dog handler. He recalls the day when he and about twenty other soldiers were sent to an MP compound near Saigon:

> "A couple of days later we were given $100 in U.S. currency and told to buy some civilian clothes in Saigon. After getting our clothes we had our photos taken in white t-shirts, with no dog tags. We were then told to turn our gear into supply, which left us only with civilian clothing. The next morning we boarded a truck to the airport and off we went in a civilian aircraft. All this time we were not told what was going on or why.
>
> On the plane we were issued red passports, with the pictures that had been taken the day before and visas to Singapore and Malaysia. We were listed as civilian construction workers! We landed in Malaysia and were taken to a military compound with an overhead sign that stated BRITISH JUNGLE WARFARE SCHOOL." [18]

Problems Keep Cropping Up

By November 1966, the two Marine scout dog platoons participated in eleven major operations that characterized both the strengths and weaknesses of the dogs.

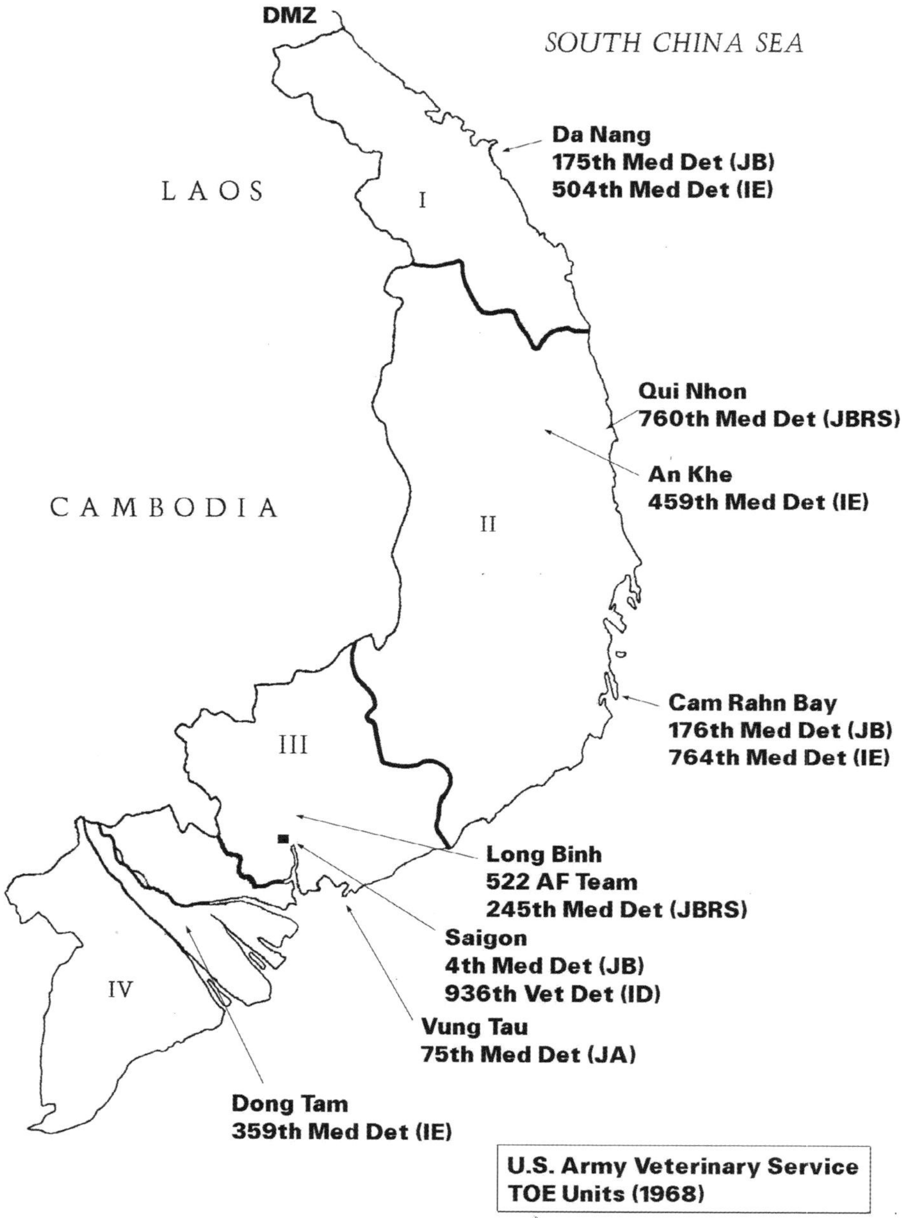

The Army Veterinary Corps was spread thoughout South Vietnam and usually close to the scout and tracker dog teams they were responsible for. *(Author's Collection)*

[19] Lt. Neubauer, reporting on activities, stated, "It has been estimated that well over 2,000 Marine lives have been saved since the insertion of the 1st Scout Dog Platoon into Vietnam." How accurate this statement is or how Neubauer made his estimate cannot fully be determined, but odds are it's a bit inflated.

The Marines ran into several problems that could easily be corrected during future training in CONUS. In training all personnel ahead of the patrols were considered hostile. In Vietnam, especially when entering a village, dogs alerted to civilians and VC as well. This meant the patrol leader needed to clear the village of civilians first and only then could the dogs effectively alert on the enemy or suspect VC. The early training thousands of miles away at Fort Benning did not consider the possibility of domestic and farm animals present in villages. Water buffalo, chickens, pigs, and other animals easily distracted the military dogs, and some went a step further wanting to cut loose and give the animals a good chase.

At first, infantrymen who were not knowledgeable about the scout dog teams distrusted the handlers and dogs. This viewpoint quickly changed after the experience of a few patrols with scout dogs out in front, which was called "working the point." It also manifested the major flaw with the concept of working scout dogs in the field; patrol members often became overconfident and many felt invincible when they had a dog team along. The scout dogs were supposed to instill confidence in patrols, but not to the point where they extinguished common sense. Their fallibility became all too apparent as dogs inadvertently tripped booby-traps or became so exhausted that they were no longer interested in working. Some dogs were not good on locating trip wires, often walking through them while in training. Like humans, each dog possessed unique characteristics and abilities that needed to be understood by the handler. They were far from flawless and when a dog failed to alert on a booby trap, one of four scenarios occurred: 1) Someone else spotted the ordinance. 2) The dogs inadvertently tripped a wire. 3) Someone else in the patrol hit the trip wire. 4) Everyone missed the booby trap entirely and continued on with their patrol.

The flood of dogs into South Vietnam brought forth a host of other problems. The buildup was so rapid during 1966 that the supply chain and veterinary support could not keep up with the needs of the dog teams in-country. Dog food supplies did not always follow the proper shipment routes and handlers often had to scrounge meals for their canine companions. With the scout dogs scattered among the different Corps areas, and sometimes shifting areas of operation, supplies were often misdirected or lost altogether.

Established kennel facilities were almost nonexistent in many areas, and many dogs spent several months housed in their shipping crates. Sometimes corrugated metal drainage pipes were cut in half and used for housing. About four feet long, they provided shade and little else. With the dogs constantly on the ground, hookworms became rampant and infected almost forty percent of the dogs in some platoons. Without proper housing with the ability to keep the dogs off the moist ground, hookworms could be controlled a bit with medication but were not eliminated. Although a big effort was made during 1966 to get dogs out into the field where they were needed, medical problems cut down the number of dogs available for missions. It seems that no one bothered to design a portable kennel that could be used in a tropical climate and there were none available in the entire United States military inventory.

The ARVN were having there own problems. As 1966 rolled along, their canine population was cut down to just eighty sentry dogs and fifty scout dogs. They procured another 210 during the year, but never came close to the 1000 dogs originally envisioned by MACV. The death rate for ARVN dogs was about twice that of American dogs and heat exhaustion and malnutrition were the prime reasons.

Veterinary support at this time was also spotty. Stan Johnson was a Navy Corpsman with the 1st Marine Division stationed at Chu Lai, where he worked triage at the base hospital. Often it was a situation of separating the living from the dead and to mop up the blood from the aftermath of battle. One afternoon a call came in. "...chopper with two wounded." Johnson had no idea what he should prepare for but was totally taken aback when the stretcher-bearers came through the doors carrying a wounded dog. A few moments later an Air Force enlisted man walked through the doors on his own legs with some shrapnel wounds and simply asked, "How's my dog?" Johnson then realized that these two were a team.

Both dog and handler received shrapnel wounds, but nothing life threatening. The medical crew debrided their wounds and set up iodeform drains. The handler then got a tetanus shot, streptomycin, and penicillin as antibiotics. For the dog the wounds were first cleaned and bandaged. Since no one had any veterinary background, it was decided to administer the same medication to the dog that the handler received, but with the dosage altered based on its weight. Once patched up, the two needed to stay for a night of observation, but Johnson couldn't decide on where to keep the dog. The handler interjected and said, "Either the dog stays with me or I stay with the dog." Both slept on adjoining cots in the medical-surgical war.

The quality of dog housing varied throughout South Vietnam. Kennels depended upon obtaining the proper materials and labor. Ideally, permanent kennels built on a concrete pad helped maintain a dog's overall medical condition. *(Courtesy of Rick Schuette)*

When permanent kennels were not available, sections of galvanized drainage pipes were cut in half to serve as shelter for scout dogs. *(Courtesy of Joseph Ertel)*

The following day someone came by with a supply of Purple Hearts, something that the military never ran out of. The officer placed one on the handler but walked past the dog. "I never could figure out that one," Johnson stated. "Didn't the dog serve as admirably as his handler? My impression of the dog and his handler was that there was a great bond that is seldom seen between men in the same unit. Maybe it's because the dog is just simply loyal and the handler knows that and loves him for it. I do know it was a unique relationship unlike any other. I envied that." [20]

During the war, veterinary services were provided by both the Army and the Air Force. The services operated independently and sometimes overlapped. In retrospect it would have been more advantageous to have a single service offering medical care to all the military working dogs. The Army had more veterinarians available and spread out in a larger area. In 1967, the Air Force fielded just ten veterinarians stationed at the major airbases and, like their Army counterparts, were responsible for the dogs, sanitation, and sometime local civic actions. This was certainly an area that may have been condensed, thus offering better support for the dogs.

Another dilemma encountered for the dogs was the necessity that they be fed daily, preferably twice each day. And although the relationship between dogs and the military goes back officially to 1942, the government still could not get some of the basic necessities right. With thousands of dogs worldwide, the United States military for the most part provided inferior food. It was often kept in the delivery system too long (sometimes up to a year) and in many cases was rancid or weevil-infested. This became so bad at one point that it took the deaths of eight sentry dogs at Tan Son Nhut, caused by spoiled food, before some action would be taken. Both the Army and Air Force inspected and purged their inventory of spoiled food and improved the storage facilities where necessary.

The Veterinary Corps provided a great service in Vietnam, often under trying circumstances. Although overworked and understaffed, they are still responsible for not eliminating the problem with dog food, a problem that had been around sporadically since 1959. The dog food manufacturer was also part of the difficulty, and indifference by the military contributed significantly to this nagging problem. In 1966, thousands of pounds of dog food were destroyed in RVN because it was infested with insects, moldy, or broken down to a powder-like substance with no nutritional value. The influx of dogs into the war created food shortages

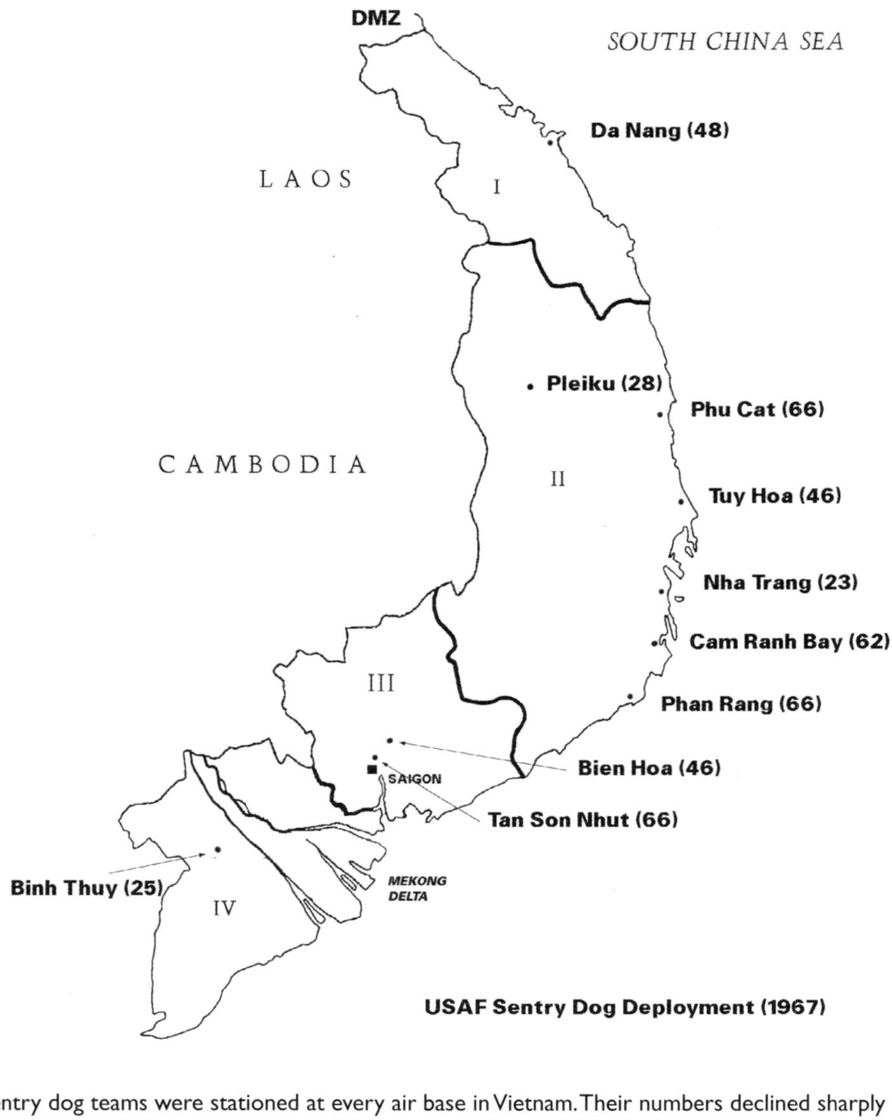

Sentry dog teams were stationed at every air base in Vietnam. Their numbers declined sharply after 1968 as the bases grew and activity increased. *(Author's Collection)*

throughout the country. Supplies were transferred from Japan and Korea, but this food was also the same brand and much of it was discarded. The food problem became so acute that many handlers were asking their parents to skip the treats for themselves and send over suitable food for their dog. If the U.S. dogs were having this much trouble getting a square meal, one wonders how those under the care of the ARVN fared. Just how many dogs were susceptible to gastrointestinal problems and other ailments brought on by bad food can never be ascertained.

Shortly after the sentry dog deaths, procurement switched from yearly to monthly. Also, the military began bringing in some civilian brands, like "Gaines Burgers" and "Prime" where possible, instead of the cereal-based dog food that was typically specified. When it was available, horsemeat and beef were added to the food to make the meal more palatable. Trouble was, horsemeat was becoming popular (among humans) in Europe and was often hard to come by. Just what a dog received for a meal varied throughout the course of the war and where they were located. [21]

When their food ran out, it was time to share your C-rations with your dog, but only as a last resort. The loss of the eight sentry dogs highlighted the problem of spoiled food within the logistics chain but did not address the nutritional value of the food and the proper diet formulation. Any military dog that is working is also under constant stress—so much so that after a six-hour tour of duty, as much as ten percent of their body weight may have been lost. The adrenal gland produces cortisol that regulates carbohydrate, protein, and fat metabolism, in effect controling the dogs' weight. According to USAF Lt. Colonel James H. McNamara, "The stress factors are so great that, on average, the adrenal gland of a five-year-old [military] dog is five to six times larger than normal…" [22]

An easy comparison is that a typical stay-at-home dog back in the states may require an intake of 25 to 30 calories/lb/day. A military working dog in the hostile environment of Vietnam expends so much energy that 32 to 50 calories/lb/day would be required. Compounding the problem was the high temperatures and humidity often found in-

Scout dog handlers prepare meals for their dogs. During the course of the war a nutritional standard was never developed for dogs by the Veterinary Corps. *(Courtesy of Robert A. Kollar)*

country. Humans control temperature by sweating, which dogs can not do; they do it by panting. Once you get above 80 degrees Fahrenheit, the blood supply to the respiratory system is dramatically increased at the expense of the digestive system. In other words, dogs cannot or will not eat much when it is hot outside, sometimes cutting back on half of the food they would normally consume.

During the course of the war, there was never one standard established for the quantity or type of dog food fed to the dogs. What was used would be determined by when you were in Vietnam and where you were based, not the service branch you were connected with. Although the bulk of the food in the early stages was of poor quality and dry, canned commercial dog food would find its way into the military system. Brands like Kal Kan and Alpo became available, along with Gaines burgers and Prime, as mentioned. Even the canned food had its problems after being exposed to high heat and humidity for a period of time; it would turn rancid. To stretch out supplies, the canned product would often be mixed with dry dog food. It would not be until the drawdown period that a new food was developed specifically for military dogs. This new formulation appears to have only gone to the sentry dogs stationed in Thailand.

For the majority of time in Vietnam, the pattern of care for scout and tracker dogs mirrored that for the troops stationed in Vietnam. The first level of care came from enlisted Animal Specialists (designated as MOS 91T), referred to as vet techs, who were assigned to each scout dog platoon. Many 91Ts were trained at the Walter Reed Army Institute of Research in Washington, D.C. Their main responsibility was to provide preventive medicine, first aid, and routine treatments. Some went further on their own, trying to perform minor surgery, often under the pressure of a handler or platoon commander who wanted immediate action. Although many technicians provided excellent attention to the dogs, some failed to perform even the simplest of tasks, such as dipping the dogs for ticks or cleaning their ears properly. Handlers, the good ones, recognized this early on and either performed the chores themselves or brought the tech's deficiencies to the attention of the platoon's commanding officer.

Graduate veterinarians at dispensaries immediately backed up the vet techs. In 1966, dispensaries were situated too far from the immediate tactical areas to provide a rapid response. Much of their organization was based on sentry dogs at fixed locations, not scout or tracker dogs scattered across the countryside that remained quite mobile. The 4th Medical Detachment (JA) would be the first to arrive and was charged with animal care for the entire country. Eventually they provided dispensary service at twenty-two locations in the III and IV Corps areas. Veterinarians also conducted (or at least they were scheduled to on paper) monthly field inspections of all the scout dogs operating in the field.

To back up dispensary care with more advanced surgical capabilities, the 936th Medical Detach (ID) established a Veterinary Small Animal Hospital on 2 September 1965. Four months later, the 936th secured its own facility at Tan Son Nhut AFB in III Corps and provided extensive medical treatment for all Army dogs from the II, III and IV Corps areas. A new hospital was planned in 1966

The Veterinary Corps provided excellent service with meager resources. Here Lux is being treated for a wounded eye that had become infected. *(National Archives)*

and was completed by year's end, except for the kennel where veterinary personnel still relied on the Air Force facilities. Marine scout and sentry dogs in I Corps received treatment at the 75th MED DET in Da Nang, not really an established facility but more like a room in the back of a large warehouse.

Of course, the Army was aware of the weaknesses of a military working dog program. And the Army liked technology and gadgets, especially in hot spots like Vietnam. If dogs could be replaced with a machine, it would be the best of both worlds. As most people know, advanced experimental technology and the real world do not always work smoothly together. Vietnam was not just a battleground of men, but it also turned out to be a proving ground for a variety of hi-tech gizmos—some useful, others just a waste of taxpayer money. Such was the case of the "People Sniffer," a device developed by General Electric that promised to be the answer to every soldier's prayer: the ability to smell enemy troops, even in a dense jungle.

The People Sniffer was brought to Vietnam and used by the Chemical Corps in a program ironically called "Operation Snoopy." Dubbed the "XM-2", it started out as a backpack unit and an air intake tube mounted on the end of a rifle. The scientific principle was that the device could locate ammonia molecules in the tiniest amount from human or animal urine. A sensor sounded a "ticka, ticka, ticka" to the operator that increased in frequency when a larger quantity of ammonia molecules was sucked into the intake tube. This would also prove to be the biggest problem with the new device. Unlike dogs, the XM-2 could not discriminate different odors. This remained the principal forte of the canine.

The XM-2 actually worked too well. It picked up signals from the enemy, ARVN and American soldiers, water buffalo, old men and women, smoke, children, and even waste from humans and animals. It was too indiscriminant to be of any use, and the false alarms proved to be problematic. After a hundred false readings, perhaps the next one would be authentic. No one knew what the sensor picked up, and those who operated the device never had any confidence using it.

The XM-2 was moved from a backpack unit to one used in helicopter sweeps. The unit was upgraded to the XM-3, and involved a helicopter rigged with the device that flew a scant fifty feet above the ground. It was supported by two helicopter gunships that flew behind the rigged helicopter to offer some protection.

It appears the device and its variations were utilized sporadically in Vietnam until about 1971, when the program was finally discontinued. Proponents of the device would say that it was an innovation "ahead of its time." Over the course of history, devices that are given that moniker never seem to come to fruition. Researchers attempted to tweak the detection system, but in the end, there was no electronic gadget that could replace the dog team on the ground. Decades later, with an incredible dearth of technological devices handed to us, we still rely on dogs on a daily basis for security and human assistance.

Small Operations and Bad Decisions

At the end of August 1966, the 40th IPSD arrived at Pleiku, further swelling the ranks of the scout dog teams already in-country. One story that emerged from the 40th IPSD occurred two months after arriving in-country and involved handler Sgt. Russell L. Castle, and eventually the attention of Senator Richard Byrd and President Lyndon B. Johnson.

There are many ways in which a dog can touch the life of someone. It may be in the subtlest form, during a moment of playing around, during one of the daily routines involving your dog, or decades after the dog is gone, just a memory and perhaps a faded photograph in a scrapbook tucked away in the attic. Knowing what dogs can do to a person's psyche, it is understandable that some people will go through to complete a journey. If dogs are characterized by the military as equipment, then what reason would compel someone to elevate them to a higher status? A good case in point is the story of a husband, wife, and a scout dog named Turk.

Russell Castle was severely injured in a skirmish near his base camp in Pleiku. With grave head and shoulder wounds, medics were able to stabilize him enough to be safely transported out of South Vietnam and back to Walter Reed General Hospital. For several months, Castle lay in a vegetative state while his wife, Josiane, stayed alongside him for many hours every week.

The two had met in Germany, where Castle was stationed at the time and was recuperating in a hospital from a football knee injury. Josiane, a native of Lille, France, was a nurse's aid when the two met. They fell in love and were quickly married. Castle originally hailed from Woodbridge, Virginia, and the couple moved back to the area before he was deployed to Vietnam. Each day in the hospital, "Josie" as she liked to be called, saw her husband in a semiconscious state. She knew how much her husband had bonded with his scout dog "Turk" and she truly believed that having the dog there with him would help in his recovery. She tried writing legislators and anyone who might assist in having the dog returned to the states. According to a local newspaper account she stated, "I hoped the dog would give him the will to live. He had never been separated from Turk since their training at Fort Benning. I knew the dog would help." [23]

According to a *Stars & Stripes* newspaper account, Mrs. Castle managed to get Senator Robert Byrd of Virginia to talk with President Johnson and try to persuade him to have the dog returned to the states. According to the same story, President Johnson issued an order for Turk to return home immediately, and within hours he was on board an Air Force jet bound for the United States. [24] Turk was accompanied on the trip home by another 40th IPSD handler, SP4 William R. Wendell. at the end of March. "It was hard for me to get them to bring the dog here, since he had saved so many lives in Vietnam and they didn't want to let him go. But when I brought him into Russ's room, I helped Russ open his left eye so he could see Turk. When he did he opened his right eye unaided, something he had not done before. It was the first time in over five months he had come out of his coma." [25] According to the report, Turk was sent back shortly thereafter to Vietnam. Three months later on 2 July 1967, Sgt. Castle died at Maxwell AFB while being transported to the Veteran's Hospital in Coral Gables, Florida. Through perseverance and the help of many others, Castle did have the opportunity to meet his dog one last time before taking his final patrol.

Several weeks after the 40th IPSD deployed, the 42nd IPSD began their move towards Vietnam in early September. This was followed by the 33rd IPSD (4th Inf Div) in October and the 34th IPSD (1st Cav Div) and 41st IPSD (4th Inf Div) in November. The 42nd completed their training with thirty enlisted, although the Table of Organization and Equipment (TOE) only allowed twenty-six. The additional four men were reassigned to several dog platoons already in-country. Like those before and

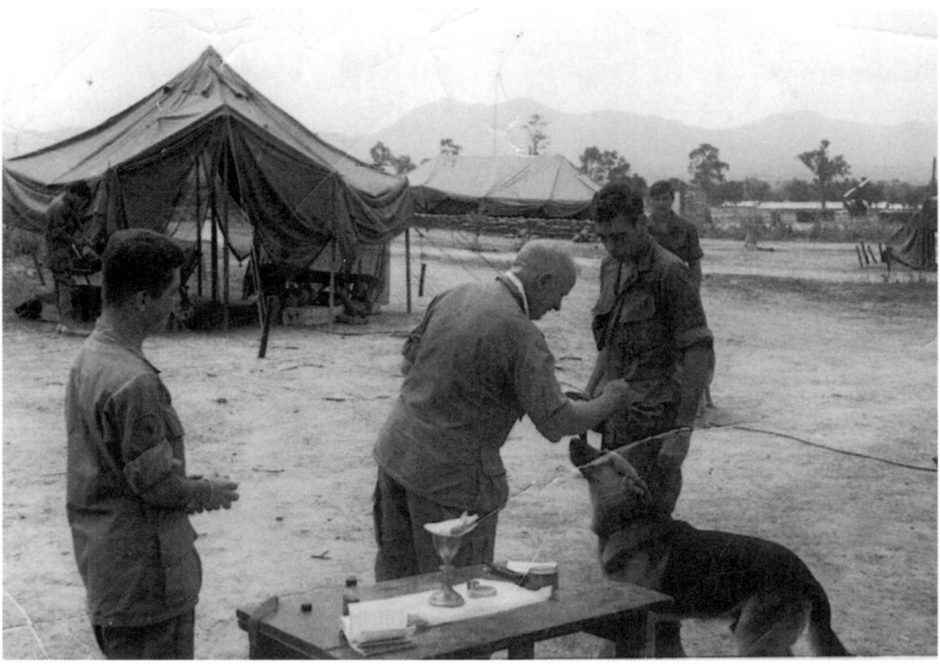

Scout dog teams sought every possible advantage out in the field. This team seeks the blessing from an Army chaplain and grace from above before heading out on patrol. *(Photos courtesy William "Twiggy" Brown, 40th IPSD)*

many to come, the Army did not always take the most direct travel route to war. The circuitous course involved the men departing Fort Benning and truck-transporting to Robbins AFB, located about ninety miles east. From there they flew to Elmendorf AFB in Alaska, on to Yokota, Japan, and finally arriving at Tan Son Nhut.

While at Tan Son Nhut, the 42nd really had no place to go, since they were not yet assigned to anyone and languished on base for almost a month. It was finally decided they would be attached to the 1st Brigade, 101st Airborne at Phan Rang. The platoon arrived at the air base on 2 October 1966. They would only stay there a week before moving out to the 101st forward camp at Tuy Hua farther up the coast, where the Song Ba River emptied into the China Sea. At the end of the month, Operation Geronimo I began and the 42nd committed fifteen dog teams. Two days later, Sarge (5X94) was killed in action and his body was brought back by his handler, PFC. Gerald Corrigan, for burial. The platoon continued with many support operations during November, accumulating 381 days in the field, and incredibly twenty-six of them were made by handler Patrick A. Copeland.

On the very last day of the two-month operation, called Operation Geronimo I, 42nd IPSD scout dog handler PFC Sidney Owen called out alerts from his scout dog, but was urged to keep moving forward. Realizing the grave situation they encountered, Owen called out a warning, but too late as the lead element was already in the kill zone set up as part of an NVA ambush. Owen took fragment wounds in the jaw, neck, and shoulder but prevented the whole platoon from being wiped out. He would later receive the Army Commendation Medal with "V" device in addition to the Purple Heart. It was just another patrol, in a growing list of scout dog team deployments that the Army would launch in the next few years. The 42nd then took a six-day break with the conclusion of Operation Geronimo I in the first week of December. Once again, they picked up and moved to Kontum, deep in the Central Highlands where the terrain was steep and thick with bamboo. For most of the month they supported Operation Pickett until 23 December 1966, when they had a little four-day break. During the month the platoon logged an incredible 204 man-days in the field.

The breaks taken by the scout dog teams were a welcome relief from being in the field. It was a time to rest or go wild, depending on what mood you were in, where you were, and what happed while you were out there. In his unpublished memoir, *Sniffer Dogs*, 42nd IPSD scout dog handler James Moore referred to this stretch, out of the field and in a rear area, as "ghost time." It was a time where you came back from the field after being out on patrol with your dog that you knew quite well—you were beat up and so was your dog—with a bunch of other guys you might have met for the first time or just a few days ago It was an opportunity to regroup, both physically and mentally, and if you had the right platoon commander, he understood. The boots came off for the first time in days and you wondered how that leech ever found its way in there between your toes. And then you realized you didn't crap for five days and you scuttle off to the toilet. You'd suck down a Falstaff, maybe look after your dog, check to see if any mail arrived, and then realize that in a few more days you'd be back out in the boonies again.

A scout dog team and radioman ham it up while on break for the benefit of a Signal Corps photographer. *(National Archives)*

Perhaps you looked at the calendar and tried to figure out how many days you had to go before you could rotate home. And what about your dog? He didn't have a calendar. And even during this slack period, if you were off base you still never forgot about your dog. You read your mail and the folks talked about a new TV program called *Star Trek*. The idea of peace still flickered dimly for Vietnam, but with Buddhist uprisings and the failing of Operation Rolling Thunder one could expect only more patrols in the bush with the coming New Year.

For most Americans, 1966 still remained a time of optimism that the war in Vietnam was going well, and based on the reports it would soon be over. Military dogs were being shipped over in ever-greater numbers and of course troops in-country acquired local dogs as mascots and they numbered in the hundreds. It would not seem advisable or even necessary to send a dog from the United States to act as mascot. But that is indeed what happened on 22 June 1966, when a dog was shipped on a commercial airliner, courtesy of Boeing Aircraft Company, to the 228th Assault Helicopter Battalion.

The employees of Boeing's Vetrol Division raised money to purchase a dog to be sent to An Khe, home of the 228th that flew the CH-47A Chinook helicopter. What better mascot, or so it would seem to the folks at Boeing, than to have a five-month old Chinook sled dog donated. The Chinook is a relatively rare breed and the pup

Handlers from the 34th IPSD take a break from the daily routine. No matter what type of recreation was available for the men, the war was only a short distance away. *(Courtesy of Joseph Ertel)*

came from Waldoboro, Maine, the only kennel in the world where the dogs can be obtained from. At the time, only about forty of the dogs existed worldwide.

Upon his arrival at An Khe, Lt. Col. Max Clark accepted the mascot from Tom Pepplet, a Boeing project manager. For a sled dog with a heavy coat, the pup appeared to tolerate the climate of Vietnam reasonable well. Named "Charger," he stayed principally at headquarters, but had free reign of the compound. Occasionally the dog would also ride along in the helicopters to different landing zones.

Since Charger was not a military working dog, he was not kenneled, nor was he tattooed for identification purposes, nor was there one person responsible for his well being. This was perhaps his undoing. Sometime in the early spring of 1967, after being in-country for less than a year, Charger disappeared. A friendly dog, it is unlikely he left the compound but was probably picked up by troops passing through. In any event, he was never seen again by anyone from the 228th.

December 1966 continued as a busy month for all the dog units in Vietnam and there was little respite, even with the traditional Christmas holiday season approaching. Six thousand ARVN soldiers attacked a VC stronghold in the Mekong Delta and managed to tally just 104 VC dead and eighteen captured. Americans continued to take on the brunt of the war and continued the bombing north of the DMZ, with missions ever closer to Hanoi. Scout dog platoon operations continued to increase as more and more troops poured into South Vietnam. The New Year was coming, yet there wasn't much to celebrate, but the Army had managed to place nine scout dog platoons into the war by the end of 1966. With several more platoons already in training, it was planned to double that number within a year.

The hospital housing the Army 504th Medical Detachment located in DaNang. Note the scale located by the entrance that was used to weigh the dogs before they entered the building. *(Otis Archive)*

A K-9 Hero Emerges

During the predawn hours of 4 December 1966, the Viet Cong launched an assault at Tan Son Nhut, the largest air base for the Americans in South Vietnam. Based on the facts it was in no doubt a suicidal mission on the part of Charlie. The airbase, home of joint USAF-VNAF operations and encompassed by a 13-mile perimeter, was at the time one of the busiest airports in the world. By 1969 over 70,000 sorties were launched from its runways each month. It was also a frequent target of enemy assaults because of its logistical and operational importance. Here on the outskirts of Saigon, the largest battle of the war involving sentry dogs teams was about to take place.

Planning for the attack began about two months earlier. A seven-man sapper team surveyed the base and decided to penetrate the perimeter where a drainage ditch, about ten feet in depth, ran perpendicular to the fence leading to another ditch closer to the runway. This outer perimeter was the responsibility of the South Vietnamese Air Force with some of the soldiers having questionable loyalty. The sappers had good intelligence beforehand about the outer perimeter and were able to cut through three fences. Running southward the enemy force of approximately ninety men planned to split into two groups and overwhelm the five U.S. sentry dog teams stationed along the runway on the opposite side of the flightline. These K-9 postings in this area were listed as Kilo-1 to Kilo-5.

The sentry dog teams were dropped off for duty at about 2100 hours the night of 3 December, A2C George M. Bevich Jr. and his dog Rex had been assigned to Kilo-1, one of the largest sentry posts on the base. Larry Laudner and his dog Cubby (612E) were assigned to Kilo-3, an easier posting that was open and could be covered with little effort. But Bevich wasn't feeling well that night and to make things easier for him the two switched postings. Between them was Kilo-2 patrolled by Dale Sidwell and Toby. On the other side of Bevich were Leroy Marsh and Rebel at Kilo-4 and Robert Thorneburg and Nemo (A534) at Kilo-5.

Around midnight the K-9 section leader drove over to Laudner's post to give him a rest break. About forty-five minutes later he pulled up to Kilo-2 to relieve Sidwell. Twenty minutes later the section leader moved on to Kilo-3 and radioed Bevich. There was no response. Getting out of the truck the section leader spotted a large group of enemy fighters running toward him. Bevich was dead. The sappers had overwhelmed Kilo-3 and left the twenty-two year old handler from Summit, Pennsylvania, dead in their wake. Hours later, security police recovered his body and found Rex nearby.[26]

Sheehan jumped from his truck just as the enemy rushed by and tossed a grenade in. The concussion and fragments knocked Sheehan to the ground as he lost consciousness. The attackers figured he was dead and lifted his wristwatch and ring and then continued on carrying their satchel charges.

George Bevich was the first Air Force sentry dog handler to be killed in Vietnam. His dog Rex survived the attack on Tan Son Nhut which took place on 4 December 1966. *(Courtesy of Ed Hobbs)*

A2C Leroy E. Marsh and his dog Rebel patrolled Kilo-4. With the breeze to their backs, Rebel didn't alert to the intruders. The two of them spotted the enemy at the same time about fifty yards away. Marsh released Rebel and was the first to call in the attack on the radio. Rebel attacked and killed one man and then was quickly cut down by automatic fire. "When I let him loose, I had a notion he might get shot," Marsh later stated. "But I had to send Rebel out there. The VC were all around. I had to throw in everything, the dog, the shots. I had to make time so the others could organize." Marsh made his way to a nearby bunker about the same time mortar rounds starting hitting near the flightline on the opposite side of the runway. Rebel had bought Marsh enough time to get to some cover.

Back at Kilo-1, Laudner and Cubby heard the mortar rounds

and dived into the ditch. Laudner listened to his radio. "Someone yelled that the enemy had reached the runway and was pushing for the flightline," he said. "There was weapons fire from almost everywhere. The radio traffic was so heavy no one could get on and you couldn't tell who was where. It was very confusing."

Meanwhile A2C Robert Thorneburg and Nemo at Kilo-5 alerted to several VC hiding in an old cemetery within the base perimeter near their post. Thorneburg released Nemo and, like Rebel, he attacked the enemy and hauled down two of them. There were several shots and Nemo's cry pierced the night. Thorneburg advanced and killed one VC before being wounded by return fire. Before the reaction team reached them, Nemo had crawled across his master's body and refused to let anyone to get near him. Finally Nemo was persuaded to move as other handlers administered first aid to both the handler and dog.

By 0125, three AC-47s (military version of the DC-3) were overhead dropping flares. It made the base turn into an eerie daylight even though it was the middle of the night. About ten minutes later, a group of VC got tangled in concertina wire placed around the runway. What they didn't know was they were heading towards two Security Police bunkers each with an M-60 machine gun and two riflemen with M-16s. The sappers were quickly mowed down and not one of them reached the planes parked on the apron.

Everything subsided a bit until around 0200. On the radio someone said the South Vietnamese were sweeping the area near Kilo-1. "Feeling the attack was over, I nonchalantly moved from the ditch where Cubby and I had taken cover and walked toward the center of my post," Laudner said. That's when I saw them. A group of twenty or so uniformed men moving straight toward me. They looked like they might be South Vietnamese soldiers but I couldn't tell for sure. "

Laudner yelled something at them, but he couldn't remember what. They didn't shoot at him either. He yelled that he had a dog but still no response. Realizing the attack was not over he got on the radio and yelled that the enemy was moving on his post. He then released Cubby. "It was very bright because of the flares. I saw him run toward the men, then I heard him make a hit. The VC he hit screamed. Then automatic fire [began] and I heard Cubby cry out."

Laudner ran back to the ditch and opened up on full automatic sweeping left to right. "I think I hit a couple of them," he stated. An Army support unit arrived to back him up. The radio crackled and it was Sidwell at Kilo-2 post. "I need help. They are everywhere." The group Laudner had fired upon moved on to Kilo-2. Sidwell was on the radio again; he just released Toby.

Laudner asked for permission a couple of times to assist Sidwell but was denied. The army unit was ordered to stay at Kilo-1. Finally permission was granted but when they made their way over to Kilo-2, Sildwell was nowhere to be found. Part of the cemetery was inside the Kilo-2 patrol area and after releasing his dog, Sidwell scurried behind one of the headstones before returning fire on the enemy. Other small firefights ensued but by 0300 it was pretty much over.

Just how Charlie got onto to the base to begin with would be conjecture for years to come. Some believed they were helped by the RVNAF sentries, but

Laudner believes many were already on site earlier in the day. "There is no way that many men, in so little time, could have made it through all the mine fields and Kilo posts without detection. There is no question many of them had settled in prior to the K-9 teams being posted."

Nemo was shot in the face, his nose a mass of pulp and flesh and his right eye was partially blown away. Apparently the round that hit him entered his right eye and exited through his mouth. Even with these wounds, he would not allow anyone near Thorneburg. They called over A2C Leonard Bryant who was working the kennels that night to come to Kilo-5. Bryant had handled Nemo before Thorneburg and was able to coax him away and bring him to the base hospital. The base veterinarian Captain Raymond T. Huston went right to work on him. "I remember they talked about putting Nemo down," Laudner explained. "But Dr. Huston decided to try and save him."

A1C Robert Thorneburg (in hospital pajamas) and A3C Leonard Bryant visit with Nemo shortly after the attack at Tan Son Nhut. Bryant was Nemo's first handler when the pair arrived in Vietnam. *(National Archives)*

"When Nemo was brought to me," Doctor Huston said, "he was in pretty bad shape. I had to do skin grafts on his face and perform a tracheotomy to help him breathe. His right eye had to be removed, but even this did not lessen his ability [as a sentry dog]. It only made his other senses, hearing and smell, more sensitive."

Nemo never did completely recover. Thorneburg and Nemo soon parted company. Nemo stayed behind while his master was evacuated to the hospital at Tachikawa Air Base in Japan to recuperate. In the ensuing months, several attempts were made to get Nemo back out on patrol but the surgeries and wounds subdued the 95-pound warrior.

Word of Nemo's exploits spread back home and many get-well cards were sent wishing a speedy recovery. Kids adore dogs and Jeffrey William White, of Seattle, Washington, sent a card along with the following note:

> Dear Nemo.
>
> My friend sent you a letter December 5. Her name is Marta Lee Coumbe. I am sending this letter because I love dogs and the last dog I had died at the age of four months. I hope you get well.
>
> Your friend,
>
> Jeff White.

On 23 June 1967, the Air Force, showing the best they had, directed that it was time for Nemo to go home. He would be the first sentry dog to be officially retired from active duty in Vietnam. A month later, nineteen months after arriving in Vietnam, Nemo, accompanied by A1C Melvin W. Bryant, boarded a C-124 Globemaster for the return trip. Stops were made in Japan, Hawaii, and California, and veterinarians checked the dog's condition along the way. The plane landed at Kelly AFB, Texas, on the 22 July. It was greeted by a Welcome Home committee headed by Captain Robert M. Sullivan, the officer in charge of sentry dog training in Lackland, who stated, "I have to keep from getting involved with individual dogs in this program. But I can't help from feeling a little emotional about this dog. He shows how valuable a dog is to his handler in staying alive." Nemo came home to the Lackland AFB to his own private kennel.

But some soldiers never truly retire. Nemo's military service continued, touring the country with Captain Sullivan to help the Air Force recruit other dogs for the war effort. He was given his own private kennel with a sign displaying his name, service number, and details of his exploit. The intent was to remind the recruits how important a sentry dog could be.

In November of 1972, in poor health, Nemo was flown to Andrews AFB for further evaluation. A month later an infection overwhelmed him and veterinarians euthanized the old warrior on 18 December. He was laid to rest at Lackland on 15 March 1973. Among his accomplishments, Nemo was perhaps the most well travelled dog in the history of the Air Force.

A1C Melvin W. Bryant welcomes home Nemo on his way back to Lackland AFB in July 1967. Nemo travelled around the country as part of the Air Force's efforts to recruit military dogs. *(National Archives)*

During a 2003 reunion of the Vietnam Security Police Association (VSPA), several members visited the 37th SFS kennel at Lackland. During the tour the group saw an abandoned cement pad with a raised border crumbling away. There were no markings at all. "I can't begin to tell you the thoughts of the handlers when we realized this was sacred ground – the resting place of sentry dog Nemo," said Bill Cummings. A group of K-9 veteran handlers came together and eventually rebuilt the kennel, restoring it to what it looked like in 1967-68 photographs of the time. The memorial site also contains a replica of Nemo's kennel house, a Tan Son Nhut "attack sign" and a memorial plaque. A water bucket and feed pan were also placed in the kennel. The kennel was officially dedicated on 15 November 2005. [27]

The attack on Tan Son Nhut would mean that George Bevich would be engraved as another name on the Vietnam Memorial in Washington, D.C. But behind every name is a person and a story. Bevich became the first Air Force dog handler killed in Vietnam and he would be accorded the Silver Star and Purple Heart posthumously. More importantly for his family, he would be remembered almost forty years later.

John Langley, a USAF dog handler who later arrived in 1968 at Tan Son Nhut, met Bevich briefly in February 1966. Bevich was part of a group of five dog handlers who, along with their dogs, were leaving Loring AFB in Maine to make the long journey to Vietnam. Langley, who later helped organize the Vietnam Dog Handler Association, traveled to the grave of George Bevich in Summit, Pennsylvania in November 2007 on the 25th anniversary of the Vietnam Veteran Memorial, where his name was read as part of the Vietnam War dead. For the family and friends of George Bevich it became a vivid reminder and quite a surprise, that someone would be remembered after so many years has passed.

The War Continues and Building a Better Dog

By the end of the year, it seemed quite obvious that the pace of the war was to be dictated by the bombing campaign against the north and not by the Viet Cong launching suicide missions. Over 860,000 tons of explosives had been dropped on the communists to date. As a comparison, 500,000 pounds (excluding the two atomic bombs) had been dropped on Japan during World War II. The doctrine of bombing North Vietnam into submission was not being successful. Most analysts agreed that the United States was extracting one dollar of damage for every ten dollars spent. We could keep making and dropping bombs, but would the communists fold before the bank went dry? As 1966 rolled toward its conclusion over 5,000 Americans had been killed and more than 37,000 wounded. There was still a lot more to come. Another truce would begin with the New Year, and U.S. troop strength would top 380,000 men with no end in sight.

As the war continued, another scout dog platoon entered action. With Lieut. Alan L. Jones in command, the 48th IPSD activated on 2 September 1966 and left for Vietnam on 11 January 1967, arriving four days later. A week later the fourteen enlisted men and Lieut. Jones moved to Tay Ninh to support the 196th Light Infantry Brigade (LIB). Tay Ninh was a bit north of Cu Chi along Highway 5 alongside the Cambodian border, and a popular jump-off point for the Viet Cong cadres that filtered south on the Ho Chi Minh trail in Cambodia.

Young prospective military dogs are checked for their reaction to pistol fire. A dog could easily be removed from the program if they continued to bark or appeared to be afraid of loud noises. Through training and positive reinforcement most dogs would be accustomed to loud noises. *(Carlisle Barracks)*

Left: Each scout dog base camp erected a sign from the local artist, who was usually one of the handlers. *(Courtesy of Bobby J. Railey)* **Right:** Some signs, such as this one, firmly stated when they arrived and unit they were attached to. *(Courtesy of Gary Zemel)*

After a short stay of just four months, the 48th moved out with the 196th to Chu Lai as they became incorporated into Task Force Oregon and eventually became attached to the Americal Division. Chu Lai is located in I Corps, on the coast midway between Duc Pho and DaNang alongside the major artery, Highway 1. This continued to show that MACV would have the scout dog platoons pick up and relocate with little consideration for the men, dogs, or veterinary services as the dog teams followed the elements that they supported. Within the next few years the 48th IPSD would move to several more locales and have the distinction of being one of the most mobile of all scout dog platoons in Vietnam.

The 44th IPSD arrived about the same time and hooked up with the 25th Inf Div and took a position in Dau Tieng. This is just south of Tay Ninh and another entry point for supplies and materials carried along the Ho Chi Minh trail and destined for VC units in South Vietnam. Two months later, two more scout dog platoons deployed to Vietnam. The 49th IPSD was attached to the 199th Infantry Brigade (Inf Bde) and worked the area out of Long Binh, while the 50th moved in a week later and was attached to the 4th Inf Bde near Pleiku. With several scout dogs platoons now in place along the Cambodian border, it became increasingly apparent that the Army wanted to choke off this VC infiltration and supply route from the Ho Chi Minh trail.

In 1966, the United States military had already deployed sentry, tracker, and scout dogs to Vietnam and more were on the way. A number of scientists in the Army Research Office, located principally at Fort Belvoir and Edgewood Arsenal, studied the problem of enemy ambushes and began looking at a different approach. Throughout history, all military dogs were trained for a specific function. Several scientists considered this an inefficient method. Most of the dogs were big and could only be successful when teamed with one handler. Genetic and animal behavioral scientists believed it was possible and feasible to breed specific behavioral and physical characteristics into a dog. They felt it was time to build a "superdog."

The program was called the "Concept for a Superior Ambush Detection Dog," and preliminary research was submitted by Ned Bayley, in the U.S. Department of Agriculture. Bayley was assistant director of the Animal Husbandry Division and he noted in the report that, "…the long military experience in the use of scout dogs commended the dog most favorably for Army needs but that the full biological potential of the dog was not being exploited." [28] The researchers went on to state, "It is clear that psychobiology has come of age, and in this area, at least, we can breed dogs better than the best available today." The USDA researchers estimated they could produce 1,000 dogs a year once the breeding program matured after several years, but could possibly provide 600-700 dogs for the Army just two years into the program. The USDA was looking to breed a smaller dog and more compact than a German shepherd, which translated into easier transportation and one that would consume a lot less food.

Army Colonel Robert W. Samuel, Chief, Research Plans Office, liked the concept and wanted to see it developed further. The war in Vietnam was going on longer than expected, and the idea of getting more and better dogs seemed to be a win-win situation. After sitting on the report for several months, Samuel notified Brigadier General

George A. Kuhn, Chief of the Veterinary Corps, about the program and asked if the they could develop their own program. Samuel wanted to go forward, but without the USDA involved. This was to be an Army operation from top to bottom.

Kuhn really liked the idea. Besides breeding dogs, he wanted the entire scout dog program moved under the umbrella of the Veterinary Corps. Of course, if a successful breeding program could be launched, it would certainly showcase well for the veterinary service to possibly assume future scout dog related training and deployment. Kuhn delegated the job to LTC Thompson, VC, and that he conduct his own background research and get back to him as soon as practical. Thompson contacted personnel at Edgewood Arsenal and also made inquiries at the Limited Warfare Laboratories and gathered information from the scout dog platoons deployed in Vietnam.

On 12 January 1967, a conference was held at the Pentagon that was headed by M.E. Lasser, the Chief Scientist from the Army concerning Research and Training of "Bio-Sensors." The seven men in attendance discussed the older USDA proposal and also the information that Thompson acquired, although for unknown reasons Thompson was not invited to the meeting. The group decided on a loose plan that would involve breeding dogs, not just for ambush detection but also for the location of tunnels. There is little doubt that the events taking place in Vietnam had a direct impact on how the Veterinary Corps program would develop. What is interesting from an historical perspective is that this is exactly what Brigadier General Frederick McCabe recommended that the Army do back in 1947.

In what appeared to be an unnecessary contract, the Canine Behavior Laboratory at the University of Maryland was hired to determine how suitable several different breeds would be for the Army's purposes. These included the German shepherds, poodles, Airedales, Labrador retrievers, and English pointers. In the end, the German shepherd won out, of course; did anyone ever believe that an Army handler would be on one end of the leash and a poodle on the other? It just didn't fit the profile of a military working dog team.

By May 1967, the main objectives of the program were ironed out and the entire project was allocated about $400,000 annually in operating expenses for the next six years. Colonel John Powell, VC was appointed as the first project director, but was soon replaced by Colonel M.W. "Bud" Castleberry, VC. Several other officers augmented the staff and the program garnered the interest of many notable civilian consultants. Everyone knew they weren't building a new breed of dog, but a "better" dog. The Air Force at this time whined that the project would conflict with their procurement responsibilities. Although no firm reason could be given, it was probably a case of inter-service rivalry that was quickly dismissed.

Temporary facilities were provided at Fort Meade and the permanent facilities would not be available (at Edgewood Arsenal, Maryland) until March 1970. Over the years the program expanded in several directions and also became involved in other research projects. It also piqued the interests of several civilians well-known in German shepherd circles, including the author and trainers such as Ernest H. Hart and William R. Koehler. The project would also extend well beyond our involvement in Vietnam—in the end it was still considered desirable to have a superior military dog, it's just that no one was willing to budget the amount of money involved in a large-scale breeding program. In 1967, the dog inventory was still growing in Vietnam and it would still be a year or two before the superdog program would be able to contribute to the war effort.

While a new designer dog was in the works, the Navy became more involved with land-base warfare. Twenty-nine sailors had volunteered during boot camp and began sentry dog training in November 1966. The training began on base and after a couple of months switched to nearby Camp Medina. The handlers were expecting a month leave after graduation, but this was short-circuited. Navy Sentry Dog Class 14126 graduated at Lackland AFB on 8 February 1967. Just a day after graduation the entire class was informed that they would be sent immediately to Vietnam to relieve various Marine sentry dog teams and infantry units pulling guard duty around DaNang.

The unit left Kelly AFB in a C-130, with the dogs tranquilized and the shipping crates piled four high in the cargo bay. It was quite a mess and stench inside. The airplane was overwhelming when the plane made a stopover in Hawaii. The dogs deplaned for light exercise but refused to board and needed to be tranquilized a second time. On 11 February, the plane landed at DaNang and the dogs and handlers moved to the 5th Marine Communication Compound where the dogs were quarantined in new kennels built by the Seabees. Since the dogs were coming in from the relatively cool Texas winter, extra care was afforded so they would acclimatize properly.

According to Navy sentry handler Tom Massey, "While the dogs were quarantined we started setting up our dog posts. We checked our posts, taking into consideration the prevailing wind direction, cover, and egress of each location. We had twelve primary posts. Eight posts at a communications transmitter site about ten miles south of Marble Mountain and four sites at the POL [petroleum, oil, lubricants] site near Hill 327." [29] For the next five months, the Viet Cong would sporadically probe the perimeter for weaknesses or fire the occasional mortar round. Like most sentry dog postings, boredom settled in on many nights punctuated with a sound or a dog alert. Like sentry duty anywhere in Vietnam, complacency could sometimes get you killed. Both men and dogs had to find the right "balance," not total boredom with the lack of activity around you or just the opposite, hyped up on adrenaline for your time on post. Both extremes had a peculiar way of burning you out in short order.

The Navy also fielded a couple of scout dogs that were attached to SEAL Team #2. The SEALs developed from the Navy's underwater demolition teams that were used during World War II and Korea and were part of the U.S. Navy special operations force. Operating on land and underwater, they were also parachute qualified. They began operations in Vietnam in 1962 as advisors and trainers operating up and down the coast and launching covert operations into North Vietnam. Most of their area of operation was in and around the Mekong Delta.

The dogs employed by the SEALS were Rinnie and Silver. Trained at Fort Benning, their use was considered experimental. Silver would also earn his Army parachute wings by making five jumps with Quartermaster Third Class Dewayne G. Schalengerg. A special harness was made for Silver that is attached to Schalengerg's harness so that the pair can exit the aircraft together and descend under a single parachute. Once the pair descended to about 200 feet above the ground, the pair would separate and Schalenberg would lower Silver on an attached twenty-foot line.

Eventually the Navy would field about 300 dog handlers during the course of the war and would incur just one fatality that took place on the morning of 22 October 1967. Fourteen handlers along with their dogs were picked up from their posts in a five-and-a-half-ton truck and returned to the kennels. Although the road used was swept for mines on a daily basis by the Marines, one mine was missed. The anti-tank mine ripped through the truck, killing FN Merle Keith Carter and wounding twelve others. If not for the size of the truck it could have been much worse. [30]

The Australian Trackers

What few people today realize is that the United States was not the only country supporting the South Vietnamese during the war. Over forty countries supplied troops, material, and money in the fight against the communists. One of the major players was Australia. As a charter member of the Southeast Asia Treaty Organization (SEATO), Australia entered the conflict in 1962 with the introduction of thirty advisors skilled in jungle warfare. In April 1965, 1400 combat troops were committed, primarily operating in the Bien Hoa area under U.S. supervision.

In 1966 the Australian government agreed to increase the number of troops committed in South Vietnam replacing the 1st Battalion Royal Australian Regiment (RAR) with the First Australian Task Force (ATF). Although initially headquartered in Saigon, the entire operation soon moved to the Phouc Tuy Province, the area known as the "rice bowl" of South Vietnam, located southeast of Saigon in III Corps. It was also an area of heavy VC activity. To the south was the ocean and to the east and north were hills populated by Viet Cong. In the west lay a thick mangrove swamp known as the "Rung Sat Zone."

Nui Dat, South Vietnam, 1967. Soldiers from the Royal Australian Regiment (7RAR) wait through a tropical downpour to carry out training with their tracking dogs, Tiber and Justin. Note that Tiber is wearing a special harness which allowed him to be inserted or extracted from the jungle using a helicopter winch. *(Australian War Memorial Negative Number EKN167/0097/VN).*

Like the British and the Americans before them, the Australian Army believed the use of K-9 tracking teams would enhance their combat commitment. Warrant Officer

Dog kennels at 1ATF, Nui Dat used by 6RAR/NZ tracker dogs D6N06 Marcus, D7N06 Milo, and D7N17 Trajan, 1969-1970. *(Courtesy of Australian Army Trackers & War Dogs Association (AATWDA))*

With just a small number of dogs, Australian handlers had no problem getting suitable kennels built. *(Courtesy of Australian Army Trackers & War Dogs Association (AATWDA))*

Class Two Robert "Blue" Carter was a former dog handler in Malaya in 1957-59, an advisor to the ARVN, and helped to establish the Tracking Wing at the School of Infantry in Ingleburn. Aiding Carter was Lt. Barry French, who gained extensive experience as the Tracker Platoon Commander of the 4th RAR in Borneo and Malaya. Ingleburn is located about thirty kilometers west of Sydney, where the first tracker dogs began their training. The dogs employed were exclusively black Labrador retrievers or crosses. As it turned out, the very best Australian Army tracker dog to work in Vietnam would be purchased for the tidy sum of just three dollars.

Although the scope of their mission would be the same as the Americans, the composition of Australian tracker teams differed slightly as they typically employed two dogs with two handlers on each mission. With a compact area to cover, just eleven tracker dogs were employed in Vietnam.

Unlike their American counterparts the dogs were not tattooed but were given a regimental identification number with a "D" prefix that was stamped on a tag attached to their collar. Carter also wanted to ensure uniformity with the dogs besides their ID number and this was through the names they would be given. Every tracker dog carried the name of a Roman emperor, politician, or general. The eleven dogs were named Cassius, Tiber, Justin, Marcus, Janus, Julian, Caesar, Milo, Trajan, Juno, and Marcian. Furthermore, they were considered "enlistees" and given a rank, and would be promoted throughout their careers while they worked in the field. Like most of their American cousins, they would never leave Vietnam.

According to Peter Haran, "The thing that we weren't prepared for and we weren't trained for in Vietnam were mines and booby traps. But on one occasion I was with Caesar, and we actually went into an area where we'd had contact with the enemy and we were tracking them, and the dog stopped and walked back and

An Australian tracker team lands and departs from a helicopter to search for a wounded VC. *(Australian War Memorial Negative Number P00800.030)*

just sat on my foot. It was only after that I found out there were four mines in front of us plus a 500-pound unexploded bomb. The dog had actually saved my life and saved the lives of all those around me." [31]

Field Operations and Hospital Miracles

One of the weaknesses of the scout dog program was that the dog was tethered to the handler by a leather leash. As any dog owner knows, the leash allows the handler total control over the animal. However, in Vietnam this could set up a deadly scenario. If wind conditions were not right, an on-leash scout dog could walk a patrol right into the enemy "kill zone" before the dog could provide a suitable alert to enemy personnel.

If the dog worked without a leash, ranging ahead of the patrol, the dog may enter the kill zone before any members of the patrol did. The idea for an off-leash scout dog began back in 1965, at the University of Maryland, and seemed to offer some merit.

A small group of handlers began training at Fort Benning in September 1966 with the first twelve weeks as standard scout dog training and the following six weeks as "off leash training." Afterward additional training was provided at Eglin Air Force Base ranger camp and training exercises were performed on Whitmeier Island. The group performed well in ambush patrols and reconnaissance patrols over a three-day period. The true test would be an evaluation period in Vietnam. The dog teams were shipped off and arrived in Vietnam on 3 April 1967.

After spending a week in quarantine with the 936th Veterinary Detachment, the off-leash group linked up with the 1st Calvary Division (AM) at An Khe. After a week of training the team participated in search and destroy missions over another one-week period. Deemed successful, they then moved to the 41st IPSD at Phouc Vinh on 6 May 1967. Here their evaluation continued as they went on additional search and destroy missions.

The concept was sound and the recommendation was that all future scout dog platoons have at least twenty percent of the handlers trained in the off-leash regimen. Like everything else in the military dog program, a lot depended on the handler and the dog. Some handlers, already in-country, began training their dog off leash. Some problems developed, especially if the dog went out of sight. The dog whistle proved an invaluable resource for recalling the dog without drawing undue attention to the patrol. In some circumstances, once the dog left the handler's sight, he was never seen again.

The impact that scout and tracker teams made in such a short period of time did not go unnoticed by Army commanders. On 12 August 1967, Chief of Staff Brigadier General Robert C. Taber heartily endorsed the working dog program and stated, "When properly employed, war dog units add significantly to the combat potential of any unit and provide a capability that cannot be gained by other means." Taber then forwarded a Combat Lessons Bulletin on the use of war dogs to commanders worldwide and even included copies to Australian and ROK forces in Vietnam.

Champ and his handler, PFC James F. Moore, were not part of the Combat Lesson Bulletin but they exemplified the assets of a sound scout dog team—and did it two days in a row. Moore and Champ were with the 42nd IPSD and worked point with the 3rd Plt. of A Co. 2nd Bn. (Abn) 327th Inf. during Operation Benton. While on patrol Champ stopped suddenly, cocked his head and sniffed the air. Two paratroopers working alongside Moore went forward and found seven NVA soldiers eating. Without giving away their position, they quietly came back and planned to ambush them later that night.

The next morning, Champ took the lead again as the patrol headed back to camp. Just fifty meters from the perimeter of the base camp, Champ alerted. No one was expecting a problem this close to home and the patrol was relaxed. Lt. Norman Fretwell signaled his men to move forward and called another platoon to cover the flank. "We moved into an NVA ambush from behind," Fretwell stated. "They were watching the trail and we were on them before they could run." A firefight ensued when the NVA eventually spotted the American patrol. In the ensuing forty-five minute fight, at least five NVA were killed while two Americans were wounded.

As the summer of 1967 wore on, it appeared that the allies had the upper hand and were winning the war, although unlike past predictions no one was willing to go out

A scout dog from the 44th IPSD, killed-in-action, is returned to base camp for a proper burial. Much like their human counterparts, dogs were recovered from the field whenever possible. *(Courtesy of John Burnam)*

on a limb to say or even hint when the conflict might end. Peace initiatives sprouted like weeds and it seemed like a new one popped up every week. On the ground, Vietnam was proving to be a ravenous monster, with a huge insatiable appetite that continued to devour more lives, resources, and money. The sheer number of military operations kept the scout dog platoons extremely busy. A good example is the 44th IPSD that hosted over 280 patrols during the month of June. There was little doubt that scout dog teams were having an impact. VC posters started to show up around the country offering "huge" rewards for handlers or dogs killed or captured.

This may have prompted the VC to attack a reconnaissance patrol of the 25th Infantry Division near Tay Ninh, along the Cambodian border, during that busy month of June. Working with the patrol was SP4 Roger Jones and his scout dog Ringo from the 44th IPSD. In a firefight with the VC, Jones and Ringo got separated and when the patrol pulled back and no Ringo to be seen, Jones figured his dog was killed. However, since no body was recovered, 1Lieut. Robert Fenner, the 44th commanding officer, had no choice but to list the dog as MIA with a nagging suspicion that negligence was involved.

What no one realized at the time was that Ringo was indeed alive, but severely wounded. During the firefight a bullet entered his nose and passed through the tongue and tore away a part of the jawbone. Incredibly Ringo did not bleed out, but had managed to survive. With a portion of his jaw blown away, he could not eat and would need help in a short period of time. Incredibly ten days later, another patrol returning to their base camp at Dau Tieng spotted a blood-caked and dirty dog following them. The dog was Ringo; he must have been driven by hunger and some inner courage to make his way back home and also avoid the Viet Cong. The dog wouldn't allow anyone to go near him until a dental technician won over the his confidence and brought him in. Preparations were made and the dental tech accompanied Ringo on an evacuation flight to Cu Chi. While there, Captain Thomas Dees, a veterinarian, operated on Ringo for several hours to help stabilize the dog's condition. Having not eaten in over a week, the dog was quite weak and had dropped twenty pounds. [32] Calls were made to round up the appropriate medical personnel and special care was given as Ringo was placed on an evac helicopter and flown to Tan Son Nhut Air Base. The scout dog was then brought to the operating room of the 936th Veterinary Detachment. Lt. Col. Donald B. Osbon, an oral surgeon, along with three other doctors operated on the dog for more than four hours. Questions arose during the procedure about the length of time he would be under anesthesia and whether or not there would be any after affects. After making the necessary surgical repairs, the surgeons properly positioned the jaw and then added a strip of denture plastic, secured with four screws to hold everything in place. The plastic strip would be removed once the jaw had healed. But this allowed Ringo to eat and drink normally during the healing process.

It was expected that he would be back for duty in about a month. This case shows not only the value of the military working dog, but also the concern of dozens of men involved during the entire episode. It required the dental tech to coax the dog home, Dr. Dees to stabilize him, and many others involved in the safe trans-

Scout dog Ringo sports a prosthetic device to help his jaw heal properly. Veterinarians often took extraordinary measures in the care of working dogs in Vietnam. This was not always a military necessity, but often compassion for a wounded comrade. *(Otis Archives)*

portation to Tan Son Nhut, where a surgical team performed an incredible operation. This was not something that could have been accomplished during WWII or Korea. If the same event had occurred then, Ringo would have been put down and become a statistic.

The 44th would continue to take a beating for the remainder of 1967, including an attack on the base camp on the night of 9 November. The handlers on base at the time were in their hootches when the camp began getting shelled. The K-9 compound was located several hundred yards within the base perimeter and when the shells started exploding all the men ran to a reinforced bunker adjacent to the kennels that was well stocked with additional weapons and ammunition. The kennels themselves had no protection except for a tin roof.

None of the handlers or the CO knew what to expect, or if the VC had breached the main perimeter, as shells

After several weeks of convalescence with the plastic prosthetic jaw support, Ringo was able to return to the 44th IPSD to resume his duties. *(Courtesy of John Burnam)*

exploded around the kennel and automatic gunfire could be heard in the distance. Interminable moments later the shelling stopped, but the night was far from quiet as the dogs, confused and several wounded, barked and howled. The men clamored out of the bunker in the darkness and ran to their companions. Among them was John Burnam who found his dog Clipper (12X3) okay but with paws bloodied from trying to escape the kennel. The kennel was a mess as men tried to calm their dogs and assess the situation. Burnam recalls:

> "On that awful night Ollie [Whetstone], who was scheduled to rotate back to the States in only a few months, found his scout dog Erik, serial number 36X3, in his kennel run bleeding to death. The dog's body had taken shrapnel wounds. Both of Erik's lungs were punctured. Ollie held his limp friend in his arms and cried. He was crushed to know that his best friend suffered painfully and was dying slowly. No one could save Erik's life. Mac [Michael McClellen], sadly, came over to Ollie and offered him his weapon. Ollie told Mac that he couldn't bring himself to use it even to relieve Erik's pain and suffering. He asked Mac if he'd take care of the terrible task. Visibly shaken with tears streaming down his face, Ollie stood on unsteady legs. Without looking back, he walked away from Erik and Mac. After Ollie left, a single shot rang out. I knew that Erik was dead." [33]

Later that same night another dog, Shadow (9X00), was also put down. None of the handlers were killed but two of them were wounded. Just two weeks later, the 44th took another hard blow when Edward Hughes and his scout dog, Sargent (6X81), were killed in action. Reportedly they disembarked from a chopper and as they cleared the landing zone, Hughes was shot point blank and his dog hacked to death. It was a full day later before both bodies were recovered, with Hughes stripped of all gear and Sargent of his harness and leash. [34]

Throughout the Vietnam War, dogs would die from booby-traps, disease, enemy fire, heatstroke, and a host of other causes that they were subjected to. Nothing short of a catastrophe could wipe out an entire platoon, but that is exactly what occurred in the fall of 1967 in An Khe. The situation would not be instigated by the enemy, but by a simple mistake made by an unfortunate veterinary technician in a scout dog platoon.

To control ticks and other body parasites, all dogs in Vietnam were subjected to a bath that contained a solution of Malathion. Malathion is a trade name for an organic phosphorus compound, yellowish-brown in color, with an unpleasant odor. Dogs are usually dipped in a bath that is typically made up of about .25% to .5% Malathion solution mixed with water. However the scout dogs of the 34th IPSD were mistakenly dipped in a solution that might have been as much as thirty times greater than normal. This toxic formula rang the death knell for fourteen dogs and sickened eight others. It became a roller coaster ride for scout dog handlers and the veterinarians involved for several weeks to come, as they first tried to diagnose the problem and save the remaining dogs.

Apparently an unmeasured amount of the chemical (a 57% concentration of Malathion) was inadvertently added to a vat that already contained an unknown quantity of the insecticide and water. Once this concoction was mixed together, the twenty-four dogs were dipped on the 3, 4, and 11 November. The first dog affected was found on the morning of the 12th, salivating and very weak, yet no one knew at the time that he was inadvertently poisoned. Veterinarians with the 459th Medical Detachment (IE) in An Khe were the first responders. A dextrose and saline intravenous solution was given by an attending veterinarian. The next morning the dog was found dead in his kennel. An autopsy discovered the dog's lungs were filled with fluid and he had an inflamed colon and intestinal tract. That very same night five more dogs fell ill.

A cold rain had fallen for five days in An Khe, and at first it was thought the problems the dogs were experiencing had something to do with poor weather. The ill dogs had high temperatures, muscle tremors, and convulsions. The three dogs that appeared to be the worst were moved into the barracks to get them off the wet cement of their kennel floors. The next day, the condition of the three dogs kept inside had not improved, but two others did seem to fare a bit better. The illness was still a mystery until a handler showed a veterinarian an empty can of Malathion and indicated that the dogs were dipped just a couple of days earlier. With the possible root cause now known, the doctors took immediate action. They began by giving all the remaining dogs a soapy bath to remove any chemical that remained on the skin and coat.

Three dogs that didn't seem to be responding to treatment were airlifted immediately to the 936th Veterinary Hospital in Saigon for laboratory tests. The patients were assigned to Captain Dennis McCurnin, a veterinarian assigned to the 4th Medical Detachment (JA) who had arrived in-country in August. A week later, after McCurnin took charge, five more dogs that had fallen ill were brought to Saigon. Despite extensive treatments all eight dogs eventually died.

An extensive treatment plan was laid out for the remaining dogs. The commitment by those involved was indeed incredible and the whole regimen lasted for 240 days. During that lengthy period, eight dogs recovered completely, fourteen died from the poisoning, and two others were euthanized. McCurnin, who was not aware of the initial history, later stated, "Since Malathion is absorbed by all body surfaces, the duration of the illness might have been shortened if each animal had been completely clipped [of their coat] before being washed with soap and water."

This case is a testament to the veterinarians who took their job seriously and often worked tirelessly caring for their patients. Although there was never a follow-up review by the military, it did indicate a weaknesses of the military dog program— that a single incident could affect so many dogs, in such a short period of time, and have such disastrous consequences. It could be compared to a bomb going off in the kennel area.

Dressed For Work

What a dog handler carried for gear varied with each man and the job at hand. Scout dog handlers and combat trackers often suited up for patrols in the field that could last seven days or more. Sentry dog handlers, by comparison, went out at night, usually for a six-hour shift, walked a fixed post, and usually were by themselves. Much of the equipment carried by the handlers would be the same, with a number of key differences.

The predominant weapon used by any dog handler in Vietnam was the CAR-15 (later designated GAU-5A/A), that is basically a modified version of the M-16A1 used throughout the war by all branches of the military. The weapon's ancestry goes back to the Armalite A-10, designed by Eugene Stoner in 1953. Redesigned in 1959, it went into production as the AR-15 and, surprisingly, was first purchased by the Air Force. When production of the rifle switched to Colt, it was renamed the M-16 and the Army accepted the rifle to replace the heavier M-14.

Lightweight and with a high muzzle velocity, the M-16 turned out to be a formidable weapon, albeit with a host of problems when it first arrived in-country. Two magazines (twenty- or thirty-rounds) were available, but filling it to capacity could possibly cause a jam because of a weak spring in the magazine. Soldiers began loading with one or two fewer rounds to prevent this from happening. Thirty-round magazines were seldom used, not only because of the increased chance of them jamming, but because it also left you more exposed, in a higher spot, when you were prone and firing. Another problem was its lack of a bolt handle. Gas pressure closed the hammer, requiring both the chamber and gas tubes to be kept extremely clean. In Vietnam, with humidity, dust, and mud, cleaning them was an on-going chore. On many occasions, the gun would jam in combat, and the only way to clear the barrel was to ram down a cleaning rod. The manufacturer replaced the chamber with a chrome one, and after issuing the proper field-cleaning kits most of the problems were alleviated.

It was still a devastating weapon, even though some instructors at Benning called it "Matty Mattel" because of its toy-like appearance. It would never gain the mythical or legendary status that the AK-47 achieved in the hands of the communists. Yet, the 5.56-mm NATO rounds from an M-16 hitting their target at supersonic speed turned a human body into a bloody pulp. It could be operated on semi- or full autonatuic (often referred to as rock n' roll), and weighed a mere 7.7 pounds. The M-16 even had a nifty in-line recoil feature that reduced the tendency of the barrel to climb upwards when firing on automatic, unlike earlier weapons of similar design.

The development of the CAR-15 for handlers seems to have originated with the Air Force, immediately after the major VC attack on Tan Son Nhut in 1966. At this time, a few deficiencies were noted with the M-16 as a dog handler weapon. The biggest change was its 11.5-inch barrel, nearly ten inches had been lopped off. With the shorter barrel, a larger and sturdier muzzle flash suppressor was required. It got a telescoping stock and sling attachments were repositioned to the top of the rifle. Easier to work now, a handler could hold the weapon in one hand while grabbing the dog leash with the other.

As late as 1968, the CAR-15 did not make it into every handler's hands. According to Sgt. Robert Kollar, a scout dog handler with the 58th IPSD in 1968, "I never saw anyone in our unit with a CAR-15, although I came across plenty at the Dog Training Detachment in Bien Hoa." Accordingly the handler, upon their reception at the dog platoon, received a CAR-15. Kollar received his M-16 at Bien

Hoa. Yet another 58th handler, Bill Denehy, stated the CAR-15 was not an option. He says, "Bond [the 58th CO] was a real asshole. For some reason we weren't allowed to have the CAR-15. In fact, we weren't allowed to even carry grenades."

Carrying a CAR-15, this handler from the 34th IPSD not only had to carry his load, but also everything his dog needed. *(Courtesy of Joseph Ertel)*

Still other choices for firearms remained. Fred Dorr, a Marine scout dog handler, was issued a Model 1911 Colt 45 pistol when he first arrived in-country. When going for something more substantial than his Colt, Dorr went with a M1A1 Thompson .45 submachine gun. "I liked it because it had a heavy-caliber round, compared to the M-16, and could tear up someone pretty good. I also knew that the Chicago gangsters had used them back in the thirties with pretty good results,"

The Thompson went into production in 1928 and became a favorite with the hoodlums and enforcers of the era, earning such nicknames as the "Chicago typewriter" or "Chicago violin," because of the case often used to conceal it. It was featured prominently on television also, specifically in the hands of Sgt. Chip Saunders on the series *Combat!,* a weekly program airing at night during the early 1960s. More recently on celluloid, the Thompson could be seen in the hands of Tom Hanks ,who played Captain Miller of the 2nd Ranger battalion in Steven Spielberg's movie, *Saving Private Ryan.*

Few if any handlers carried a Colt 45 automatic pistol even as an additional sidearm. Some sentry dog handlers were issued a Smith & Wesson .38-caliber as a backup sidearm. With a 4" barrel and limited stopping power it was more suitable for an urban cop back in the states. In 1966 some handlers had no choice and carried it as a primary weapon while on duty at various airbases in-country.

Also typically carried were anti-personnel hand grenades, commonly referred to as a "frag." Early in the war these may have been the MK2 type, the classic "pineapple" grenade from World War II. Made of cast iron and filled with flaked TNT, they had a fragmentation radius of about 10 meters. The problem with them was that sometimes parts of the grenade would be blasted even farther, possibly even injuring the guy who threw it.

The more common grenade was the Mark 26 that replaced the MK2. Made of thin-walled sheet metal, it weighed only fifteen ounces and threw out 1,000 fragments in about a ten-meter radius. Of two-piece construction it resembled a baseball, had a four- or five-second fuse delay, and could be tossed about forty meters. One variant of the grenade enabled it to detonate on impact. It was perhaps the one item that poised just as must danger for the handler as for the enemy. For added safety, some men would take a pipe cleaner and twist it around the head and the spoon. Many times, when going through heavy vegetation out in the field, you would get hung up on a branch or a vine (often called a wait-a-minute vine, because the barbs grabbed your clothing and you asked everyone to hold up while you released yourself), so it added an extra measure of safety to keep the pin from pulling out. In and out of helicopters, hitting the ground, or just getting into a jeep, there was always a chance for an accident, and there were many during the war.

Robert Himrod recalls, "I carried two frags most of the time and had a very healthy respect for them; they were damn dangerous! Once out in a dry paddy on patrol, two B-40 rockets were shot at us from some area that was just napalmed. No other shooting or contact. Apparently some fragmentation set off a frag on this guy's belt and killed him. Another time I threw a frag down an overgrown trail to 'recon by fire' and it didn't go off. Of course, we still had to go down the same trail. Luckily I found it a few yards away but it took me three shots [from the CAR-15] to set it off."

Many sentry dog handlers also carried the M-26 frags and expressed much of the same anxiety about them. "They were a cause for concern ever since it was dis-

Handler Roland Romanchek (39th IPSD) is weighted down with a full pack. Romanchek is waiting with Major (668M) for a helicopter to take them out for another patrol. *(Courtesy of Johnny Mayo)*

covered that a new guy had almost completely straightened the ring pull pins on his grenades," says Ed Hobbs "Many times there was a lot of chaos on the posting trucks with muzzled dogs trying to fight and handlers with a lot of gear bouncing in the bed of a truck trying to navigate a bumpy dirt road. One wrong movement by this guy with that pin slipping out could have wiped out everyone on the posting truck."

Sentry dog handlers had an easy time determining what to carry since their posting was at night and for a fixed amount of time. Craig Lord was at Phan Rang during 1968 and 1969 and stated his standard issue for a normal post consisted of a

> "...CAR-15 with twelve magazines, two flares, flak vest, helmet, radio, web belt, flashlight, poncho, and of course a canteen of water and c-rats. Personal stuff usually carried in a small bag were a sterno kit, homemade stove, extra clips, and *real* toilet paper. After January 1969 we carried some non-standard items including a bandoleer with 15 clips, two extra flares, and if working a listening post (LP) a Winchester Model 12 riot gun, unplugged, with five rounds or an M-79 with high explosive rounds. In all instances we carried the CAR-15."

The flares carried were parachute illumination flares, sometimes referred to as slap flares that were housed in an aluminum cylinder about one inch in diameter and approximately nine inches long. To launch it you removed one end and placed it over the other and then slammed it down on a hard object. It was usually your helmet, after you took it off.

According to Hobbs it was mandatory to carry the flak vest to your post but your own choice to wear it while working. Scout and tracker dog handlers seldom if ever wore a vest in the field; there was enough load to hump and the flak vest, weighing in at eight pounds, was among the first items to be taken off the list.

The rain poncho supplied by the military was large, hooded, and snapped together on the sides. "It was very effective and a big aid during the heavy monsoon rain," says Hobbs. "Walking and standing in these torrential rains all night could be rough without some protection. Your feet stayed wet, but your upper body stayed reasonable dry. Of course your dog got wet, and all German shepherd dogs smell bad when they are wet. All German shepherd dogs also believed you brought the poncho for them."

Besides a choice of weapons, a major consideration for handlers was how much water to carry. Sentry dog handlers, working for a fixed amount of time at night, usually carried one or two canteens of water. Tracker and scout dog handlers had to consider how long they would be out in the field, the terrain, any resupply by chopper, and of course the weather. A typical three- to five-day mission may find a handler carrying eleven quarts of water, distributed in two one-quart canteens, a couple of two-quart canteens, and a single five-quart, plastic, collapsible bladder. A dog could go several days without food, but not without water when you consider that half the dog's weight is made up of water. The consequences of coming up short for your dog could easily mean heatstroke, death, or, in the case of Butch (38M6), a missing dog.

Butch was an off-leash scout from the 33rd IPSD handled by PFC Charles C. Rowe. On 25 April 1969 they had been working a patrol with A Company, 2nd Bn., 35th Infantry, near Ban Me Thout in the delta area of IV Corps, along with another scout dog team. They had gone for two days without food or water when Rowe lost sight of his dog. A few minutes later the other scout-dog team had an alert, which turned out to be the scent of water. Rowe continued to search the immediate area but turned up nothing. Back home, it would probably be no problem, as you can call out for your dog. This was Indian territory and you could not just yell out and catch your dog's attention without the enemy taking notice. Butch was carried as an MIA on the books and was never seen again. Obviously this was a tough loss for a young handler arriving in-country just two months earlier. It also served noticed for the men who worked their dogs off leash of a potential and devastating problem.

By most accounts, the scout-dog handler had one of the heaviest loads of any patrol member that went into the field. What was brought with him depended upon several factors: the length of time spent in the field, the terrain and weather, and what the handler deemed necessary. There was a great distinction between what the handler would *like* to carry and what he *could* truly hump on a lengthy sojourn. Newbies or "cherries" (the FNGs) packed heavily, but with experience and time they lightened their loads considerably. Eventually, every dog handler had his own list of materials he carried into the field. Everything the dog team needed to survive would be carried in the rucksack or on the pistol belt. A typical five-day mission, circa 1970-71, would probably include many of the following basic items, besides the CAR-15 and water that was discussed earlier:

Scout dogs were worked both on and off-leash out in the field. Off-leash dogs were more susceptible to take off after something and never return. No matter how well-trained a dog is, the dog might follow ancient genetic instincts under some circumstances. *(National Archives)*

- Helmet. For every soldier in Vietnam, the brain bucket was the standard issue M1 steel helmet. Inside was a nylon liner that came in one size and had an adjustable headband. It took some time to get use to the weight (3.44 pounds). A cloth helmet cover with a disruptive camouflaged pattern was worn on the outside. A camouflage elastic helmet band was also provided to hold small pieces of foliage. More often it held in place a pack of cigarettes, an extra magazine, or insect repellant, all in easy reach and not likely to get wet except during a monsoon. In later years many guys opted for the soft "boonie" hat.
- Military spec rucksack and pistol belt. The rucksack was often called an Alice. After hefting the load for several hours deep marks would often appear on the back of a grunt. Some vets still wince at the thought of them.
- Combat knife if you were lucky to find one.
- 2.2 pound block of C-4 high explosive for cooking purposes.
- Bottle of water purification tablets and canteen cup.
- Roll of trip wire. An item that had many purposes.
- OD (olive drab) towel, extra bootlaces, and two pairs of socks.
- Two or three bottles of insect repellent for both the handler and dog. It was also useful for getting leeches off the skin.
- One meal a day for the dog. This consisted of three to four Gainesburgers with four extras just in case, although many handlers also secured cans of horsemeat. By 1970 many handlers were issued LRPs (Long Range Patrol meals). A total of seven meals would be carried and perhaps a small bottle of Tobasco sauce or mustard to kill the taste of the LRPs. Even then some simply weren't very palatable. Randy Kimler (42nd IPSD) said the chili con carne was the worst. "I once gave it to Prinz (K047). He never went near it again."
- Also, two or three cans of "real" food picked up at the PX would be carried along, with packets of coffee, sugar, and milk. Some guys cut the taste of the water with Kool Aid, while other guys didn't bother, figuring it just made you thirstier.
- Metal dog comb. It was often shared between the handler and dog. About the only things not shared with the dog were your toothbrush, toothpaste, and the supply of toilet paper.
- A pair of six-foot leather leashes (in case one broke), leather collar, choke chain collar and scouting harness.

Synthetic materials were hard to come by and seldom used. Leather deteriorated quickly in the moist conditions prevalent in Vietnam, as Gary Zemel (25th IPSD) found out one day when his dog Tux broke the lead and got into a fight with another dog in the compound kennel. As Zemel relates:

"Our kennel is usually quiet, but any unusual event, visitors, or local dogs, starts our dogs barking, straining their chains. Sometimes, coming or going with Tux sets off the kennel. Tux and all the dogs have leather leads. Tux's lead (leash) is fairly old, it probably came with him in 1966 [two years earlier]. I'm taking Tux out of the kennel. I unclip his chain, clip his lead to his collar and exit the kennel. All of our dogs bark at Tux and me. As we move between dog shelters, each dog strains his chain and barks at us. Tux aggressively tugs and barks, in turn, at each dog. I'm annoyed! I give Tux a good correction: I yank his lead hard and it snaps. I almost fall on my ass. Tux and King [another scout dog] are at each other. I hesitate, then wade in and part the dogs. All this takes only seconds. I'm shaken. The dogs are fine. My broken lead finds its way to Atom, the platoon "wheeler dealer." He contacts the riggers who are the guys who package equipment for transport. He trades dog food and the riggers sew nylon webbing into dog leads. That's how I invented the nylon dog leash."

Full gear, excluding the dog, could extend beyond seventy pounds, and for the new guy with no experience could approach a hundred. In comparison, a typical load carried by an infantryman in Vietnam was fifty to sixty pounds. One good reward for the dog handler is that the load was a lot lighter at the end of the mission, as the rations and dog food were used up. Yet a great disparity existed between

Bill Bodnar (42nd IPSD) chows down with chili carncarne and rice, often described as the worst c-ration ever devised. *(Courtesy of Bill Bodnar, 42nd IPSD, 1969-1970)*

what was SOP and what men usually took to the field. Randy Kimler recalls that he never worked a patrol with a helmet on. "It was stupid, just plain stupid," Kimler recalls. "The helmet kept shrapnel from entering your head. I always wore a boonie hat (officially called *hat, tropical* or *hat, hot weather*), probably because it was more in defiance of the order than anything else." Although the boonie hat began to see widespread use by the end of 1967, when Gen. Creighton W. Abrams became MACV commander, he hated its "unmilitary appearance" and attempted to stop shipments and place tighter restrictions on their use.

What irked Abrams even more than the wearing of what he called the "jungle hat" was how the men were embellishing it. Abrams specifically stated, on 25 September 1971, "Subject hat was designed to be worn by all personnel on field operations for protection against climatic conditions (rain and hot sun), bugs, and mosquitoes. The hat was not intended as a carrier of grenade rings."

Like everyone else, the dog handler carried a pair of dog tags. There are a couple of reasons why and how they were carried. Many men carried them around their neck and typically the edges had a rubber cover or were taped to keep them from clanking around while on patrol. Others separated the pair, as Kimler recalls. "I wore one in the boot laces on each boot. Less trouble that way, I didn't have to worry about them making sounds or getting in the way. Also, if I got blown up with a booby trap, chances are they would find one of the dog tags better than if both were around my neck. Most of the grunts I worked with wore them in their boots that way."

A notice was issued stating: "A recent check by the graves registration unit showed identification tags were being found on less than half of the deceased upon arrival at the mortuary." The last thing anyone wanted was to tick off the folks over at graves registration. Besides the requirement of dog tags, they expected you to mark each article of clothing to make identification that much easier. As everyone knew, marking your boots lasted about a day in the field.

Although many dog handlers carried similar equipment, the scout-dog handlers also had a small piece of paper that was not issued to those who worked with sentry or tracker dogs. Sized to fit into a wallet and crammed with so much information that it was difficult to read, it contained the briefing instructions for handlers to provide platoon leaders on the capabilities and the limitations of scout dog teams. It was SOP for all handlers to receive these cards, entitled "Briefing Guide for Scout Dog Handlers" while training at Fort Benning. Instructors urged their students to carry them along on their visit to Vietnam. Like so many other things, both before and after, the briefing guide didn't make it into the hands of every scout dog handler in Vietnam.

Tom Sykes, a handler with the 48th IPSD in 1967 and later an instructor at Benning, called them a "crib sheet" for briefing unit commanders and NCOs in the field. "It was handy to have a hard piece of paper to show a unit commander what a handler was saying wasn't pie-in-the-sky." Although all infantry officers were supposed to have training on the proper use of scout dog teams, the card was there to serve as a reminder so that the teams were not abused. Many of the scout-dog handlers who received the briefing cards never had to resort to using them in the field. Kimler states:

"I never had a problem with me or Prinz being pushed too much. The grunts were always glad to see us because it meant they wouldn't have to work point while we were there. I never had trouble with officers in the field either - the highest one I ever had to deal with was a Captain. Some officers were very familiar with dogs and their limitations from working with them before. Some officers didn't know anything about dogs so I just told them what Prinz and I could and couldn't do. You did have to be forceful. It wasn't my home unit of course so I was a little more independent than one of the grunts in the infantry units. A handler could refuse to walk point if his dog was too tired, hot, or sick. It was the handler's call and only his - as far as we were concerned, we could overrule an officer and it did happen. A dog was a very valuable piece of government property and the Army made sure handlers knew it. We often felt the Army thought the dogs were more valuable than we were! We were expected to protect this Army property. I never thought about using the briefing cards like this [showing it to an infantry officer of platoon NCO], but it would give a handler more ammunition for his argument - an appeal to higher authority - an official document to back you up."

Although just a small piece of paper, for a green handler arriving in Vietnam it would be a resourceful tool, more so than lugging around the Army FM 20-20 scout dog manual. Yet the briefing card did not reach everyone's hand. Those who learned the scout job trade OJT in-country were never issued one (officially at least). Apparently many class graduates from the scout dog school in Benning never received one either. Both Robert Kollar and Lee Stewart, who graduated together as part of the 58th IPSD in 1968, stated they never saw one or heard of

Randy Kimler (center with moustache) with the 41st IPSD, stands with several local women who were employed by the handlers to help with daily routines and housekeeping. Handlers not only came home with memories of their dogs and fellow handlers, but also with civilians that had helped them while in-country. *(Courtesy of Randy Kimler)*

their existence during their entire tour of duty. [35] The Army felt a more comprehensive pamphlet desirable and printed a second card titled "USARV Scout Dog Platoon" that was provided to a number of handlers in-country.

Scout dog handlers did not need to be in the field to have problems with those in positions of higher authority. Trouble with leadership could be closer to home in your platoon commander or platoon sergeant. There was not a formal aptitude test for someone to lead a scout dog platoon, and for many officers it was a stepping stone to another position, yet commanders and sergeants were part of the military working dog program in Vietnam. When a veterinary technician, someone who is keenly aware of a dog's condition, complains about leadership, something needs to be addressed and not taken likely. Such was the case with the veterinary technician from the 41st IPSD who wrote in 1967:

> "I have a few complaints to make [and] also a suggestion. My complaints are the dogs are being overworked, the moment they come off one patrol, our platoon commander and platoon sarge has them already committed to go right back out. The kennels have not been built yet. Dogs that have been on medical hold have been taken off without my knowing it and sent to the field. I don't know if anything will come of this, but let me know if there is anything I can do or say to stop this." [36]

Dog Art

Left: Scout dog handler SP4 Dane Robertson (unit unknown) is shown with his scout dog. This painting was probably done towards the end of the Vietnam war, although both the artist and date are unknown. *(Center For Military History)* **Right:** An early watercolor created by an Army artist, depicting a scout dog team in 1967. *(National Archives)*

Left: The military dog was sometimes depicted by the combat artist. This montage (artist unknown) shows several views of a sentry dog. *(National Archives)* **Right:** Cartoonist Hal Atkins, who often contributed to The American Legion Magazine, takes a poke at a scout dog team from the 58th IPSD. *(Courtesy of Robert A. Kollar)*

Prelude to Tet

During the final quarter of 1967, little changed on either side of the war, although the Americans did not realize that North Vietnam had a few surprises in store after the calendar turned to a new year. Operation Rolling Thunder continued to pound targets north of the DMZ. At the end of October, Nguyen Van Thieu and Nguyen Cao Ky were installed as the President and Vice President of Vietnam, with the hope they would provide some political stability.

Sentry dog teams continued their night patrols and scout dogs still took the point position in the field. Although there would be few sentry dogs lost in combat, a death from an accident can be devastating for a handler. Such was the case with a dog from the 12th SPS at Cam Ranh Bay while exiting the posting truck. The dog caught its paw between the bed and the tailgate breaking all the bones in its foot. The dog was brought to the base dispensary and Captain Caraway, the USAF base veterinarian, set the paw and leg in a cast. The prognosis was not good and eight weeks later it became apparent the bones would not heal properly. This meant that the dog needed to be put down, which is a task no one wishes for.

Elsewhere, newly formed tracker teams pulled fifty-five missions but took a heavy blow when CTT #2 was ambushed on 15 November. [37] Over two dozen men were lost from the 25th Infantry Division along with the tracker team, in an operation named Barking Sands. The tracker team comprised SP4 Robert Brede,

CPL Mark Howard, Sr. SP4 Arnold Johnson, SP4 George Koon, and the tracker dog Bodie (4A75). Apparently the team was tracking at a good clip and entered an ambush site with no time to react.

Day-to-day life went on back home in the states amidst the turmoil generated by Vietnam. The St Louis Cardinals bested the Boston Red Sox in seven games and the "Impossible Dream" was ended. Earth Day was celebrated for the first time, along with the Super Bowl. Norman Mailer and Joan Baez were arrested at a couple of Vietnam protests, and in San Francisco, Scott McKenzie's hit single beckoned everyone to come to the city and wear flowers in their hair. As in most conflicts, events at home contrasted sharply what was taking place in the war zone.

For Americans, Christmas and New Year's are particularly special times, especially for those fighting overseas and far from home. It didn't matter where you were in Vietnam, getting mail in-country was a Godsend for many soldiers—just as much a benefit as having someone to write letters home to. Jim Stewart was a sentry dog handler stationed at Tan Son Nhut with the 377th SPS who worked with Dobe (7X49), who did not quite fit the profile of a typical sentry dog. According to Stewart, "Dobe hated the muzzle. He was a dog fighter and was always causing trouble on the posting truck. He would reach out with his paw and grab the dog across from him by the back of his neck and attempt to pull him closer so he could bite him."

With this aggressiveness toward other dogs, Stewart wasn't sure he wouldn't attack someone while on post with the muzzle off. "In the training ground I would have him muzzled and release him on a guy running away from us (without attack padding). Dobe would take off OK, but about twenty yards into the attack he would stop, put both [paws] under the bottom of the muzzle, and try to force it off his face. This ended the attack." Of course, what takes place in Vietnam sometimes stays in Vietnam. Stewart was not about to let his parents worry about his situation. One can sense the balancing act and underlying tension as Stewart recognized where he was but displaced any sense of danger in his letters. On the last day of the year 1967, shortly before Tet, the following letter was posted home:

> Dear everybody,
>
> Enclosed you will find some pictures, which are explained on the back. I am finally getting out from under my Christmas fan mail. I didn't realize that I knew so many people. I only have about 20 letters left to answer. I should be able to rap them out in a month or two. Ha.
>
> I had a little too much Christmas cheer, but am stable again. Ha. We had a party at the section after we all got off work on Christmas morn. We will have a New Years party this morning, but most of us are cutting down the consumption of liquids and are concentrating on the steaks.
>
> I have kennel C.Q. tonight and have had it for the last two. I strained the muscles in my back while training dogs the other day and have a light duty excuse. Will be ready to go back and rid the world of communism on Tues. Dobe is fine but still hard headed. We have a slight disagreement about whether his muzzle should stay on. So far it has remained in place, but he tries to pull it off every night [on the posting truck].

Mom, you said that you heard the V.C. were fighting about 25 miles from Saigon or as far as from Montrose to Flint. When they get to Cow Corners is the time to start digging! Ha Ha. Really, I'm being watchful and didn't take any unnecessary chances. I'm healthy and getting fat. I'll have to start playing ball or something. Have a Happy New Year!

Love,

Jimmy

You won't find Cow Corners, Michigan, on any map. But those familiar with the area know it is located about two miles from the Stewart family house. As the Air Force handler penned another letter home, another Christmas truce ended the day before. Hanoi also softened their stance (by appearance), as they often did around the holidays and publicly stated that talks with the United States would resume once the bombing was halted. As one "truce" ended, another New Year truce emerged and Ho Chi Minh declared that there would be many victories for the communist cause in the upcoming year. President Lyndon Johnson had little to celebrate as the year ended and did not make any declarations that the war would be over soon.

Like every other night during the year— New Year's Eve was no exception— throughout the country as the sun began to set sentry dog teams loaded up on the posting trucks and drivers fired up their engines. In a few minutes they were dropped off at their assigned posts where muzzles were removed from their dogs and the two of them walked and worked alone during the hours of darkness.

Airman James Stewart (377th SPS) worked with Dobe (7X49) at Tan Son Nhut AB, although some would argue it was the other way around. Stewart was typical of most men in Vietnam (i.e., get the job done and get home). Most Vietnam vets would tell you that their time in-country was the most significant event of their lives. *(Courtesy of James A. Stewart, O.D.)*

4

Is This Any Way to End a War?

"As this long and difficult war ends, I would like to address a few special words to ... the American people: Your steadfastness in supporting our insistence on peace with honor has made peace with honor possible."

President Richard M. Nixon

A Turning Point

As the calendar page turned to 1968, the faint glimmer of peace in Vietnam still shined for the United States. Another New Year's truce emerged and North Vietnam considered going to the bargaining table if the aerial bombing of their homeland ceased. There is little doubt that the U.S. still had the upper hand in the war and just two months earlier President Johnson stated, "We are inflicting greater losses than we're taking...We are making progress." Oftentimes, as history has shown, progress in a war of attrition is just an illusion.

Tet is the lunar New Year on the Vietnamese calendar. The NVA and Vietcong had planned months in advance for massive attacks across the South during this period. The communists expected the operation to advance a popular uprising in the civilian population and the quick collapse of the ARVN. Like a political campaign slogan, Ho Chi Minh's cry, "Defend the North, Free the South, and Unite the Country," would sound a bit hollow in just a short period of time. As it turned out, after the all-out attack the civilians did not rise to the communist cause and for the most part the ARVN were able to hold their ground. The basic core objective of the enemy was to attack Saigon, Tan Son Nhut Airbase, the ARVN compounds, and air bases at Long Binh and Bien Hoa—what was known as the

Saigon Circle. Attackers were also planning to seize Cho Lon (the predominantly ethnic Chinese district of Saigon), MACV headquarters, communication centers within the city, and the fuel and ammunition depots.

A classic military diversion was set up prior to the major offensive with an attack at Khe Sanh, that had the purpose of drawing both U.S. men and materials away from the primary targets. General Westmoreland didn't realize it was a tactical distraction at the time, but took it as an opportunity to decisively engage the enemy using the 6,000 Marines there as "bait." To a limited extent, the diversion worked, even as it developed into a siege. President Johnson did not want another Dien Bin Phu, nor did he want a Texas-style Alamo. Ultimately, the entire battle of Khe Sanh would dovetail with the country-wide offensive that took place beginning on 30 January.[1]

Like any army in the world, the Viet Cong suffered from communication and coordination problems. A full day before the planned nationwide attack, the VC prematurely began their assault on Da Nang and eleven other cities. The Tet holiday ceasefire abruptly ended and all American and ARVN personnel went into full alert. The next day, the major offensive began as an all-encompassing assault by the NVA and the Viet Cong, involving thirty-six of the forty-four provincial capitals and sixty-four of the 242 district capitols.[2]

Nineteen suicide commandoes held control of the U.S. Embassy in Saigon for six hours before they were all killed. For the television viewer and armchair generals back home in the states, it seemed like everything that came out of the Johnson administration was a lie. We weren't winning the war at all. Just look what was taking place on the six-o'clock news.

The Viet Cong decided to send their 275th Viet Cong Regiment and the U-1 Viet Cong local Force Battalion to attack Long Binh, the largest U.S. Army base, located twenty miles north of Saigon. With paved roads and rail spurs spread out over twenty-five square miles, it was home to more than 50,000 troops, and that included elements of the 199th Light Infantry Brigade. Long Binh also had the largest contingent of sentry dogs in the country, to provide security for the 3rd Ordnance Battalion's ammunition supply depot. This was definitely not the area where sentry teams suffered from boredom. Outside the wire, the handler and dog needed to contend with VC snipers, mortars, and RPG fire in their direction on a routine basis. Backing them up was also no safe haven, with a huge ammo dump that could be lit up at any time. The Viet Cong attack turned up a major weakness in the command structure, as the 720th Military Police Battalion provided security for the post and the 95th Military Police Battalion looked after the ammo dump. To coordinate their work more effectively, the 212th Military Police Company (Sentry Dog) was released from the 95th and assigned to the 720th.

When the attack began at Long Binh, the VC 274th Regiment started their assault at Bien Hoa, just a few miles north. Killed at the beginning of the engagement were Pfc. Gordon Leroy Currier, Jr. and his dog Satch (M164). Reportedly, Currier had tied his dog to the ladder at the base of a watch tower and ascended to help his fellow MPs. When the tower was nailed, an RPG killed the both the occupants and the tethered dog, Satch.

A second wave of attacks took place during the first week of May, as a follow up to Tet. Once again, Bien Hoa took more than its share of hits, since it was adjacent to the VC supply line that fed south from Cambodia to Saigon. Like every aspect of Vietnam, a million stories could be told from actions taking place all over the country. Jerry Matthews, 3rd SPS, and his dog, Caesar (104M), were posted at the west end of the base about 600 feet between the perimeter fence and the south runway the night of the attack. When the rockets and mortars began to rain in, the pair were caught with no cover nearby, except for a manned bunker near the taxi-way.

The manned bunkers comprised little more than sandbags that were quickly built after the Tet offensive in January. Most were manned by a single Air Force security enlistee. During the attack, Matthews and Caesar ran to the bunker as he yelled over the din to the sentry holding the position that they were coming in. God only knows what the soldier thought. Mathews yelled for him to go to ground and cover himself. Caesar, not the friendliest dog in the area, was coming in too.

Matthews later stated, "Putting your collar on your dog is like having your CAR-15 locked and loaded." There was an obvious concern that Caesar would attack the soldier. Matthews piled on top of the sentry and pulled Caesar along to make sure he had some protection from flying shrapnel. If the dog knew the sentry was there he never took notice. "The dog looked at me as if to say, "Thanks, pal," Mathews said. About five minutes later, the all-clear sounded and the dog team moved out of the bunker, thanking the sentry for the company. The sentry hugging the ground never moved or said a word the entire time. Just a few yards away there was a reminder of the attack, as a three-foot piece of metal from a 122mm Soviet rocket stuck out of the earth. With the night once again quiet and dark, Mathews and Caesar went back to their post and worked until daybreak, finishing their shift without further excitement.

Although the VC military operation impacted just about everyone in-country, it also set the tone for those back in the states who knew they were headed for Vietnam. An example is Herman "Rusty" Allen, who at the time was training with the 47th IPSD at Fort Benning. Allen recalls:

> "We were all scared and I remember watching the news in the dayroom. What made it so bad was that we knew we were going to be there in a short time. Sometimes it looked so bad that I thought they may send us on without finishing training. The Army made it clear they could do anything with us that they pleased. All in all, it was a very worrisome and confusing time." [3]

From a military standpoint, Tet was a military disaster for the Viet Cong and North Vietnamese, but it turned out to be a propaganda victory for the communists. It didn't matter how well our men did on the battlefield during the offensive, when a photograph by Eddie Adams depicted the gunshot "seen" around the world. The black-and-white photo shows Nguyen Ngoc Loan, chief of police of Saigon, shooting a VC suspect with his hands tied behind his back. The execution photo was released without any background information and it cast Saigon in a bad light, in total disregard for the Geneva Convention. [4] Out in the field, a massacre of Vietnamese

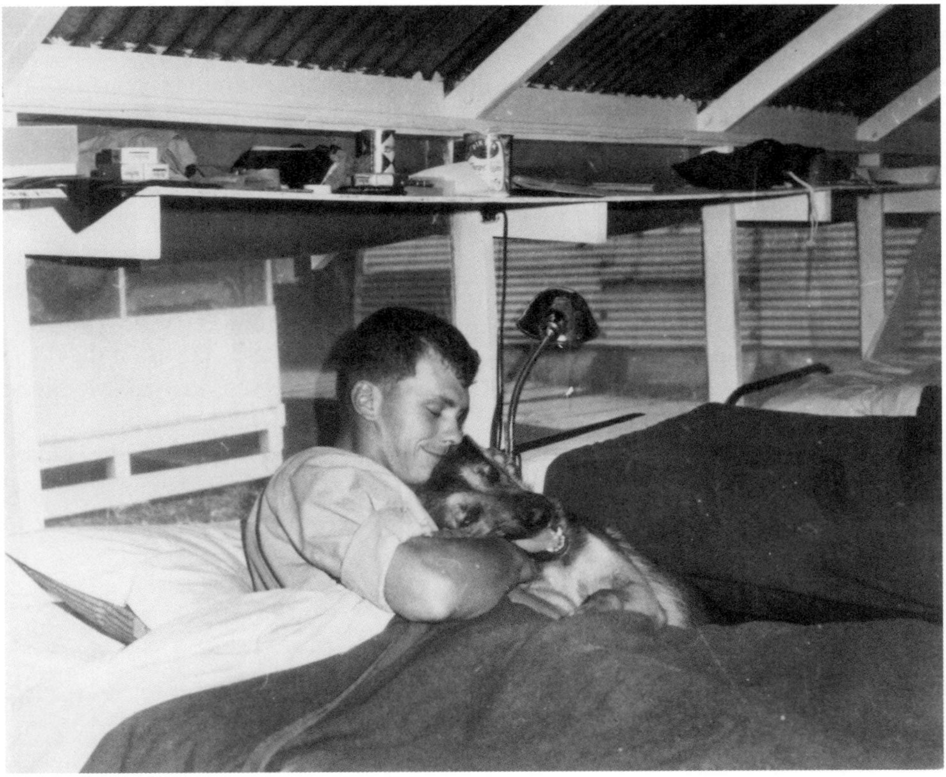

Happiness radiates from the face of Marine Sgt. Robert Sabo as he embraces his scout dog Hans. The two were reunited after Sabo was wounded on a patrol. *(National Archives)*

civilians took place at My Lai, but it was another eighteen months before Lieutenant William Calley was brought up on related charges. President Johnson took the political fallout back home, and on 31 March, on national television, announced to the nation that he would not seek re-election. The man wanted a way out of the quagmire, but had no clue how to accomplish the task. At the same time, Johnson announced limiting air attacks on North Vietnam and that preliminary discussions for peace were once again expected to begin in the near future.

Dog Platoons Are Everywhere

At the beginning of May, 1968, another wave of Viet Cong attacks began with an aborted attempt to take control of the capitol city, Saigon. By the end of the month, twenty-one scout dog platoons were in place throughout RVN attached to various divisions as needed. Over 175 booby-trap devices were discovered by scout dog teams in the first five months of 1968. To say the scout dog platoons were "in place" is like saying each unit had a permanent home base in South Vietnam. For most scout dog units it was pick up and move to follow a particular division to another location. For several scout dog units, their platoons would be split among several different positions. For this and other reasons, dog handlers were never really part of any one group and seldom did they work with the same people over a long period of time. This would inherently be another weak link in the scout dog program. As such, dog teams would occasionally work patrols with officers familiar with K-9 operations and who knew their limitations. Other handlers would be saddled with inept leadership or with line companies where the grunts either were doped out, didn't care, or did not work professionally as a team in the bush. At the end of May another, albeit weaker, attempt emerged to take Saigon with heavy fighting in the Cholon suburb. Many events taking place around the country did not affect dog handlers—their world was simply everything they could see around them and nothing more.

Constant movement of scout dog platoons would also take its toll on the dogs. Many would be quartered in temporary kennels and Army veterinarians would be challenged in locating and treating dogs that seldom stayed in one location. A good example was the 58th IPSD that completed their training at Fort Benning on 31 January 1968 and deployed two weeks later to Vietnam. Like so many before them, they flew in a Hercules C-130 to Tan Son Nhut and then moved about thirty miles northeast to

A critical mission for scout dog teams was to search villages after all civilians were removed. Often VC hiding spots or munitions were located during these sweeps. *(National Archives)*

Phuoc Vinh. Here they were attached to the 3rd Brigade of the 101st Airborne Division (Airmobile). The first few weeks entailed additional training before starting operations in the field. Half of the platoon moved south to Cu Chi. The remainder of the men and dogs, along with the headquarter element, remained at Phouc Vinh.

Meanwhile, the 1st and 2nd Brigades of the 101st were located far north in I Corps around Hue. In September it was decided that the division should be re-united. Men, dogs, and equipment were loaded onto a C130 aircraft that flew up to Phu Bai Air Base. They settled-in at Camp Rodrigez, just a mile from the 42nd IPSD who supported the 1st Brigade. A little farther north was the 47th IPSD supporting the 2nd Brigade. Once again, the 58th settled into the area, built bunkers and training lanes, and picked up and moved again on 1 November to Camp Evans. Evans was formerly the division base camp for the 1st Air Cavalry Division that was moving south to III Corps, at Bien Hoa and Phuoc Vinh. The 3rd Brigade of the 101st Airborne, including the 58th IPSD, moved into Evans, which was a short truck-ride north and situated halfway between LZ Sally and Quang Tri. It was home to the 1st Cav, but most of the unit moved south to Bien Hoa and Phouc Vinh. The 58th took over an area originally occupied by the 34th IPSD that moved out with the 1st Cav and took up residence in Phouc Vinh. For the remainder of the war, the 58th stayed put. Only at Phuoc Vinh did the 58th have actual kennels built on a concrete slab. At Camp Rodriguez and Camp Evans, the dogs were housed in their shipping crates. During their entire time in-country, the 58th never had permanent kennels and the dogs remained with their shipping crates or in cut-down

Helicopters played a critical role during the Vietnam war. *(National Archives)*

With helicopter deployment, scout dog teams could accompany patrols on short notice. *(National Archives)*

galvanized drainage pipes. A concrete slab for a kennel was poured in June 1971, but a month later the platoon stood down. 1,250 days after it first arrived in RVN, the 58th departed and the kennels at Camp Evans were never completed.

The movement of scout dog platoons was just one component of a musical-chairs scenario. Handlers rotated out as either their time was up or they were wounded and removed from duty. Platoon leaders, mostly 1st Lieutenants, would stay no more than a year. Replacement handlers would arrive from Benning, locally from other scout dog platoons, or the USARV Dog Training Detachment in Bien Hoa after receiving on-the-job training.

Scout dog teams were expected to support whatever Army element requested them. In many cases it involved a group of men with focused operations and objectives, known as "Lurps." In May of 1964, the Special Forces established five teams, comprised of six men each, to operate independently deep in enemy territory. The contingent of specially trained volunteers was denoted as Long Range Reconnaissance Patrols (LRRP), hence they were simply known as "Lurps" in-country. Often they worked for five or more days in the field independently, ten to forty miles from their base camp. This meant that they rarely had the support of artillery to back them up, should they get in trouble.

Weighted down with Claymores, M16s, M26 hand grenades, and additional water and rations, the men usually skipped wearing such "non-essentials" as flak jackets and steel helmets. Many recon members even went so far as to carry

Helicopters also enabled tracker dogs to be delivered in quick fashion so that the teams could acquire a fresh scent. *(National Archives)*

AK-47s and don green NVA floppy hats, to confuse the enemy even more if they happened to be sighted in the bush.

The main job of the Lurps was to gather intelligence on enemy activity. Secondarily, their priorities included taking prisoners and setting up ambushes along VC or NVA trails. Since support was limited or non-existent during their operations, recon teams relied on themselves if the enemy hit them while working in Indian country. Lurps earned a great deal of respect in-country, along with legendary status; much of it was deeply deserved.

Just like riding in cars, most dogs relished the opportunity to fly in a helicopter. *(Courtesy of Joseph Ertel)*

Operating in the enemy's backyard took skill, courage, and a fair amount of luck. It often proved an ideal situation for Lurp teams to have the benefit of a seasoned handler and scout dog tagging along. Problems can crop up during such operations. LRRPs were always inserted and extracted by helicopter. The chopper needed to hover or

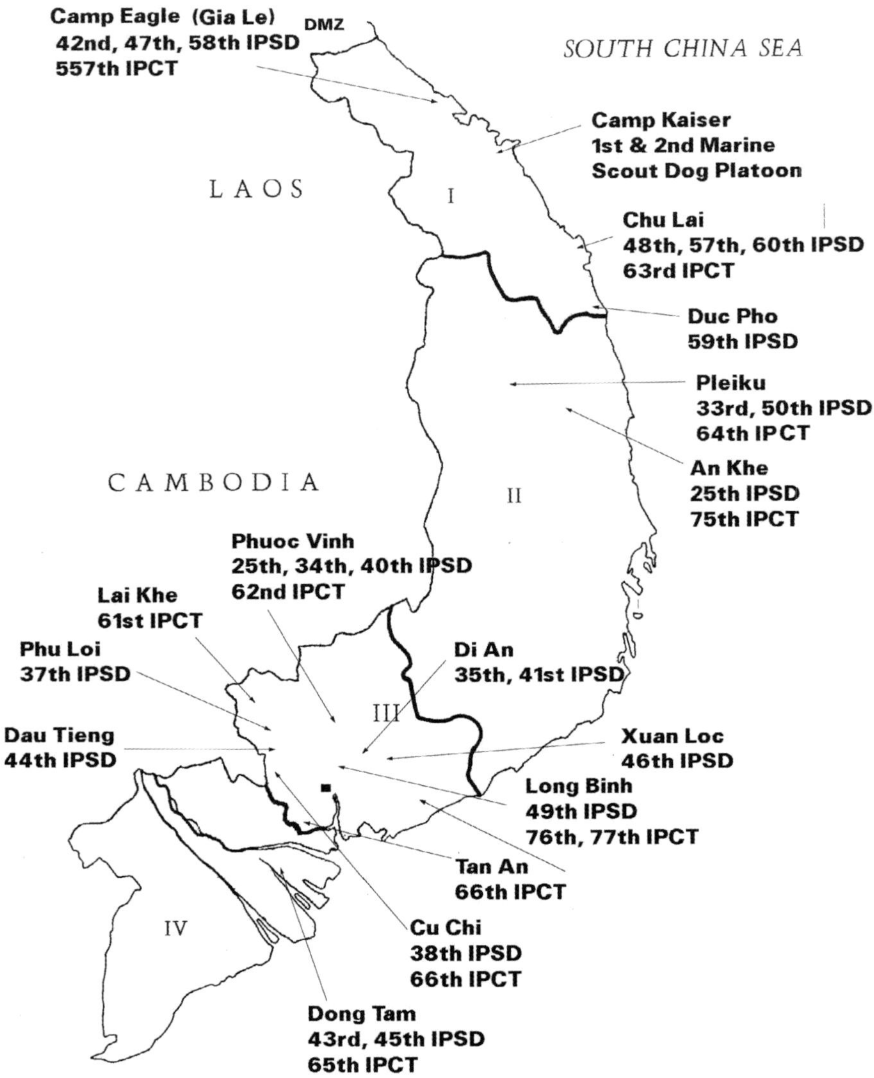

Tracker teams were deployed across Vietnam in the same fashion as their scout dog counterparts. Fewer in numbers, they were expected to cover the same territory when called upon. *(Author's Collection)*

touchdown on the landing zone (LZ) so the dog could exit or enter by jumping. In some cases, handlers lowered or pulled their dogs by their working harnesses. This was not only uncomfortable for the dog, but could induce a serious injury. Sometimes a "McGuire rig" was fashioned from a blanket or poncho that made transport easier and safer for the scout dog. During the course of the war, no formal extraction harness was developed for scout dogs; apparently no one was ever given responsibility to develop ancillary equipment for military dog teams.

The number of dog teams that supported LRRP operations during the Vietnam War is not known. 1Lt. R. W. Menig, CO of the 33rd IPSD, related both the effectiveness and problems of using scout dogs in his reports during the spring of 1968. At least two dogs and handlers assisted LRRPs from E Company, 20th Infantry (Abn), and it was expected more requests would follow.

Two dog teams from the 33rd worked with Recon Teams 33 and 34 during Operation Oasis III in the last three weeks of February 1968. In mountainous terrain with thick vegetation, the dog teams needed to work behind a point man, allowing him to break trail with a machete. In this manner the dog would not tire so easily and would have better endurance. On one patrol, SSG Rose and his dog, Ringo (7X91), accompanied Team 24. The dog started working immediately after jumping from the chopper at the LZ. Team leader SSG Ralph Resch later reported:

> "During the mission, the dog alerted us to man-made objects and to animals. He also alerted to well-used trails in the area. My men and I all agree that we would rather work with a Scout Dog Team than have an additional man in the patrol. I, SSG Resch, believe that the dog knows the men in the team and that if the situation ever occurs, any man in the patrol team could handle the dog. I would like to have the dog and his handler stay with my team as long as possible."

During another action with Recon Team 23, PFC Jeffrey Dick called an alert from Nicki (40X1). The patrol set up a hasty ambush as they heard voices draw closer along a trail. The patrol was spotted as they moved into position and a firefight ensued. Nicki remained quiet but wanted to attack the enemy. After breaking contact, the team headed back for the LZ. The dog continued to make alerts to the flanks and allowed the team to keep changing direction before another quick firefight broke out. Fortunately a forward air controller (FAC) flying overhead appeared on the scene and directed the patrol to the nearest LZ. During the entire time, Nicki kept working until the team was safely extracted. [5]

Since a LRRP patrol could stay out in the field for several days, food and water for the scout dog needed to be distributed among several team members. The biggest potential problem was the safe extraction of the dog with the other team members. With the right dog and handler along, early silent warning of the enemy proved a valuable asset. Unfortunately, this potential was not realized, so LRRP teams usually operated independently without support from a scout dog and handler.

When LRRP patrols began to use scout dogs in the field, Major George M. Massey, at Fort Benning, believed the officers and senior NCOs who led platoons in Vietnam should become proficient with scout dogs themselves. Massey instituted a program to accomplish that in August 1968. It is not known where the order originated, but it gave officers a better appreciation for the job the dogs and handlers needed to do.

More handlers and dogs were needed in Vietnam. Following on the heels of the 58th IPSD, the 47th and 59th landed at Tan Son Nhut in May and became operational two months later. The first day the 47th became fully operational, Jimmy Powrzanas and his dog, Pal, located a couple of bunkers and a trip wire; two days later Otis Johnson sustained shrapnel wounds in his leg. A week later, an infantry

Sgt. Frank Spano and his scout dog Lobo completed the first ever tandem jump of a man and a dog in Vietnam. Although the exercise never took place during a combat situation, it did reinforce the capability of a scout dog team. *(National Archives)*

CO unfamiliar with war dogs kept pushing Jonathan Harraden and Major (3M47) forward, after the dog kept throwing strong alerts. This pressed the patrol into an ambush and several guys were wounded when a command-detonated, Chicom (Chinese-Communist) claymore exploded. Harraden recovered from his wounds and rejoined the unit in December. The day after Harraden was wounded, the platoon suffered its first dog killed in action when Willie (6M11) was blown up by a booby trap and his handler, James Youtz, was severely wounded in the arm. The 47th was getting beat right out of the gate in a bad neighborhood, and they didn't even finish their first month out on patrol.

Having a scout dog improved the chances of getting out of Vietnam in one piece, but it was no guarantee. Not every dog was built the same or had the best instincts; training continued on a regular basis. At base camp, training lanes were set up with trip wires, decoys, and dummy booby-traps for handlers to work their dogs and hone their skills. Robert Kollar, with the 58th IPSD, worked with Rebel and was preparing to go into the field for his first patrol. In a letter home to his wife, he wrote:

> "Rebel did worse today. I think he learned the lane as he did so well yesterday. However they moved the wire positions and he hit two. Damn if he hits one out there! But he did pick up two others and two decoys they had out and picked them up by scent alert. So I'm not entirely unhappy with him today. I'm hoping he'll be ready when it comes time to go out (but will I ever be ready?)" [6]

Such are the problems and anxiety faced by scout dog handlers who will eventually lead a patrol. Regardless of the confidence handlers had in their dogs, you could never trust them 100 percent. Many men just hoped and prayed that when the time came, their dog would be the best in the country and come through in the clutch.

As proficiency of scout dog teams increased in Vietnam, the success of the combat tracker teams dictated that training needed to be established in CONUS, especially since the agreement with the British could not be extended indefinitely. In November 1967, the combat training mission for trackers was authorized and assigned to the Military Police School at Fort Gordon, Georgia. A slow start-up meant the first six teams trained would not be ready until September 1968.

The biggest boost the school could get was the five seasoned British instructors assigned to start the training program. This team included two officers, Major Huia Woods and Captain Donald Hall-Smith; along with NCOs Sgt. Joe Little, Sgt. Bob Wilson, and Sgt. Ron Adie. Their experience was superb, including service in Syria, Egypt, Libya, Tunisia, Palestine, Borneo, Kenya, and Malaya. Fully developed and operating at maximum capacity, the school was projected to turn out 60 dogs and handlers along with 250 visual trackers every three months.

By the middle of 1968, fighting in Vietnam clearly showed that Americans had the upper hand in this war of attrition. In June, General Westmoreland was replaced by General Creighton W. Abrams, who planned to continue the program, but did not make grand statements that would prove to be false in the future. The move at the top of the command chain seemed to reinforce the notion that there still was no clear-cut policy for the United States in Vietnam. Protests continued against the war, but those who participated sacrificed little, such as the 200,000 students in New York City who refused to attend college lectures. After much deliberation, Paris was chosen as the host city for peace talks between the United States and North Vietnam.

Sentry Dogs in Thailand

Thailand was one of the forty countries that supported the RVN, by first providing pilots and aircraft mechanics in September 1964. The Thai government sent a reinforced battalion the following year, and in 1968 a full division was in place at III Corps near the Bien Hoa and Ben Cat area. By the end of 1968, more than 12,000 Thai combat personnel were participating on the ground in South Vietnam. The biggest contribution from Thailand was the air bases from which strategic bombing operations were launched over both North and South Vietnam. The U.S. used the Royal Thai Air Base (RTAB), and it was supported by United States Air

Force sentry dog teams. Some early-arriving handlers helped pave the way for fifteen handlers and twenty dogs from the 635th SPS who arrived on 24 March 1968 and deployed to the base at U-Tapao. As the buildup continued throughout the year, handlers and dogs included the 388th SPS (Korat), 56th SPS (Nakhon Phanom), 355th SPS (Takhli), 8th SPS (Ubon), and the 432nd SPS (Udorn).

A strong ally of the United States, Thailand occupies a central position on the Southeast Asia peninsula. Twenty percent larger than California, Thailand is bordered to the west and northwest by Myanmar (formerly Burma). To the north and east, the main border was the Mekong River, separating Thailand from Laos. To the south is the Gulf of Thailand and to the southeast is Malaysia, with Cambodia providing separation from Vietnam.

In July 1968, the U. S. Air Force presented the Prime Minister of Thailand, Thanom Kittikachornn, with five grown female dogs and four puppies, as a gift of appreciation from the United States of America. The female dogs arrived at U-Tapao (RTAB) with the first elements of the 635th SPS. The puppies were whelped on 25 April 1968, when sentry dog Lita (9M71) delivered a litter of five (three males and two females) at the Security Police kennels at U-Tapao. One of the puppies died on 14 May 1968. The gift was to assist the Thai military in starting a military working dog program and to establish a Royal Thai Palace Guard Kennel, at Korat RTAB in Bangkok. At the turnover ceremony at U-Tapao, Thai military officials accepted the gift of canine warriors.

Thailand's location afforded only a small margin of protection from the Viet Cong and NVA forces. Numerous sapper probes were made, despite extreme

Sentry dog teams such as this one provided security at air bases in both Vietnam and Thailand. *(Courtesy of Larry Chilcoat & Geisha (A871) USAF)*

distances covered by the enemy. Ubon, where the B-52s launched bombing raids against North Vietnam, was a favorite target. Three full-fledge attacks, almost suicidal in nature, took place during the course of the war.

The first assault took place on 28 July 1969. At around 0130 hours, sappers managed to penetrate the base and plant satchel charges. However, their escape was blocked by the K-9 team A1C Kenneth O'Dell and Shaeffer (X846). O'Dell and Schaeffer both were wounded, but both recovered. The sapper team escaped into the jungle, dumping most of their gear along the way.

Another attack took place on 13 January 1970, in the early morning hours. The sentry dog team Larry Bridges and King (A642) alerted to a group of sappers; Bridges released the dog, who promptly chased down the enemy. A response team laid fire on the intruders, as another sentry dog team alerted to intruders closer to the main runway. Sgt. Thomas Cartwright Jr. released Jodie (89X1) and dropped down to open fire on the enemy. One sapper was dropped dead, but Cartwright took a round in the leg and Jodie got hit in the neck. The sappers were quickly knocked out by the response teams after just a few minutes.

Within twenty minutes, all known sappers were dead. What was not known was that the dog King, wounded during the initial encounter, had pursued the VC insurgents across the runway. He was hit again from an enemy round but continued crawling after his quarry. This proved to be King's undoing; he was shot by the quick reaction team that mistook him for a crawling sapper. No one was to blame; it was the luck of the draw. Cartwright and Jodie were evacuated and both recovered from their wounds. King was dead, but had displayed the loyalty and qualities of a sentry dog who never gave up.

Canine Friends and Foes

Not only American dogs poised a headache for the Viet Cong. Based on documents captured by members of the Ninth U.S. Infantry division, local dogs also caused problems for the VC in the countryside. The communist District Military Chief (VC), Nguyen Bao, issued orders on 10 September 1968 that all local dogs within the area of the Ben Tre Provincial Military Command be exterminated.[7] The city lies near the mouth of the Mekong River, surrounded by Giang, Vinh Cong, and Tra Vinh. A foiled attack on American forces precipitated the VC orders, a week earlier. Apparently local dogs started barking outside the village of Phu Tuc, enabling the Americans to open fire first and inflict heavy casualties on the guerillas. The VC military order stated:

> "Considering the common interest of the Revolution and that of the majority of the masses, with a view to ensure our victory over the enemy [United States] in all circumstances and protect our forces , the Military Committee hereby orders :
>
> 1. That all localities in the three areas should thoroughly exterminate dogs and in no circumstances go back to raising dogs.

2. The liberated areas and contested areas should eliminate all dogs not later than September 25, 1968; all localities should thoroughly carry out this order upon reception.
3. Warnings are to be issued to all disobedient elements that keeping dogs is acting against this military order, that once blood is shed due to this act, the perpetrators are liable to answer to the masses and bear all the consequences.

The effect of such an order was based on the influence the Viet Cong held over a particular area. Over the course of the war, the VC pursued this type of tactic throughout the country where they were able to intimidate the local populace. Obviously the VC understood how dogs could be advantageous during a conflict, not just in a defensive posture. With scout dogs being fielded by both the ARVN and U.S. forces for several years, strong anecdotal evidence indicates that the Viet Cong attempted to field scout dogs as well. It is possible that the American and ARVN scout dog teams made an impact on Charlie. Events at the beginning of 1969 in II Corps seem to confirm this, although no VC dogs were ever captured or killed.

In February 1969, 1Lt. Brian J. McGee, 39th IPSD, reported what appears to be the first incident of the VC possibly employing their own scout dogs. While on patrol in the Tuy Hoa area, handler PFC Compton and scout dog Fritz (5X72) called constant alerts to an unknown enemy. Although no contact was made, the VC seemed to be just a few steps away. McGee thought they were working with a scout dog, but none was sighted to confirm this.

A sighting did occur a month later outside the Cu Chi base camp perimeter. On 25 March 1969, SP4 John Rice was working an ambush patrol with an element of the 25th Infantry Division. Rice spotted a small Vietnamese dog about 1500 meters outside the base perimeter wire, along with other movement. The enemy was between them and the base camp, but they were not engaged. Other patrol members also confirmed Rice's observation.

If Charlie attempted to use scout dogs, it was not to great extent. It is doubtful that adequate training could be accomplished in the circumstances they worked in. Since the NVA had never established dog program, it is doubtful the dogs were brought down from the North. If dogs were employed, they probably were mongrel strays or captured ARVN dogs. Several American dogs were listed as MIA over the years, and after going hungry and thirsty for a couple of days, any dog could be coaxed and befriended with food and water. As a matter of survival, they should not be considered traitors, just practical. It is doubtful that an American dog trained to locate the Vietnamese would accept the same people as friendly.

The VC had no background employing scout dogs, but the United States Army may have inadvertently provided formal education. According to Sgt. Jesse Mendez, shortly before the Tet offensive, three ARVN officers were brought to Fort Benning for extensive instruction on the use of scout dogs. Like everything else in this crazy war, it is possible that one of the men may have been VC, or at least a sympathizer. There is a possibility that several ARVN handlers held VC connections. Mendez suspected one of the officers as being VC, but had no proof; only an innate suspicion from his previous experience as an advisor in Vietnam. [8]

An event at the Filhol rubber plantation near Cu Chi confirms that the VC tried to employ a scout dog. A forward air controller for the 25th Infantry Division, Major Bogue Harrison, spotted a large dog in an open field. Harrison took his twin-engine Cessna O-2 down for a closer look and saw the dog run to a small stand of trees. Immediately he fired a smoke rocket and watched as a squad of nine guerillas sought new cover.

In the vicinity of this encounter, two Air Force B-57s circled and the FAC directed them for a low-altitude, attack profile. The bomb run killed all nine VC, yet the dog escaped unharmed. Harrison guessed the dog to be a VC pet. Based on Charlie's tactics and their resources, this seemed unlikely. Capabilities of the Viet Cong may have been exaggerated over the years, but it is doubtful they would have a pet and even more unlikely they would have taken an untrained dog out in the bush.

Walking on Charlie's Ground

Some two hundred years ago Lord Byron stated, "War's a brain-spattering, windpipe-slitting art." Although thousands of advances have been made since then to effectively send your enemy to their maker, the end result is pretty much the same and oftentimes just as gory. Hand-to-hand combat will always take place, but technology usually keeps antagonists at a distance while killing each other. In Vietnam for a good portion of the war, guerilla activity included the prolific use of mines and booby-traps. The person who planted an explosive device or trap could be miles away from his victim or already dead. It could also be that he (or she) could be just a scant few meters away holding an electrical detonator waiting for soldiers to come walking by in the sweltering heat of a sunny day.

Science and technology have advanced tremendously in the detection of explosive mines and ordnance since World War II. Even with the vast arsenal of sophisticated electronic equipment developed by the military, little could be done to detect explosive booby traps that were used extensively by the NVA and Viet Cong forces in Vietnam. The cruder and simpler the device, the more difficult it was to detect with highly engineered gadgets. Booby traps posed an unseen terror for the American soldier and the ingenuity that the VC displayed in their deployment cut deep into the soldier's psyche. In many cases booby traps were not set to kill immediately. The VC set shrapnel explosives aimed for the head or groin that had enough explosive force to provide a lifetime of disfigurement or blindness. These nasty little devices were often referred to as "bouncing Bettys." Punji pits held sharpened stakes of bamboo capped with feces that an unwary soldier could step or fall onto. Other devices planted in the ground were called "toe poppers," even though they blew off most of your foot.

These devices proved very demoralizing for the many troops that patrolled the landscape of Indian country. In 1967, booby traps and mines accounted for more than 4700 casualties and seventy percent of the losses for tanks and armored personnel carriers (APC). There was no longer anything that could be considered a routine patrol. Routine came to be known as a patrol where you didn't encounter the enemy. Otherwise, you just walked along, either in a rice paddy or a "friendly" village. Even then, just one misstep could results in an explosion that ripped the silence into a God-awful day, and someone would start screaming in agony. As a soldier, you could be walking along and miss every booby-trap planted, if there was even one to begin with. Just when you thought everything was safe, a VC could pop out of a well-camouflaged spider hole. Every patrol member would have his back toward him and the entire platoon could be mowed down in seconds by a chattering AK-47.

The question was, "Can anything be done?" From a technological standpoint, not much could be offered from the Army or Marines. A minesweeper, which really was just a metal detector, would catch the big ordnance. But they were useless if it was a monofilament trip-wire or booby-trap device slung from a tree. The same held true of a grenade stuck in a can with a vine attached or a man who buried himself underground. How do you deal with something that cannot be seen, smell, or heard? Morale was declining and men were refusing to go out on a patrol. American soldiers do not fear a fight, but like every human being there is fear of the unknown. American technology and spirit would only carry so many burdens. Ahead of his time, at least for the men fighting in Vietnam, was a French poet and writer by the name of Alphonse de Lamartine, who stated, "When man is in trouble, God sends him a dog."[9] We had made the atomic bomb and were preparing to send men to the moon. Yet, with the entire technological prowess that the United States possessed, the military turned to dogs to solve a vexing problem in the countryside of Vietnam.

The United States military wanted to bring back mine-sniffing dogs, known as "M-dogs," from the World War II era. The M-dog program was the first of its kind established for training dogs to locate concealed explosives. Although under actual field conditions the ability for dogs during that war to locate mines ultimately proved to be a failure, it was because researchers and trainers did not know how to properly train dogs to locate hidden ordnance. The military in the late 1940s knew dogs could do it; but how would they enable them to perform the function and achieve acceptable results? After WWII was concluded, the British launched a similar program at the War Dog Training Centre at Melton-Mowbray, England. Once again the testing proved inconclusive. Like the American program, the British based the motivation for the dogs finding the mines on positive stimulation and a food reward. But just like the Americans they trained the dogs to locate soil that was turned over in planting a mine or booby trap instead of locating the actual device.

In the fifties, Stanford University studied the problem and tried "fear motivation" to train dogs to locate buried mines. This entire exercise turned into an abysmal failure. Regardless of the animal to be trained, and the same holds true for most humans, positive reinforcement will provide the best results.

In Vietnam, besides locating mines it would be desirable to have dogs alert to booby traps, tunnels, and enemy personnel. The US Limited Warfare Laboratory (USALWL) was expected to produce results, but did not have the resources or qualified people to turn out a positive result. Instead, the agency looked to farm out the project and considered a couple of organizations that might meet their

BSI also developed training for dogs that helped to locate enemy personnel hidden within tunnels that were prevalent in several locations in Vietnam. The dogs' job was to locate the entrance but not enter it. *(National Archives)*

needs, including the University of Maryland, which had helped to develop some of the basic training regimen for scout dogs. Ultimately, they turned to a small start-up company called Behavior Systems, Inc. (BSI).

BSI did not fit the typical mold for a military contractor. Founded by Dr. Robert E. Lubow and Dr. Eugene E. Bernard, North Carolina State University professors, BSI had focused its attention on training pigeons to guide missiles. This background was strictly limited to the classroom and never advanced to actual trials in the field. What the two had going for them were contacts they had cultivated at the USALWL as they discussed future programs with people within the Biological Sciences Divisions, such as John Romba, Max Krauss, and Milton Cutler. When an official request for a proposal (RFP) was made public for training mine dogs, much of the wording came directly from Lubow and Bernard, showing that they had the inside track. In today's parlance, it would be considered a sweet deal that netted the university professors a contract to develop an initial group of fifty-six M-dogs at a cost of $625,000. First and foremost, twenty-eight dogs needed to be trained and evaluated before the contract would be awarded.

Lubow and Bernard secured a short-term loan from a local bank for start-up funds and began scouting for land suitable for training and housing the dogs.

They found it in Apex, North Carolina, fifteen miles west of Raleigh. Since they were both full-time professors, much of the work was farmed out to two graduate students who became principals within the company. Finding suitable labor turned out to be quite easy. Lubow stated:

> "We found that in and around the college community there was an unexpected manpower resource for this work: college dropouts, members of the local drug culture, non-drug-using hippies all looking for a non-routine, non-office, non-factory job; a job that was not identified with Western industrialized urban ideals. What could be better than working with dogs in the beautiful, green, North Carolina countryside? Although the work was clearly defensive in nature, it still was related to the war in Vietnam. On this basis we had expected a considerable problem in recruiting personnel from the available population. However, to our surprise, the anticipated difficulties never materialized."[10]

In just under two months, personnel were hired, kennels were built, dogs were procured, and the training trails were laid out. Strictly speaking, the goal was to produce dogs that could detect ordnance buried in six inches of earth, hanging up to five feet above the ground, or located ten feet to either side of the trail. The dogs could be worked on-leash or off-leash, but were expected to alert by sitting about two feet away from the booby trap. Food was the reward and it was provided as a positive stimulus. Each dog received basic obedience just like any other war dog—one big difference would be the "sit" command. It was never used for the obvious reason that this was the key indicator that a mine or booby trap had been located.

The instruction was intensive and formed the basis for every explosive detection dog trained since that time. All those who were part of the training regimen knew what was at stake. Developing a dog that could efficiently and accurately locate mines and tunnels ultimately took seven months. By the end of the program, fourteen dogs were trained for mines and another fourteen for tunnels. All were cross-trained to locate trip wires that were part of a booby trap, but that did not necessarily include explosives.

The test to show how well the BSI-trained dogs performed took place on 18 July 1968, at Fort Gordon, Georgia. The dogs were carefully scrutinized by the military, as were the hippie handlers who worked them efficiently, even though an air of open hostility was ever-present throughout the demonstration. But one cannot argue with success. Under a scorching sun, the handlers and six demonstration dogs performed superbly, and in short order the contract was awarded to BSI to develop twenty-eight dogs for the Army and twenty-eight for the Marines. Bigger facilities were sought and a new training site, comprising 1,500 acres, was leased in Shotwell, North Carolina. The ranks of the company swelled to 150 people. Dogs would be trained, but it would cost about $10,000 each; then again, what price do you put on potentially saving a man's life and those around him? Additional trainers needed to be employed, along with vet techs, data clerks, kennel laborers, and a host of other people who needed to make an operation of this size run smoothly.

Also at this time, the two principals of BSI, Lubow and Bernard, made the classic business mistake. There was an unwritten understanding that if the contract were satisfied, BSI was to get the next group of dogs under contract and train them for the military. This proved to be a critical business error fatal for many future handlers. Once the training program had been well documented, the military grabbed the program manual and decided to go it alone. But handling dogs was not something that could be learned from a written manual, and the Army had yet to learn its lesson. It was tragic for all involved, a classic military blunder, which proved that the armed forces did not possess the intelligence or commitment to handle a working dog program to its best potential.

BSI conducted their training at Fort Gordon and in August 1968 activated the 60th Infantry Platoon (Scout Dog)(Mine/Tunnel Detector Dog). [11] From the very moment that BSI personnel tried to enter the grounds of Fort Gordon, problems mushroomed. Many of the trainers were college "peaceniks" and there was open resentment between many of them and the soldiers they were meant to train. Among the BSI personnel was Charles Fasanaro, who was against the war and more importantly against American GIs being blown up. Fasanaro proved to be an excellent point man for the military contractor and was able to mend fences and bring the two groups together. The conflict started simply when he began eating c-rations with the platoon members, when he didn't have to. Eventually tensions subsided and the training commenced in earnest, as the members expected to be deployed to Vietnam the following year.

After the completion of training, the 60th IPSD (Scout Dog)(Mine/Tunnel Detector/Dog) arrived in Vietnam to begin operations, and their evaluation, on 22 April 1969. It would be a two-pronged assessment: first three months with the 25th Infantry Division around Cu Chi, and the next three months up north in Chu Lai with the Americal Division. Two dog teams were also sent to work with the First Marine Division for three weeks. After a ten-day quarantine period for the dogs and an in-country orientation course for the handlers, a check trial was made that determined the dogs needed refresher training. The first dog team to deploy on a tactical mission took place on 10 May, at which time the evaluation officially started.

As with every other military working dog program in modern warfare, the mine and tunnel dogs had many successes as well as its share of problems. At the conclusion of the test period, eighty-five percent of the patrol leaders involved gave a positive response to the program. Although the 60th had a twenty-five percent casualty rate, no handler losses were due to the dog's performance. Problems were somewhat the same as any mission, with or without a dog.

One handler was injured on his first support mission. The mine dog successfully alerted to three trip wires attached to booby traps and made another alert when the handler approached and keeled over from heat exhaustion, tripping the booby trap. The grenade exploded wounding two patrol members; it was later determined that the dog had been deafened by the explosion.

By the time the platoon moved to Chu Lai on 28 July, seven dogs were lost, yet the results with the 25th looked good. Artifacts were missed and the dogs seemed to have problems with ordnance that had been emplaced for a long period of time. [12] Mine dogs were available sixty-nine percent of the time and tunnel dogs eighty-one percent, figures that were quite acceptable considering the typical losses from sickness and injury for both dogs and handlers.

Many of the recommendations from the evaluation followed typical military doctrine and the majority were sound. Since mines were a bigger threat, fewer tunnel dogs were required or they could be cross-trained, and a wider variety of artifacts could be available during the training period. There was no field manual available, nor were any qualified instructors on hand who could reinforce training or catch mistakes so fatal errors in the field could be cut down.

The House Appropriations Committee studied the results of mine/tunnel dog use in Vietnam. Based on testimony received and the overwhelming support of the patrol leaders interviewed, continuation of the program was assured. This was accomplished by having the Marines conduct their own in-country evaluation in I Corps, where the enemy was using an ever-increasing amount of booby traps and mines. In July 1970, the mine/tunnel dog program shifted to Fort Benning, Georgia, partly as a consolidation move but also with the stipulation that the dog's effectiveness and training techniques employed were to be continuously improved.

The success of the mine/tunnel dogs in Vietnam is attributed to the Department of Defense. The real credit belongs to Behavior Systems, Inc. and their dedicated employees who nurtured the program in its infancy. This company developed the initial group and wrote the training manuals for future handlers and dogs. Success does not always breed future contracts, as borne out as the Department of Defense dumped BSI in favor of the Army for future program development.

As the conflict in Vietnam rolled along, the performance of these dogs began to diminish. Many people deviated from the original training regimen. New handlers rotated in and each one had less experience than the previous one. This also precipitated the idea "I have a better way to do it." The strict training regimen required was often abandoned and many handlers tried to employ their personal techniques. Consequently, some mine/tunnel dog teams worked efficiently, others so-so, and the remainder accrued a dismal record. Occasionally this led to dissatisfaction with the dogs and, naturally, to a higher casualty rate for patrol members and working dog teams.

Project Aquadog

Sporadically throughout the Vietnam War, a threat emerged from enemy surface or underwater swimmers placing demolition charges at key locations. Military installations in riverine areas, specifically bridges and harbor facilities, could seriously be damaged by the explosion from a satchel charge or underwater mine. For the most part, protection of these areas was made from the shore or in boats by visual observers or with the use of sophisticated acoustical detectors. Both swimmer countermeasures had their weaknesses and the Navy seriously considered the use of trained military dogs to function as swimmer detectors.

The scenario for this type of operation ranked high for any limited war situation and particularly so in Vietnam. The Viet Cong could easily train and equip a swimmer/sapper with minimal resources and still achieve spectacular results. One only has to look back to World War II to see the accomplishments of U.S. Underwater Demolition Teams (UDTs) and the success they achieved in Europe and particularly in the Pacific.

In September 1968, the Naval Ship Research and Development Laboratory (NSRDL/PC), located in Panama City, Florida, proposed that a project be established in Vietnam to evaluate the use of dogs as an effective defense against enemy swimmers. The coordinator of the East Coast Vietnam Laboratory Assistance Program (VLAP) and the Chief Navy Research and Development Unit - Vietnam (NRDU-V) both agreed to the proposal. Before jumping right in-country, researchers decided to do a feasibility study in CONUS first. The tests would be conducted in waters around Florida with Air Force personnel and then move to Vietnam for further study. The Navy called the evaluation "Project Waterdog."

Although the idea of having dogs detect humans in water is a common procedure today as part of many civilian search and rescue operations, this appears to be the first time anyone had attempted the practice. For some unknown reason it took almost a year before the Navy began their tests. Patrol dogs and their handlers came from Lackland AFB to begin the program. These sessions took place during October and November 1969, near Panama City, Florida. Further investigation was made in Key West, Florida, during January and February 1970.

What the Navy found out was that the dogs could detect swimmers on the surface and those underwater using open circuit scuba and snorkel in excess of 500 yards. The dogs alerted either by barking or displaying a very aggressive nature. By placing both the dog and handler in a low draft motorboat, a large area could be covered, and once detected, the swimmer could be prevented from carrying out his mission or escaping. Once a swimmer was detected, searchers could use either rifle fire or concussion grenades to eliminate the threat. Be assured that the most expedient means would be employed.

Overseeing the entire effort was Project Officer LCDR A.F. Barta. A few delays ensued, but the waterdog teams and support personnel arrived in-country at Tan Son Nhut air base on 19 March 1970 to begin a two-month evaluation. Civilian Project Coordinator, Paul M. Eisenhauer, from NSRDL/PC and the four Air Force handlers (TSGT James H. Edmundson, SSGT Thomas G. Deloach, SSGT Francis L. Flynn, and SSGT Leo H. McRee) remained in the Saigon area while the four German shepherds acclimated to the heat and humidity. [13]

This tight-knit group soon moved to Nha Be, just south of Saigon—a large operation area for the Navy and a launching point for many operations carried out by Navy SEAL teams within the area. It was also a place where the VC had conducted a number of swimmer attacks, some successful and some not. All operations were to be coordinated through the Rung Sat Special Zone (RSSZ) Tactical Operations Center (TOC) or the Nha Be District Sensitive Zone TOC, with support from the Naval Support Activity Detachment (NSAD).

Phase one of the evaluation involved refresher training for the dogs and detection of friendly scuba divers. Even though this training usually took place in the cool early morning hours, all combat search operations would take place at night. Training commenced near the Nha Be fuel facilities and involved Vietnamese swimmers provided by an Army advisor attached to the Commander of the Nha Be District Sensitive Zone.

Once this instruction was completed, the group moved to the Advanced Tactical Support Bases (ATSB) at Gau Dau Ha and Ben Keo on the Vam Co Dong River to conduct riverine operations. Both locations consisted of ammo-barges moored in the river that had been the subject of previous sapper/swimmer attacks. Neither location afforded a suitable land area for a kennel, so one was constructed on a barge. It featured a concrete floor and screened sides so there was adequate ventilation for the dogs. This also meant that the kennel facilities could be moved quite readily to any desired location by the connecting waterways in the immediate vicinity.

Within the last six months since the waterdog team arrival, there had been at least three swimmer attacks. The last one was most successful, incapacitating the bridge crossing the Song Vam Co Dong River that carried traffic along highway QL-1 into Cambodia. A pontoon bridge needed to be constructed upriver to carry vehicles as part of the Cambodian offensive. Everyone felt this area was primed for another attack and the waterdog teams were called on to patrol this area. But with just four dogs, it would be impossible to provide coverage on a round-the-clock basis. This really wouldn't be necessary, since swimmer attacks would in all probability take place in the dark of night.

On 8 April 1970, the handlers and dogs attempted to patrol the river. These sorties began at 1950 hours and lasted until 0530. Each dog worked for about two and one-half hours before being relieved. It wasn't pleasant duty as there was a lot of activity in the area and the waterdog teams had to keep ducking from friendly small arms fire. Not everyone was informed who was out on the river, and the recent flare-up of VC activity kept everyone trigger-happy. Because of these problems, the patrols were quickly discontinued and the barge-kennel moved to ATSB Ben Keo on 16 April 1970.

Conditions at Ben Keo weren't much better. The waterdog barge was one of six barges tied up alongside each other on a river that spanned a scant 125 to 150 yards across. Each barge was 180 feet in length with a fifteen foot beam. Often, other river patrol craft were tied up alongside the barges. Just four weeks earlier, three swimmers were killed attempting to plant C-4 charges at this location.

Beginning on 16 April, the team began night patrols commencing at 1930 hours and winding up at 0530 in the morning. On the third night of patrolling, a 107mm rocket just missed hitting the waterdog barge. The next night, the VC launched ten rockets that hit the Vietnamese Training Center only a mile away.

About a week later, Navy dog handlers arrived and alternated with the Air Force handlers in patrolling activities. This continued until 5 May, when the Navy took over the entire operation and moved everything north to Cam Ranh Bay. Two weeks later, one of the dogs, Topper (3A36), died of heat stroke. It was decided at this point that they would get one of the Navy handler's sentry dog, Fritz (79X3), from DaNang and retrain him. An above average sentry dog, it took a mere three weeks for Fritz to be retrained as a swimmer detector.

On 1 July, Pete (72M8) also died from unknown causes. He was exhibiting some acute stomach bloating and weakness in his hindquarters. Within two days he was dead. Consideration was given at procuring another sentry dog, but it was decided to send the three remaining dog teams to the Cua Lon River where there was sapper/swimmer activity taking place.

The three teams continued to work in the area until 1 September. Based on all the available data, the program was considered successful. It was recommended that additional operational units be trained and deployed. However by this time Vietnamization was in full swing and no one was interested in putting more resources into another dog program in Vietnam. The South Vietnamese showed little interest in taking over the program and the dogs were eventually turned over to the USARV dog training detachment in Bien Hoa to be re-integrated as land-based patrol dogs.

IHS – How Our Dogs Were Almost Wiped Out

Theoretically on paper, the military dog program in Vietnam appeared to be a solid winner as summer turned to fall in 1968. Missions pulled by Army scout and tracker dogs mounted in frequency, sentry dogs continued to be a positive presence in thwarting the Viet Cong, and mine and tunnel dog teams worked diligently. There were weak points for sure within the framework of the military working dog program in Vietnam. Some of the difficulties were being addressed, while other persistent problems were simply ignored in hopes they would go away. Quietly and with no warning, the entire K-9 effort in Vietnam was threatened with complete failure, yet no one at the time or even for years later really knew or understood just how close a complete disaster was at hand and how deeply the combat effectiveness of the dog teams were impaired. The enemy this time was not the NVA or the Viet Cong, but a small parasite that had the potential to kill and never be caught.

Like many medical catastrophes, the events did not occur with a bang but a whimper. It all started with one dog having a simple nosebleed. In clinical terms it is called a unilateral or bilateral epistaxis; in other words, the dog has a nose bleed from either one or both nostrils. It didn't stop at just that. In a very short time other dogs experienced the same symptoms and some dogs died within a day, others within a week. Those that did recover (or appeared to) often loss weight and had a decrease in stamina, vomited frequently, and displayed weakness in their hindquarters along with many other problems. In the end, the dogs afflicted eventually died.

The first reported clinical case of this disease appeared to have originated with a sentry dog from the 212th Military Police Company in Long Binh on the 24 July 1968. Around the same time, the 48th IPSD over at Chu Lai lost a dog and three others died at Tan Son Nhut while under the care of the 936th Medical Detachment. An epidemic of some type was ramping up, except no one knew it at the time. The deaths occurred in different parts of the country and under different commands, hence those familiar with the problem only knew it on the local level.

Several veterinary officers were meeting in Saigon in a restaurant one afternoon when one happened to mention losing a dog to a nosebleed. Another recalled the same thing. A couple of more came forward with similar stories and after a few beers and further conversation the group realized that an epidemic was at hand. The first five deaths from the mysterious ailment were reported by Major

Jerry S. Walker, Chief Department of Veterinary Medicine, 9th United States Army Medical Laboratory, Vietnam, on 12 October. The deaths had occurred between mid-September and the first week of October.

Three days later, a shipment of sentry dogs arrived in Okinawa from Vietnam for retraining with a group of new handlers. Retraining would often take place in Okinawa when handlers rotated home and the rookies took their place. It often took a couple of weeks for both man and dog to get acquainted and come to a mutual understanding. A new case emerged on the island on 29 October and that dog died on 8 November. By the end of January the following year, there would be an additional nine deaths and an additional ten suspected cases. No one knew what the root cause was and it was given the name "ideopathic hemorrhagic syndrome" or the acronym IHS.

At the beginning of 1969, the disease was given a name and a better profile of the affliction had begun to emerge. It appeared to be very similar to a disease reported a year earlier in the Labrador retriever tracker dogs obtained from the Jungle Warfare School in Malaysia. Fortunately, the dogs in Okinawa were quarantined, which helped slow the spread of the disease. Animals could still be received at Okinawa from Vietnam, but none were shipped from Vietnam to other Pacific commands or back to CONUS. Whatever the problem was, the Veterinary Corps intended to keep it contained within Vietnam and Japan. Quarantine would limit the spread of the disease, but it was much more important to find the cause.

When a dog from Lackland arrived in Okinawa and then contracted the disease, there was real cause for concern. This meant that what was causing the problem was both infectious and contagious and could strike quite fast. This prompted the Staff Veterinarian, Colonel W. Vacura, to contact Colonel Earl W. Grogan at Walter Reed Army Institute of Research (WRAIR), the Armed Institute of Pathology, and LTC James Fowler at the 406th Medical Laboratory in Japan. Both men were unfamiliar with the disease described by Colonel Vacura. The general consensus among the veterinarians was to begin the collection of blood samples and have them examined by WRAIR and also a SEATO lab in Bangkok, Thailand.

Back in Saigon, Captain James E. Varley VC and Captain Michael J. Reardon, 176th Vet Det (JB) began to draw blood samples from infected dogs and those suspected of harboring the disease. LTC Fowler arrived from Japan to assist in the collection, packing, and quick shipping of samples back to WRAIR. The first results from the tests were discouraging. All samples were tested for known viral and bacterial agents and came back negative. No magic bullet or cure would evolve at this early stage of research. Colonel Arthur L. Hogge of the 44th Medical brigade was a bit more optimistic and stated, "We have the first team in and that it will only be a matter of time till we have an effective vaccine."

Additional help came to Okinawa during January 1969 with the arrival of Major Paul K. Hildebrandt from WRAIR and Major James Ferguson, who was already in Vietnam. A breakthrough of sorts came during the first week of February, when a dog at WRAIR that had been injected with infected blood began to get sick. Its hematocrit (the percentage by volume of packed red blood cells in a sample of blood after being spun in a centrifuge) dropped and the white blood cell count went down to 4,000. The researchers at WRAIR seriously considered a blood-sucking insect could transmit the contagion.

A fissure began to open between the veterinarians in-country and the researchers working back in Washington, D.C. More samples were being asked for, yet little information was being sent back to Vietnam. According to Major William J. Kelch, "It was observed very early that all affected dogs were either kenneled at Long Binh or Saigon, or had been exposed to other affected dogs in the Long Binh or Saigon area." The doctors in RVN suspected that the disease was being spread from dog to dog and not by some external force from their surrounding environment. Yet for the time being, WRAIR insisted on ruling out chemical poisons, bacterial toxins, and even radiation, thus prolonging the investigation.

To close the communication gap and invigorate the research, the WRAIR sent Captain Bradford S. Goodwin as a field representative. Goodwin worked with the 936th Veterinary Detachment and got to see the effects of the disease first hand. He also helped the veterinarians with the 552nd Veterinary Detachment (AF) in Saigon in gathering information and brought feedback to those in the field from the researchers working at WRAIR.

For the vets on the front lines, the continuing research was fine, but the dogs under their care were still dying. Many attempted to combat IHS with antibiotics, vitamins, sulfonamides, hematinics, and whole blood transfusions. Some dogs hung in a little bit longer, but in the end they still died. Veterinarians Captain Rodney F. Taylor, Unit Commander of 936th Med Det (ID) in Saigon, and Captain Byron L. Wilson, Unit Commander of 459th Med Det (IE) in An Khe, tried every trick in the book. They both pumped the dogs with Vitamins A, D, B complex, C and iron, a broad spectrum of antibiotics, as well as coagulants to help stem the internal bleeding. Blood transfusions were given every day and usually lasted for an entire week. By that time, if the dog didn't respond it was time to call it quits. "When the dogs die despite everything you do, it gets very disappointing," said Taylor.

One handler came in every day to Taylor's hospital to bathe and groom his dog. While attending to his companion, the dog died. Taylor recalled, "He was with the dog when it happened and he came to me with tears in his eyes, and said, "Doc, my dog's dead." He held onto the dog's body like he didn't want to let him go." It would be times like these that many veterinarians vowed to continue the fight for a cure.

The spring of 1969 brought forth the second breakthrough and, although strictly by accident, it sent the investigation on the right course. The British in Malaysia related to their American counterparts that they have had problems with their dogs in the past, principally Labrador retrievers. It first showed up in late in 1963 at the RAF station, Change, Singapore, and then the following year at the Fifth Gurkha Dog Compound also located in Singapore. The problem went away for a short time only to reappear in September 1965. The disease picked up a variety of names, such as "Tracker Dog Disease," "Ideopathic Epistaxis," "Ideopathic Hemorrhagic Disease," "Canine Hemorrhagic Fever," and "Tropical Canine Pancytopenia."

The British determined that the disease fell in line with a tick problem they were experiencing. In 1965, ticks had become resilient to the insecticide they were using.

These handlers training in Malaysia had no idea that their dogs may have been carrying ticks that would eventually bring a new disease to challenge the Veterinary Corps in Vietnan. *(Courtesy of SFC Robert Himrod USA Ret.)*

Instead of attacking the disease, the British attacked the source. Malaysian kennels were fumigated with methyl bromide and a new insecticide produced by the American chemical manufacturer Union Carbide, called "Sevin" was used. To learn more, the Army dispatched Colonel Richard B. Morgan, Staff Veterinarian for the 44th Medical Brigade, to consult with his British counterparts and investigate the situation further. What information came forth changed the name of the disease from ideopathic hemoraghic syndrome (IHS) to tropical canine pancytopenia (TCP). Eventually the organism that carried the dreaded disease was identified as *Ehrlichia canis*.

If 1968 and the Tet offensive was the most decisive year for American ground troops, then 1969 had to be a pivotal point for the K-9 forces. A tick-borne disease did what the Viet Cong and NVA could not: diminish the combat effectiveness of dog teams dramatically, strain manpower resources to the maximum, and cost the Americans several million dollars in associated expenses. The disease had killed the dogs, but the problems went well beyond that. Handlers did not go into the field because they had no dog to work with. And when dog teams did not go into the field, many patrols were left without scout dog support, mines would not be located, the VC could not be tracked, booby traps would be tripped, and tunnels could not be detected. Dogs afflicted by the disease that could still work showed a diminished stamina and work ethic; they may have been sent out to the field, but their productivity would be limited.

There is no way to estimate how many more casualties may have been averted had the K-9 teams been at maximum strength. After all, veterinary personnel did not report the disease's effect on military operations nor was there any responsibility dictated within the armed forces. Dog units, whether they are sentry, scout, tracker, or mine and tunnel, only reported that so many canines were not available for duty. Each military unit worked within their domain and had no idea what effect the disease had on each other across Vietnam. It is something that needs to be considered when men and dogs are thrown into future battles on foreign soil. Had veterinarians not been present, it would be a safe conclusion that most dogs would have been wiped out by TCP and the entire military working dog program in Vietnam, within all service branches and for all practical purposes, would have been extinguished.

Dogs were routinely dipped in a Malathion solution in an effort to keep ticks from biting and attaching themselves. *(Courtesy of AATWDA)*

Although there was no "home front," just consider what the American public would think if it knew "their" dogs were being decimated by some mysterious disease in a distant land. It would be a public relations disaster of the first magnitude. For the American public, already disenchanted with the course of the war in Vietnam, it would be like throwing gasoline on a fire. Long after the crisis had passed and the exodus of troops continued, a soldier wrote a letter to the dog's owner. It might seem trivial to some, but it reaffirms the bond established between the handlers and their dogs. As written on 29 December 1972, it is about a dog that saved at least one life, but would not be returning home.

> Dear Sir:
>
> I just got your address and wanted to let you know how Cappy--D002 did in Viet Nam. Cappy was an outstanding dog in scouting and endurance. I worked him for eight months and he was the best scout dog I've ever seen and many others would agree.
>
> Sir, at one time Cappy was credited with sixty kills. Because Cappy was such a good dog no man on any mission, which Cappy was on, was lost to hostile fire or booby traps. I myself did not receive a wound and credit this to Cappy one hundred percent.
>
> I was out of service for 13 months and did not know your address or anyone who did, or I would have contacted you sooner. I met SSG. Woodworth and he gave me your address.
>
> Sir, I want to thank you for the fine job you did with Cappy, for he is the reason I'm here today. As bad as I hate to tell you this Cappy was put to sleep in March of this year for TCP.
>
> Sincerely,
>
> Sgt. George V. Coleman
> 423-64-3305 HHC 197th Inf. Bde.
> Fort Benning, Georgia [14]

During the fall of 1968, the disease began to truly inhibit the combat effectiveness of the K-9 units in Vietnam. There were 210 suspected cases in the Army, Air Force, and Marine units. Some scout dog platoons could barely maintain fifty percent of their authorized strength, while thirty percent of the dogs within the Marine units were affected. The disease also began to appear in both the ARVN and civilian dog population. Another twenty-nine cases popped up in Okinawa. The epidemic was in full swing.

As 1968 closed out, the communists up north could look back at the year with a grim satisfaction. Granted they took heavy casualties, but these were primarily Viet Cong forces in the south. They were able to oust a United States president and open some deep wounds in the American people. The election for a new leader of the United States did little to quell to the protests back home. In November, the Students for a Democratic Society (SDS) at Grossmont Junior College in El Cajon, California, threatened to "napalm" a dog in protest. SDS spokesman Ken Happel said, "People won't mourn for human deaths but would for a dog's death." [15] For the dog teams in Vietnam it was a mixed bag of satisfaction for a job well done and realization of how deadly this war was, with no end in sight. No matter how well everyone did and what contributions were made, there still seemed to be little progress to ending the war.

Take for instance the actions of one combat tracker team, the 61st IPCT. During 1968, this unit was responsible for eliminating 120 enemy soldiers while capturing thirty-five. Throughout this year they contributed to the destruction of over 300 enemy bunkers and recovered over a ton of rice. Many men had to ask themselves, "What are we accomplishing? Are we really making any difference?" These questions have been asked thousands of times when it is a war of attrition and not one of territory gained or cities captured. Unlike World War II, Vietnam had no benchmarks to gauge success or failure; it was a daily grind to keep the enemy off balance and keep yourself alive. The 61st conducted themselves with valor, like most dog teams in Vietnam. During May and August they conducted more missions than any other combat tracker platoon in Vietnam.

While the 61st was showing success in the field and posted 219 missions during 1968, the 62nd faced the same dilemma other tracker teams encountered: how the teams should be effectively deployed. 1Lt. Richard Baumer stated in his monthly report:

> "The major problem encountered this month [August, 1969], as in the past, was the elapsed time from the actual contact, to when the mission was actually laid on. Many units do not realize that time is the biggest obstacle that Combat Tracker Teams encounters. Too many tracks are 7-10 hours old and the enemy exfiltrated before the team was even inserted. Additionally, in most cases, even with tracks two hours old, units are reluctant or unwilling to deviate from preplanned lines of march to pursue the enemy. Hence, the Combat Tracker Teams have only rarely been utilized to their true potential." [16]

Baumer recommended that all Brigade operation sections be briefed again for the proper employment and utilization of Combat Tracker Teams. This problem was never truly resolved during the course of the war. If anything, operations were even more haphazard in the remaining years, when infantry units resisted going into the field because American withdrawal was in full-swing. With few exceptions, combat and scout dog teams faithfully pulled their weight to the very end, but they would always be subordinate to the units they worked with.

The Beginning of the End – 1969

On 26 January 1969, the 37th IPSD arrived in Vietnam as the twenty-second scout dog team to be deployed. One more Army platoon had yet to arrive, but this would be comprised of mine detector dogs. The winds of change were already blowing when the American presidency was passed from Lyndon Johnson to Richard Nixon, who also inherited a death toll to date of over 30,000 Americans. In the upcoming years, Nixon wielded an iron fist with strategic bombing of North Vietnam, but also introduced "Vietnamization" to the war, enabling the ARVN to fight alone against the communists. Vietnamization also made possible the withdrawal of troops over a long period of time, although it did not pacify everyone in the United States, but it was never intended to.

The same evening that the 37th IPSD arrived, a large-scale mortar, sapper, and rocket attack was made on Phan Rang Air Base. Although no Americans were killed, fourteen were wounded, four of them being dog handlers. A couple of F-100s were destroyed and several other aircraft severely damaged, while fourteen enemy were KIA and one was captured. Dog alerts were made during patrols on several nights before the attack, but nothing was ever found. It appears these alerts were a precursor to events about to take place. VC insurgents captured later stated they knew little about the sentry dog detection capabilities and believed they were just trained to attack.

While Nixon was being inaugurated, the U. S. Marines launched their last major offensive of the war, dubbed "Dewey Canyon," that took place north of the A Shau Valley in the Da Krong Valley. Within a month, the CO of the 37th, 2Lt. Robert Crowder, started his newly arrived dog teams on missions for the 82nd Airborne Division that included many hot spots with names like "Iron Triangle," "Hobo Woods," Pineapple Region," "Parrot's Beak," and "An Son Valley."

February marked the last USAF sentry dog killed in action. On the night of 22 February, Rex (5A77) was felled by small arms fire during an attempted penetration at Phan Rang. The attack was preceded a month earlier by a larger and more intense encounter that had obviously been planned by the VC well in advance. During that encounter, Fritzie (763F) was killed and four handlers were injured.

Not all heroic actions by handlers involved their dog. Robert Hartsock was killed on the night of 23 February 1969 at the Dau Tieng base camp where three perimeter bunkers were manned by men of the 44th IPSD. On this particular night, a long-planned attack by the Viet Cong took place.

The VC did not attack from outside the wire, but tunneled into the center of the base where they popped up and immediately set up a machine gun nest. Another tunnel had been dug near the airport runway. The sapper attack that Hartsock encountered was from the tunnel near the headquarters. Hartsock fired on the sappers

Only 246 recipients earned the Medal of Honor in Vietnam. SSGT. Robert Hartsock would be the only dog handler to receive (posthumously) this commendation. *(Author's Collection)*

and was seriously wounded by a thrown satchel charge. Still he kept firing, allowing other men to get in close and repel the attack. The twenty-four year-old from Flinstone, Maryland, died soon thereafter. Posthumously, he was awarded the Medal of Honor with the citation reading:

"For conspicuous gallantry and intrepidity in action, at the risk of his life, above and beyond the call of duty, SSgt. Hartsock, distinguished himself in action while serving as section leader with the 44th Infantry Platoon, Scout Dog.

When the Dau Tieng Base Camp came under a heavy enemy rocket and mortar attack, SSgt. Hartsock and his platoon commander spotted an enemy sapper squad that had infiltrated undetected. Realizing the enemy squad was heading for the brigade tactical operations center and a nearby prisoner compound, they concealed themselves and, although heavily outnumbered, awaited the approach of the enemy. When they were almost upon them, SSgt. Hartsock and his platoon commander opened fire on the squad. As a wounded enemy soldier fell, he managed to detonate a satchel charge the he was carrying.

SSgt. Hartsock, with complete disregard for his life, threw himself on the charge and was gravely wounded. In spite of his wounds, SSgt. Hartsock crawled about five meters to a ditch and provided heavy suppressive fire, completely pinning down the enemy and allowing his commander to seek shelter. SSgt. Hartsock continued his deadly stream of fire until he succumbed to his wounds.

SSgt. Hartsock's extraordinary heroism and profound concern for the lives of his fellow soldiers were in keeping with the highest traditions of the military service and reflect great credit to him, his unit, and the United States Army."

Day-to-Day the Fight Goes On

During summer months enemy operations wound down, but the VC still managed to launch attacks against 150 targets throughout the south. Scout dog teams still went to the field, with the toughest patrols being the first ones for the newly arrived FNGs. Even when the first mission was the worse, some managed to pull the best from a situation. Such was the case with Brian Taras, who left home in Walnutport, Pennsylvania, and wound up with the 39th IPSD in June 1969. The 39th was located at LZ English in the Central Highlands and was attached to the 173rd Airborne Division. In August, Taras and his dog, Gretel (X399), posted an alert of a claymore mine that was a good ninety meters off the trail that they walked. Later, the during the day, the pair managed a 100 meter alert on a tunnel and a rice cache; the tunnel was found during a village search. However, on his second patrol Taras was slightly wounded by an M-79 round and was on medical leave for a week.

Taras and Gretel would make a great two-some, as just a couple of months later the pair located a battalion-size VC headquarters chock full of ammunition, rockets, and explosives. The VC moved out quickly and left behind an enormous cache of material and exposed their tunnel system as well. A week later, Gretel once again alerted to a hastily evacuated VC hospital about sixty meters off the trail. This scout dog team truly exemplified a first-class handler and dog in sync with each other out in the field.

Years later, Taras recalled when Gretel made a large and rather strange discovery. "We were patrolling the perimeter of a base that had just been attacked. The dog found a notebook containing names of people in South Vietnam that the enemy could go to for help. The notebook gave the military an insight on who could not be trusted," he stated. [17]

No doubt the folks listed were promptly rounded up. Over the years scout dogs not only discovered documents, but also food, medical supplies, buried bodies, money, and anything else associated with odors that they knew to be foreign or associated with the enemy. From 1966 to 1972, Army scout, tracker, and mine dogs were responsible for locating over 500 tons of rice, three tons of corn, and two tons of salt. In the big picture, this was probably just a drop in the bucket, but it did put a crimp on the VC that had supply problems for foodstuffs during the course of the war. The war dogs also delivered over 400 pounds of documents. Some of these documents were surely of importance if the enemy had put it down in writing.

To honor their fallen comrade, the 44th IPSD named their kennels in memory of Robert Hartsock. *(National Archives)*

Shift to Patrol Dogs

Sentry dogs were formidable creatures as trained by the Air Force. They not only provided a physical and psychological deterrent against an unseen enemy, but sometimes also for their handlers and anyone else they met. Having a very aggressive dog was a burden and liability for all personnel involved. Sentry dogs have been known to attack their handlers, vet techs, and kennel personnel. If the enemy (real or not) were present on the other side of a concrete wall, some dogs would attempt to scratch and bite their way through the wall. Problems arose when handlers rotated back home. New handlers sometimes feared losing their own body parts to the aggressive dogs.

These problems forced the Air Force to begin experimenting with a new category of sentry dog in 1968. In a fresh approach they began to recruit and train patrol dogs—canines more adapted to working in a variety of situations and with a diverse set of people. The Air Force contracted with the Metropolitan Police Department of Washington, D.C., to train four patrol dog teams. Their initial trial began at Andrews Air Force Base, Maryland, and these tests were wholly successful.

Replacing a sometimes vicious canine, was a dog that could work perimeter defense, even while unmuzzled and off-leash, and the handler could easily command it to attack an intruder. This meant that the dog could achieve a multi-purpose role, including crowd control, tracking, and escort service. Stationed worldwide, some of these dogs did find limited service with both the Air Force and Army in Vietnam.

The Strategic Air Command (SAC) came to the same conclusions at the end of a 120-day test in March 1969. This experiment involved thirty patrol dogs. Six of the dogs were formerly trained as sentries and twenty-four were new recruits. Observers stated that they were "far superior to the sentry dog." Other tests were conducted at Castle AFB and Vandenberg AFB in California, and Davis-Monthan in Arizona. One advisor involved in the new program said, "With the sentry dog, the handler could only look forward to spending his time in isolated areas. With the patrol dog, a much broader spectrum of security police activity is open to him." Shortly after these tests finished, the Air Force adopted the patrol dog as the standard military working dog for perimeter defense.

Withdrawal

Although sounding Johnsonian in many respects with the war in Vietnam, President Nixon was committed to reducing U. S. presence there and he began turning the war over to its rightful owners, the South Vietnamese. All it would take would be time, material, money, and of course a few more American lives. By April 1969, the death toll for American troops in Vietnam exceeded those killed in the Korean War.

Removal of the first men from Vietnam under Nixon's withdrawal policy took place on 8 July and involved personnel from the 9th Infantry Division. The 9th was located in Dong Tam, well south of Saigon and deep in the Mekong Delta region.

Seven days later their combat tracker team, the 65th IPCT, stood down. Technically speaking, the mine and tunnel dog teams of the 60th IPSD stood down on 20 October 1969, although the teams were dispersed to other scout dog platoons throughout RVN. While many sentry and scout units were slowly withdrawn from RVN in the near future, plans were still in the works to bring in at least one additional scout dog platoon.

On 10 November 1969, the 55th IPSD was scheduled to be activated and deployed to RVN, making it the 23rd scout dog platoon to be brought in. The Army then changed its mind and decided to send the unit to Korea. This would have been the first scout dog platoon deployed to that country since 1951. Either a change in requirements or in budget ensued, and the deployment was never made as the Army deactivated the platoon on 10 February 1970. [18]

Although withdrawal was underway, it would still be several years before everyone came home. These were perhaps the toughest years for those serving in Vietnam. People were leaving and many more would still be sent over, yet everyone was expected to keep up the fight and sacrifice themselves as necessary. It was a recipe for disaster as morale plummeted, drug use soared, and those who had to carry on the battle were disillusioned about the task at hand.

One thing that did not change during the war is that Western Union seldom delivered good news to the home front. Sergeant Dixon's parents must have been somewhat relieved when they received the following telegram on 29 Jan 1969:

> THE SECRETARY OF THE ARMY HAS ASKED ME TO INFORM YOU THAT YOUR SON, SERGEANT LAND S. DIXON JR., WAS SLIGHTLY WOUNDED IN VIETNAM ON 28 JAN 1969 AS A RESULT OF HOSTILE ACTION. HE RECEIVED FRAGMENT WOUNDS TO THE BACK AND BOTH LEGS. HE WAS ON COMBAT OPERATION WHEN HIT BY FRAGMENTS FROM HOSTILE COMMAND DETONATED MINE. HE WAS TREATED AND (HOSPITALIZED IN VIETNAM) ADDRESS MAIL TO HIM AT THE HOSPITAL MAIL SECTION, APO SF 96381. SINCE HE IS NOT REPEAT NOT SERIOUSLY WOUNDED NO FURTHER REPORTS WILL BE FURNISHED.
>
> KENNETH G. WICKHAM MAJOR GENERAL USA C3996 THE ADJUTANT GENERAL (1224)

It's amazing how the Army can understate things in a left-handed way. In truth, Dixon's wounds were far more serious than stated in the telegram and he required a hospital stay in CONUS for nine months before finally being discharged. At least he was out of Vietnam, alive, and relatively intact. He would be awarded a Bronze Star Medal with "V" Device, and in a small way his scout dog, Shack, shared the medal. The citation read in part, "…Dixon and his scout dog led an infantry company for more than 30 hours through enemy infested territory which had been heavily mined by the hostile forces. He enabled the friendly force to avoid the explosive traps and warned them when the enemy was near until he was seriously wounded by a Viet Cong mine."

It was determined quite some time ago that dogs within the United States military should not receive the same decorations as their human counterparts.

Although dogs could be cited in text and under general orders, the United States, unlike other countries, did not have any specific awards for military working animals. To display how some awards are acquired, in 1970 two dogs (or perhaps the same dog) were awarded Bronze Star medals in South Vietnam. Smokey M. Griffin and Griffin M. Canine were among the "men" listed in General Order 10260 for heroic action against an overwhelming force. However, the order was revoked on 19 November 1970 when it was determined to be a hoax. [19]

The military still did not understand the dynamics of teaming men with dogs. Even with all the information and empirical evidence at hand, they still believed that in a short period of time a handler could be assigned any dog, get along well, and do an adequate job. Training manuals provided plenty of useful information, but nowhere would you find reference to the bond that needs to be established between a man and his dog. Too many times during the course of the war, you would find dog teams trained stateside and discover that only the handler would be sent overseas, leaving "his" dog behind.

Steve MacRobbie, 212th MP, volunteered to be a sentry dog handler. He knew he would eventually be sent to Vietnam and trained extra hard with his dog, Keechi. For over a month they worked together day and night so well that he could give hand signals to Keechi at twenty or thirty feet in the pitch black. When it came time for MacRobbie to leave for Vietnam, Keechi was left behind. MacRobbie says,

> "To this day I'm upset about that. It made no sense. We had trained together for months and were a great team. Why not go as a team? I'll never forget how incomplete and incompetent I felt arriving in Nam. A dog handler without a dog." [20]

Since there were several service branches involving thousands of personnel throughout South Vietnam, it would be difficult to find any consistency within the military working dog programs. There were so many diverse techniques were being developed, some of which were counterproductive. Some officers still resented the use of dogs to begin with. Colonel W. H. Brandenburg, United States Army Provost Marshall and Commander of the 18th Military Police Brigade from 30 August 1968 through December 1969, was among them. In one report [regarding sentry dogs] he stated:

> A. The Brigade has two sentry dog companies with a third one in the process of activation [the 595th Military Police Company (Sentry Dogs) at DaNang]. Dogs are stationed at ammunition supply points, airfields, tank farms, outposts and similar areas. The efficiency of sentry dogs is difficult to determine. Sappers have successfully attacked installations guarded by dogs (e.g. Qui Nhon Ammunition Depot), and they have been detected at others, (e.g. Tay Ninh and Ban Me Thout). Although doctrine prohibits the use of dogs as deterrents, it is possible that dogs do deter attacks. Dogs are deployed in a number of locations that have never been attacked. While cause and effect cannot be established, the possibility is not unreasonable. Nevertheless, dogs are expensive.
>
> B. Veterinary care must be available. Training must be continuous. Care and grooming are extremely important, especially in the Vietnam climate. With all this

attention dogs can only work sx hours out of 14. Thus his handler remains on post only six hours also, whereas the average security guard and military policeman works a twelve hour shift.

C. A number of dog posts in RVN were established simply to humor senior commanders. It is a fact that good dog posts are difficult to find in RVN. Continuous activity at most key installations creates a cacophony of sights and sounds that virtually negate a sentry dog's ability.[21]

A year later, Colonel Paul M. Timmerberg assumed the position Brandenburg had had, yet a report he issued was in stark contrast. He wrote:

> "The employment of sentry dogs in physical security functions was highly successful and represents one of the outstanding achievements of the military police in Vietnam. They were programmed into country during the initial phases and have been retained to the present. They have been efficient, economical, and effective in protecting property against theft and providing security against attack. They have also produced substantial savings in manpower." [22]

TROUBLES ON AND OFF THE FIELD

By 1969, veterinary care at every level was well established throughout South Vietnam. Injuries sustained by sentry dogs were never an issue, as a base dispensary or hospital was nearby. Scout, tracker, and mine dogs that received combat injuries out in the bush posed a different problem. It was the responsibility of the platoon to get the injured dog to a local dispensary. If dogs needed further hospitalization or major surgery, veterinarians had to find creative ways to get the dogs from the dispensary to a hospital. Too often a handler waited with his dog at an airfield to catch a flight that would bring them to a hospital. The dog team could board a chopper or airplane that was evacuating wounded men if space was available.

In February 1969, when Major General Hal B. Jennings took command of the 44th Medical Brigade at Long Binh, he expressly forbade the use of brigade helicopters to evacuate wounded dogs. This policy was overturned in July when Brigadier General David E. Thomas replaced Jennings. It was determined that any dog requiring more than seven days of treatment (later reduced to five days) needed to be evacuated to a hospital, and more chopper flights would be available.

Another bug in the system was the use of Air Force planes to evacuate wounded Army dogs. Air Force regulations dictated that all dogs are to be crated or muzzled. Of course, this was not always possible. A dog with a broken leg would be a stretcher case and a muzzle was not always available. The pilot could simply refuse the dog to board his plane.

Apparently the problem of transporting scout dogs hit a raw nerve with 1Lt. Daniel McIntosh of the 57th IPSD. This was not just about dogs requiring medical attention but also included the handlers. Angered by the attitude of the Air Force, McIntosh lashed out in his monthly report:

> "The Air Force is interfering with the transport of scout dogs on passenger flights again. Contrary to existing regulations, they have repeatedly refused in a belligerent, rude, and condescending manner to transport my personnel and dogs. When presented with the regulation itself, they have defied my personnel to try and board their aircraft. This unbecoming conduct extends from the most junior airman to crew chiefs to aircraft commanders. Some of these individuals – to include Lieutenant Colonels – have acted in an extremely reprehensible manner without regard for my personnel, my dogs or their mission, in defiance of Air Force regulations, which were quoted to them." [22a]

The ongoing scourge of IHS also created a domino effect on the treatment, evacuation, and hospitalization of dogs. At Cam Ranh Bay, the clinic of the 764th Veterinary Detachment (IE) was upgraded with a surgical suite and prep space along with an x-ray room and additional offices. It shared the area on the base with the seventy-five sentry dogs from the Army's 981st MP Sentry Dog Company. When news of the tick-borne disease spread throughout RVN, the MPs virtually kept out any other dogs except their own. This kept the sentry dogs safe and secure, but forced all other patients in both I and II Corp to be evacuated to the 936th based at Long Binh.

Another problem, that first arose with the dogs in May 1969, was acute glossitis or "red tongue." Although not lethal, it was quite painful and the afflicted dogs had great difficulty eating and drinking. A first sign of red tongue was excessive salivation followed by inflammation and erosion of the tongue's surface. During a six-month period, red tongue accounted for the largest loss of duty time and was more troubling than TCP. At its peak, about sixteen percent of the scout dog population was afflicted and some cases popped up with sentry and tracker dogs. In late 1970, some dogs acquired the condition within two weeks of arriving in-country.

The cause was believed to be a type of photosensitivity, but no one could explain why the condition never appeared back home in the southern United States. Antihistamines and anti-inflammatory drugs did not help, but some reports indicated that steroids and antibiotics were somewhat effective. The best treatment seemed to be keeping the affected dog out of direct sunlight and rested for seven to ten days. For those involved, it was a perplexing affliction that was never resolved during the course of the war.

A continuing problem was the consistency of training at Fort Benning and proficiency of the handlers and the dogs that were arriving in Vietnam. A good example is two handlers who arrived on 12 March 1969 and were attached to the 43rd IPSD in Dong Tam. SP4 Eric Cobb and Moose (702M) and SP4 Billy Toft and Dusty (23M8) were trained as off-leash handlers, but neither team was trained at Benning for booby traps. Both Cobb and Toft told the 43rd CO's 2Lt. Karl Lunkenheimer that they had been trained to work at a fast pace and no work was done with booby traps, since they were told there were none in Vietnam.

Neither dog team had had any remedial training within the past two months and the first time out in the training lanes they did not even respond to basic commands. Moose was even scared of his own handler when he held a rifle. Over the course of the next month, the two dog teams received careful re-training with special emphasis

Wherever a handler was expected to go, the same went for their dogs. SP4 Michael Lutz (43rd IPSD) and Dusty take their turn getting wet. *(National Archives)*

on booby traps. Once they became operational, they had excellent success alerting to enemy personnel, ambushes, and booby traps. Lunkenheimer stated, "It is my opinion that these results are due to the high caliber of the dogs and the work of the handlers, not to any special training they received at Fort Benning. I consider the teams to have been successfully OJT'ed here on booby traps." [23]

Lunkenheimer was understandably angry that these handlers were not given any training on booby traps at Benning. A 9th Division report that covered his area of operation noted that 758 booby traps were found during the month of April alone. He was also incensed to learn that an instructor at Benning was disciplining the dogs with a rubber hose, and Lunkenheimer forwarded a recommendation that this instructor be relieved of duty.

Down in the Delta, Lunkenheimer was not satisfied with the "off-leash" dogs received from Benning but results across the board were not always the same. Far north in Chu Lai, the 57th IPSD received dramatically different results from the two new "off-leash" scout dog teams they received. Initially there were some difficulties with Vietnamese locals and livestock, yet 2Lt. Mark Zirngibl, the CO of the 57th stated, "The dogs are all exceptional in their ability to alert on enemy personnel over great distances. Their ability in detecting caches, mines, dud rounds, and trip wires is also above the usual performance expected of an "on-leash" dog."

The differences can be attributed to the initial training received. The dogs from the 57th seldom worked twenty-five meters ahead of the handler, usually within fifteen meters if the terrain was open. Zirngibl was adamant that the dog not "zig-zag" over a large area, but stay immediately in front of the handler. Neither handler needed remedial training after arriving in-country, which reinforces the fact that superior training yielded the best dog teams in the field.

Regardless of how well a dog could be recalled, there remained the underlying risk that he could bolt while off-lead and quickly disappear. Such was the case with a scout dog from the 47th IPSD named Sarge (X052). In June 1969, Sarge and his handler, SP4 Ronnie McCrary, were working near Firebase Veghel with Alpha Company, 1st BN, 502nd Infantry. McCrary recalls, "We were on a small hill when Sarge alerted to something in the stream at the bottom of the slope. I didn't have the leash on him and he took off down to the stream." McCrary ran down the slope and called after the dog, but he didn't come back. "It was like he vanished," McCrary said.

Just having your dog disappear in the field like that is a blow to any handler. McCrary stayed with Alpha Company for two more days before he returned to his unit at LZ Sally. Everyone figured the dog was finished. Yet the following day, three days after taking off, Sarge was outside the perimeter of Firebase Bastogne barking away. He was brought in and handed over to personnel of the 58th IPSD. After several calls were made, Sarge was returned to the 47th where he belonged.

For some handlers, having their dog alongside them saved their lives. SP4 William Huskie from the 47th IPSD was working with the 101st Airborne about twenty-two miles southeast of Hue. The patrol was hit by a sniper as Huskie and his dog, Little Joe (223M), dropped to the ground to get some cover. Little Joe got hit by two rounds that surely would have hit his handler. After the sniper was taken out, Huskie asked for a medevac chopper for his dog, but the jungle was too thick to bring one in.

A good handler never forgets his dog. Huskie carried Little Joe for eight hours before a helicopter could be brought in. This was no easy feat, given the terrain and temperature. He later stated, "There is no doubt Little Joe saved my life today plus a hundred other times by sniffing out the enemy before they spotted us. If I could, I'd take him home with me and treat him like a king. Joe deserves it." Little Joe was placed on a medevac chopper but, like so many dogs before him and many more to come, he never made it. [24]

The results achieved from scout dog teams are well documented: potential ambush alerts, enemy killed, caches and booby traps located. It is more difficult to substantiate the effectiveness of the various sentry dog teams in place throughout Vietnam. The Army Concept Team in Vietnam began a short-term evaluation of sentry dog teams in-country on 1 September 1969, to determine if their employment was effective. The two-month evaluation included the sentry dog units with the 212th at Long Binh and the 981st at Cam Ranh Bay.

Highlights of the review revealed that although many postings were undesirable for several factors, the psychological presence of the dog teams contributed to the overall security. It was also determined that a six-hour posting was too long; the performance of both handler and dog diminished accordingly. The recommendation was that the teams work four hour shifts and that communication systems be standardized and improved. Finally, it was suggested that dog teams be surveyed for their performance on a quarterly basis.

Sentry dogs from the various services worked every night, yet their results can't often be quantified. There is no doubt that quite a few sapper attacks would have taken place had the sentry dog teams not been in place. There is no way to determine how Charlie's orders to "avoid the dogs at all costs" resulted in men and military equipment being saved.

A good indicator of the scout dog's performance was published in a Marine periodical called *Sea Tiger,* in January 1970. It provides several hard numbers on the results of Marine dog teams, specifically from the period January 1968 to October 1969. Included are the early detection of 1,181 ambushes, 509 enemy captured, and 137 taken prisoner. Also mentioned is the location of twenty-three tons of rice, seventy-one NVA base camps, fifteen VC camps, and thirty-four enemy hospitals. Dog teams also uncovered 1351 enemy weapons, 351 sets of documents, and thirteen radio relay stations.

Exactly where these numbers are derived from is not known. They seem reasonable based on the number of Marine scout dog missions over this period. During this same time period, dog handlers were awarded four Silver Stars, fourteen bronze starts, fourteen Navy Commendations, and twelve Navy Achievement awards. Other awards were presented to dog handlers after returning from Vietnam. What should not be overlooked is that these accomplishments did not come without a price.

Come December, Ho Chi Minh was dead, the fighting slowed down a bit, and President Nixon

The enemy realized and respected the threat the American scout dogs posed and they became a primary target for sniper fire. Marine Corporal Isaihah Martin comforts his dog shortly after being hit by an NVA round. *(National Archives)*

ordered the withdrawal of another 50,000 troops. The troops killed in Vietnam topped 40,000, even as Vietnamization was taking a greater hold. There was still a long road ahead and ultimately the war would be expanded into Cambodia before the troop pullout would be fully completed.

During this same period General William R. Peers began his investigation of the My Lai massacre and whether or not there was indeed a cover-up by field commanders. Peers decided he needed to personally view the hamlet where the incident took place. The immediate area was still seeded with VC and NVA soldiers, and prior to his visit the Americal Division took at least five casualties from booby traps. The general still made his trip, but was accompanied by a mine detector dog team from the 60th IPSD. During his inspection, Peers went to each hootch during his search and although the accompanying dog team did not turn up any booby traps, it was still a confidence builder that the Army really did believe in the capability of the detector dogs.

While the military had confidence in the dogs working in Vietnam, this did not necessarily extend to many of the men in uniform. Drug use escalated dramatically after the Tet offensive and the DoD would later estimate that seventy percent of the GIs in-country used an illegal drug at least once. The most popular drug of choice was marijuana, followed by amphetamines and opium or heroin. Most of the drug users obtained the habit before arriving in-country and were thrilled to find that a joint cost a dime in Vietnam. A gram of heroin, almost ninety-five percent pure, could be had for just two bucks. Back home, the same amount would cost a hundred dollars.

Drugs were easy and cheap to come by no matter where you were in Vietnam. For many it helped relieve the boredom, while for others it took them away from the stress and horror of the war, if only for a short period of time. The military would deal with drug use much like the civilian police back home and probably with the same effectiveness. One thing the government didn't want was for cheap drugs to be smuggled back to the states. There simply was too much baggage being shipped home to have it all properly searched by hand, unless of course dogs could be trained to sniff for illicit narcotics; then it may be a worthwhile endeavor.

SFC Enos Cooper spent time as an ARVN scout dog advisor, but would later serve as the one of the first trainers for dogs to detect marijuana. After a sixteen-week training course, two dogs, named Cookie and Smidget, were ready for duty. This involved screening thirty potential dogs and accepting seven for training, before eventually training just two for duty. Handlers SP4 John Burnett and SP4 Cleveland Murphy of the 18th Military Brigade arrived at Tan Son Nhut in September 1969. The pair conducted demonstrations at Tan Son Nhut and Long Binh before they went to Dong Tam to begin sniffing luggage and packages bound for the United States.

1970 and the Drawdown Continues

Another group of thirteen BSI-trained mine dogs arrived in DaNang along with eighteen Marine handlers on 7 March 1970. The official reports state that fourteen dogs shipped out, although Perry Money, a Marine dog handler who worked with Missy, would later state it was only thirteen.[25] This was followed by a second group of twenty handlers and fifteen dogs on 30 May. All of these movements were part of a 270-day field evaluation to establish their operational suitability and to determine if the dog teams fulfilled the needs of the Marine Corps. At this stage of the game, it seemed evident how useful dog teams could be, regardless of what role they served. It appears to be incongruous, with the imminent withdrawal, to post another evaluation that would make absolutely no difference in the final outcome.

In several aspects, both the Marine Corps and Army evaluations of mine detector dogs was nonsensical. The only comparison to be made regarding the location of booby traps would be by a patrol led by a dog and a patrol that did not have one. Neither evaluation took that into consideration. In both evaluations, dogs were faulted when they missed a mine or booby trap. Over the years, hundreds were overlooked by men who worked point on patrol that did not have a dog in the lead position. A better comparison would be when a dog did alert to a mine or booby trap, would that same device have been detected by a man?

Mine dogs used by both the Army and the USMC were all trained by BSI, although there would be a slight change of policy once the dogs were deployed. It would appear that the Army mine detector dogs were put into use if there appeared to be a good possibility that mines or booby traps were positioned in place by the enemy. The USMC sent the mine dog teams out on patrol just as they would with any scout dog. From a tactical standpoint this made little difference, as each team could expect to encounter explosive devices anywhere along the trail. The added insurance would be that all the dogs worked off leash and gave some margin of safety for the handler.

Although the Marine mine detector dogs began to accompany patrols in March 1970, and would continue throughout the year, the small unit patrols carried out in I Corps still suffered enormous casualties. During the year, 1,868 Marines were killed or severely wounded by booby traps. The dogs proved useful, if not invaluable,

The USMC MBT and sentry dog kennels at Camp Kaiser, Da Nang during the summer of 1970. Like many buildings with galvanized roofs, sandbags were added to keep them from blowing off during a storm. *(Courtesy of LCP1 Perry C. Money USMC)*

although there were only a limited number of mine detector dog teams available. Hundreds of patrols were conducted during the evaluation period, yet there would only be thirteen negative reports for the use of detector dogs out in the field.

When a mine or booby trap was located, the standard procedure was to "blow it in place." It was not wise to tamper with or disable the device. In the event you triggered the device, you perhaps had four seconds to react, unless the fuse was shortened by the VC. If a mine on the trail was detected, your best bet was to turn 180 degrees and jump – not always practical if you had a leash wrapped around one hand with a German shepherd at the other end. Still it was better than nothing.

Scout dogs not only accompanied patrols, but took on special significance as part of the Marine Combined Action Group (CAG) teams in I Corps. CAG teams comprised seven to ten Marines who lived with villagers in small hamlets for short periods of time. The villagers were taught how to defend themselves and their families from small detachments of Viet Cong, who would try to penetrate the village for food or supplies to support their various missions.

Having a scout dog as part of these groups proved extremely effective. John Denecke was a Marine handler who worked with Rex (5A31). Denecke stated, "The most important effect Rex had when working in the villages was the psychological one. Since the enemy worked in small numbers when trying to penetrate a village, they would avoid one where they thought a dog team was working, because they knew the dog's capabilities for early detection and also the dog's eagerness to attack if the handler thought it was needed. Never staying in one village for a long period of time was also an advantage, because the enemy was never sure where you were and the dog worked best in strange areas." [26]

Sometimes Army scout dog teams would also support the CAG function. When the 43rd IPSD sent along a dog team to support one mission, it resulted in one VC surrendering as part of the Chieu Hoi amnesty program. The former VC stated that he feared the dog would lead U.S. forces to [his] position. The CAG team members believed the constant presence of the scout dogs with their elements was responsible for the VC giving himself up. [27]

April proved to be a very busy month for the 981st Military Police Company (Sentry Dog) at several locations. On 1 April 1970, at the Phu Tai Ammunition Base Depot, SP4 Lawrence Bowman was walking his post along the eastern edge of the base when his dog alerted. Bowman then saw a small group of sappers trying to penetrate the perimeter and opened fire, killing three of the enemy while the remaining VC fled the area.

Just two weeks later at Pleiku, sentry dog Brutus (44M9) was found missing from his kennel run sometime around midnight. Although the neighboring area was searched, the results were negative and Brutus was listed as MIA. Apparently the dog became frightened from nearby artillery fire and scaled the chain link fence of his run and escaped between the small space at the top, between the fencing and the roof. He was never seen again.

With more troops being withdrawn in ever-increasing numbers, the dog teams that were attached to them also stood down. In April, the 61st CTT, along with 41st and 35th IPSD, closed up shop. Handlers with time left were moved to other units. The Army dogs, with little chance of rotating home, were either moved to units that were short due to medical losses or began to fill the ranks of 4th War Dog Company (Provisional) or the 34th War Dog Company (Provisional). Other dogs were brought to the USARV Dog Training Detachment in Bien Hoa and were dispersed from that location. The Air Bases were still fully employed at this time. Although the dogs and handler positions were not being refilled, they primarily stayed in position.

As dog handlers left the country in ever-increasing numbers, the dogs were not being rotated out or handed over to the ARVN to date. Medical issues facing the dogs did not decrease, but there were fewer people and hospitals to deal with them. And it wasn't just the routine problems that needed to be dealt with, but some unique ones as well.

A good example is a sentry dog known as "Old Rex" among the Air Force handlers at Cam Ranh Bay. Rex was down right sick, had dropped thirteen pounds and would no longer strike on command by his handler, Sgt. Patrick Higgins. The staff of the 483rd USAF hospital insisted it was kidney failure and that the dog had to be put down. Things were quickly winding down at this point in the war and there was a surplus of sentry dogs. It made sense to a lot of people, but not to Captain Vic Anspaugh.

Captain Anspaugh was a veterinarian assigned to the 483rd who disagreed vehemently with the assessment by his superiors and believed the weight loss was caused by gastritis brought on by severe dental problems. Rex had fractured both of his lower canines, probably from the chain link mesh in his kennel. Knowing that his superior, Colonel Eugene Jones, would be gone for the weekend (taking the "milk run" to Saigon) and not be back until late Monday, the young vet decided to take action and sought help from his hoochmate, Robert Engelmeier, an Air Force dentist.

Engelmeier had free use of the dental clinic since he was DOD for the weekend and agreed to look at Rex. Anspaugh brought over the anesthesia machine from the vet clinic and Higgins brought in Rex. Once under the gas, Engelmeier determined that Rex ripped out his two front canines exposing the pulp. The dog also had a very large cavity in his lower right tricuspid. Canine dentistry was not a common practice during the war, but the treatment would be the same as a human: two root canal fittings on the fractured teeth and prep them for crowns. [28] The tricuspid would need to be extracted, and it proved to be the toughest extraction Engelmeier would ever do in his career. As later stated, there would be numerous obstacles still to be surmounted:

> "Over the next week, I waxed-up the crowns with help from a dog anatomy book I had found in the hospital library. My real dilemma came when it was time to cast the crowns. It never crossed my mind to use anything other than gold! After all, that was how I was trained. Our clinic laboratory technician refused to have anything to do with this case but did agree to issue me enough gold (over two troy ounces) if I gave him properly completed paperwork.
>
> Without hesitation I took a form 513 and filled it in. I used Rex's actual service number, gave him the rank of Airman First Class, the full name of Rex Harrison, and boldly signed it. I completed the casing and polishing of the crowns at night. Two

> weeks after the first appointment, Rex was covertly knocked out [anesthetized] for cementation of the crowns. After a little occlusal adjustment he was good to go." [29]

Rex quickly gained back the weight he had lost and resumed training. Engelmeier figured that would be it and a good story to boot. Yet two ounces of gold does not go unnoticed in the military. Just two weeks later he was to face Colonel Jones and account for his actions. Engelmeier later stated, "That day the colonel added a new word to my vocabulary; Leavenworth." Fortunately what saved Engelmeier was the fact that Rex did get better and returned to duty.

The Draft

Scout dog teams answered to their military masters and had to go where they were told and with whom they would be working. Some groups, line companies and LRRPS alike, were great to work for and even went out of their way to make life easier for the handler. These men recognized that this guy and his dog were there for them and usually walking the point. Even so, not every operation could work so smoothly. Problems arose even more in the later stages of the war, when drug use in the ranks skyrocketed proportionately with the increasing drawdown of American troops. It was times like this when a dog handler working an operation with a line company just wanted to finish the patrol in one piece and get out of there with his dog.

In the bush there were a few unwritten rules about scout dog teams. Perhaps the most important one was that you did not mess around with the dog. Some dogs could be quite friendly, but this was perhaps the exception rather than the rule. More often, the dog and handler bonded and could count on each other under any circumstance. Probably for the best, the dog seldom trusted anyone else.

One example is an experience Charlie Cargo (48th IPSD) and his dog, Wolf (66M0), had in 1971. When Cargo, a native Californian, received his draft notice, it was a welcome relief and a way out of a life going nowhere fast. Orphaned at twelve, Cargo did have some experience with German shepherds as a boy that would set him down later in life with good company. Like thousands of others before him, he came in-country, arriving 10 December 1970, with an MOS (11-B-10) that denoted infantry, plain and simple. As the newbie or FNG (fucking new guy), he either found himself walking point or carrying the radio while on patrol. Either one made you a good target for the VC and the guy most likely to trip a wire or draw enemy fire. In other words, low man in any popularity contest. Five weeks after Cargo started walking point, he was in Xuan Loc when someone came into camp looking for dog handlers. [30] About forty guys heard the pitch and just about everyone walked away saying "no way" or "bullshit." Cargo and a couple of guys who stayed behind pressed for more information. The others should have at least listened to what the guy had to say. Three guys volunteered and eventually went to the rear to work as sentry dog handlers with the military police. The sergeant who gave the speech learned that Cargo had some knowledge of shepherds, so pushed the idea of his becoming a scout dog handler. "At first I thought, what am I doing?

Never, ever, volunteer," Cargo said. "Then I figured, if I stay here I'm walking point anyway and I might as well do it with a dog." Cargo signed on.

In January 1971, he began training in Chu Lai with the 48th IPSD and was assigned Wolf. They began three weeks of intensive training. Wolf had been without a handler for about two months and was eager to get back to work. The pair worked well together, yet they would later find during this tumultuous period that it was not always the enemy or booby traps that could give you problems.

While working with the 1/46, an outfit characterized by Cargo as "...a bunch of rejects and losers Most of them just out of LBJ [Long Binh Jail]. Never one of them cared about anything. They'd set off their own trip flares when picking them up in the morning. I've even seen them blow their own Claymores. Just lucky they were pointing out from the perimeter. Just unbelievable!" The friction and frustration would finally manifest itself. Cargo relates that during one encounter:

> "A colored guy got bit by the dog [Wolf] when I told him many times, '...when we are in the middle of the perimeter, don't walk around within six feet of this tree where the dog is tied up to.' He comes walking by and the dog bites him. He came back with his weapon [M-16] and clicked that sucker on semi, pointed it at the dog, and I clicked mine on automatic and pointed it at his head. "You kill the dog, I'm killing you. And I don't give a God damn." It didn't take long that we had the weapons up at each other when the Lieutenant and half the people there came between us. Think I gave a damn - I didn't give a shit one way or the other. I'd blown that son of a bitch away in a New York second. Just because... that was my dog. And that dog - at that time when I was in Vietnam - was the only living thing I cared about. That dog was my ticket to get out of that stinking shit hole alive. And he was." [31]

"You Can't Bring Your Dog Home"

Very simply put, DEROS means the "date eligible to return from overseas." It was indelibly impressed in the conscience and mental fabric of most grunts in Vietnam, except for the few infantrymen or handlers who extended their tour of duty. DEROS was marked on calendars in the hootches and on the cloth cover of a soldier's pot helmet. It was a day that the freedom bird arrived and whisked you away from the land of nasty stuff and back to the country of plenty.

The war dogs of Vietnam did not keep a short timer calendar marking the days that they would return home. This was due to two reasons. First dogs can't tell time, at least not the way we sound off the minutes, hours, days, weeks, and years. For dogs, time is probably measured in intervals: when the next meal is coming, when do we go out on patrol, when will I return to my kennel, and when will I be loved? It is the basic tenant of survival. Dogs live in the moment. These triggers of thought may limit how far a dog sees into the future, but as humans we would not relish the idea of keeping time like this. Dogs live with it and it becomes their calendar, one that we as humans may try to comprehend but never imitate or would we wish to.

Secondly, for dogs to keep a short timer calendar they would have to know when they would be going home. With just a few exceptions the war dogs of Vietnam would never return to our world. Their life was all they could see and feel about them. For most of the war dogs, Vietnam would forever be their home.

In the manner that dogs relate to time may have been the best blessing for our canines in combat. It meant that they wouldn't falter in their work ethic from the same problem that inflicted many of the troops who would be in-country for a short period of time. Air Force and Army personnel could count on just twelve months (the Marines thirteen) of presence in Vietnam. This, of course, is assuming one did not get killed or severely wounded in the course of their duties. Dogs did not carry the stress that went along with those who fell short. The terminology or the idea of just a little time left in this God-forsaken patch of earth would vary widely among the troops. Some felt that the time to rotate home could be counted in days or weeks. Still others could feel the tug of past experiences back home pulling and gnawing at them even though there were still six months of duty to be completed. Dogs were not saddled with those thoughts that often carried a heavy burden on the soul. As such, dogs did not reflect on how they conducted themselves on a day-to-day basis, in essence keeping themselves and their handlers from being killed.

Dogs, unlike the men in Vietnam, were in for the duration. Now here was a phrase not used in many years, since World War II to be exact, the phrase "in for the duration." A couple of decades earlier, during the Second World War, the war was considered over when Germany, Italy, and Japan were defeated and each surrendered unconditionally. Both men and dogs would keep fighting until the job was done. In a specialty unit like the China-Burma-India (CBI) dog team detachment, a common slogan in 1944 and even in 1945 was, "The Golden Gate by 48." [32] For most men, the plan set forth was to be in for the duration plus an additional six months of duty. And it is a known fact that the war dogs were expected to come home with the men as well.

DEROS proved to be a double-edge sword. It played out in Korea, another unpopular war, and seemed the politically correct thing to do for Vietnam. In some ways it meant a better chance for survival if you're a grunt, just one year of combat compared to being in the line of fire for perhaps several. In another aspect, it probably cost quite a few lives. DEROS stated in a quiet way that the United States was prepared to fight a "limited" war, but not fully mobilize all available forces against the enemy. It also meant that many career officers (of which there was an inordinate amount) would resort to "ticket punching." Ticket punching had officers rotate very quickly in and out of combat commands. The experience would be gained and then abruptly lost while another officer took his place. It did look good on their resumes, but did little for the war effort. This is why troop leadership waned as the war dragged on. More and more officers achieved less and less experience. Toss into the corrupt nature of battlefield awards, drugs, race relations, and demonstrations back home, and it's easy to see why morale for many soldiers in Vietnam nose-dived within a short time after Tet.

World War II was unlike Vietnam in so many ways. American citizens donated all the dogs that saw service from 1942 to 1945, even if many of them were conscripted from pounds and shelters. Numerous owners sent their dogs into the military just to get rid of a headache or an additional household expense that they couldn't afford. Anyone who donated a canine that was accepted by the military would receive a certificate that stated:

> Appreciation is expressed for your patriotic action in donating your dog __________ for use in connection with the Armed Forces of the United States.
>
> If the dog were found to be suitable for training another letter would usually be issued from the war dog reception and training center stating:_________
>
> We are happy to advise you that your dog, with name, brand, and breed as follows, has arrived at this Depot in good condition.
>
> At this time, we are not able to predict your dog's capability to the rigors of Army training. You will, of course, understand why the interests of the military secrecy will be served if further information is withheld from this point forward.
>
> Thank you for your generous donation at the time of this national emergency, I am,
>
> (Signature of Commanding Officer)

For those involved, it was expected that after the conclusion of hostilities the dogs would be returned home, either to their original owners, their handlers, or a family that wanted to adopt a K-9 veteran. Richard Zika, a World War II handler with the first dog unit in Burma, knew that as fact. "It was expected when we returned home, the dogs would be going with us. If anything else happened, well, let's just say there would have been a mutiny." [33]

Although the Army or Marines never stated that the dogs donated would be rotated home, the United States government did make good on the unwritten deal. Over 6,000 dogs were retrained with the knowledge that they would return to civilian life. For more than two years, well after the war was over, American citizens still wrote to Dogs For Defense, the civilian agency responsible for the procurement of the dogs, for the opportunity of bringing home a canine veteran.

After World War II, Dogs For Defense disbanded and the procurement of war dogs was solely within the military establishment. Although a relatively small number of dogs were used during the Korean conflict, once again the disposition of the war dogs was raised as a potential problem. On 8 April 1952, a United Press story that originated from Korea stated that "…six scout dogs who have saved at least three Allied patrols from ambush will be destroyed when they are no longer useful, instead of being sent back home to the United States, their handlers said."[34]

The story originated with scout dog handler Corporal James G. Heffron who stated, "The dogs have been guiding patrols for about two months, and will probably stand up to the strain for about 18 months. The Army intends to destroy them. I guess they do not have any way of getting the dogs back home." The Army refuted the story very quickly, just two days later, in a press release. "No scout dogs used in Korea have been destroyed to date, and there are no plans to destroy any. Although no dogs have been returned from Korea yet, it is expected that if they pass the medical examination, they will be returned to Japan initially."

Although they did not specifically state that the dogs would be returned to the United States, they made every indication that they would, after passing the appropriate medical examinations. This did not stop a number of complaints from concerned citizens that the Army (and the President) received within the next couple of weeks. Major General K.B. Bush responded to at least one letter and stated, "The only circumstance under which dogs would be destroyed would be if they had acquired an incurable disease." [35] It is not known how many of the scout dogs employed in Korea were finally returned stateside. York, who was cited in several order and commendations, would be one of them. Even during this period, the disposition of a few dogs could illicit such strong emotion from civilians and such a quick reaction from the military.

None of the handlers serving in Vietnam knew about York and what the dog teams accomplished in Korea. Many of them may look back on the events of World War II and the dog return policy of that time with incredulity. But consider how dogs were both treated and characterized during their service in World War II and what was expected from them. Vietnam changed much of that. Dogs, now classified as equipment and a surplus commodity, especially as our troops were withdrawing, needed to be dealt with. Several options were available and talked about; including mass euthanasia, but this extreme operation was never exercised. And considering that most of the soldiers returning from Vietnam were never welcomed home, is it any surprise that the dogs could possibly share the same destiny as their World War II predecessors?

Many handlers in Vietnam still fought to have their dogs returned. One example is USMC Corporal Daniel "Dano" Miller, who went after the establishment the best way he knew how and received this reply:

> "This is in response to your inquiry of 13 April 1970 concerning the retention of a scout dog by his handler, Corporal Daniel Miller, USMC. In view of the camaraderie that develops in a combat environment between a handler and his dog where so much depends on a relationship of mutual trust and confidence, I can readily understand the deep devotion and sense of attachment that Corporal Miller feels for "his dog." The Marine Corps has received numerous pleas from handlers and former handlers to bring "their" dogs home. The Marine Corps position, prohibiting the return of military dogs to the United States, was initially taken in 1966 and no exceptions to this policy have been made to date. The Marine Corps policy is based on the following:
>
> a. A militarily trained dog is conditioned to operating in a noisy, violent, and sometimes confusing combat environment. Experts in the field of training such dogs have stated that a military dog cannot be completely d etrained. The danger always exists that, while a dog may appear docile, a loud noise or other outside stimulus may cause the dog to react in a violent manner thereby resulting in severe injury to persons in the immediate vicinity. To place such an animal in a civilian community would be most hazardous and could ultimately lead to serious human injury or death.

b. The communicability of canine diseases that dogs may acquire in the Republic of Vietnam is a subject about which little is known. Study on the effects of the Southeast Asian environment on military dogs is being continuously conducted by the U. S. Air Force to the extent that a military dog, an Air Force sentry dog, was returned to the United States for medical research and recruiting purposes.

c. Each military dog once in Vietnam is an asset of unquestionable value in the conduct of military operations. There have been many instances of scout dogs saving entire patrols from disaster. Furthermore, military dogs are selected by he U. S. Air Force only after meeting rather stringent requirements as to bone structure and disposition. Due to these stringent requirements, the procurement of acceptable dogs is a continuing problem. In addition to the procurement costs engendered by such a program, there are training, equipment, and transportation costs which make the individual dog a substantial investment once in Vietnam but the value of a human life, many of which have been saved by these dogs, cannot, of course, be overestimated.

In view of the above and in substantiation of the basic soundness of this policy, it should be reiterated that it is not feasible to detrain the military working dog with the intent of converting him to a pet suitable for civilian environment. The rotation or return of military working dogs from overseas theaters to the Continental United States is also inadvisable because of the inherent possibility of introducing contagious diseases. The major overseas commander will determine the local disposition of military working dogs based on current policies and mission requirements. Upon reassignment of a handler, the military working dog will normally be assigned to another handler.

Sincerely,

Major General C. B. Drake, USMC" [36]

Major Drake stated a number of good reasons why military dogs could not be returned. One would also have to take into account everything that was not said. Few, if any handlers knew the "complete" history of war dogs in the United States military. Hardly anyone in Vietnam was familiar about the dog return policy of the military at the conclusion of World War II. This is understandable on several accounts, the number one consideration being that Vietnam dog handlers were never told of the history of military working dogs or of the dog return policy in the past. In all the manuals provided and instruction given to the Vietnam dog handlers, not one iota of information is related about how dogs were retrained and returned to civilians at the closure of World War II.

Drake also goes on to state that "Experts in the field of training such dogs have stated that a military dog cannot be completely detrained." Once again, if all the literature is reviewed during this period, not a single "expert" is quoted. It is assumed that the experts Drake is referring to would be the instructors at Lackland AFB and Fort Benning. In one respect, dogs are like people – neither can be "detrained." The proper terminology is "retrain." If a dog is trained to attack someone who raises his arm against a handler, that same dog can be retrained to do something else under the same set of circumstances. Granted, many dogs, particularly very aggressive sentry dogs, may not be retrained to function in daily life, yet the same problem would not be encountered with scout dogs, originally trained to alert silently, or tracker dogs that followed a dead scent. These are reasons why police dogs that receive similar training in the United States are retired to civilian life with few or no problems.

The idea of communicable diseases in dogs that could be brought over to the United States is just a red herring. Certainly no consideration was ever given to the men who served there and the potential for spreading a deadly disease among the American population. The importation of dogs from all over the world is allowed into the United States, once sufficient testing is performed and after they have passed through a suitable quarantine period. The two considerations that should be addressed are the cost of returning a dog from overseas and whether or not the government would face any liability should something go wrong.

Dan Miller tried to get his dog returned through Marine channels. He found out, like so many others, that it is usually easier for a government agency to say

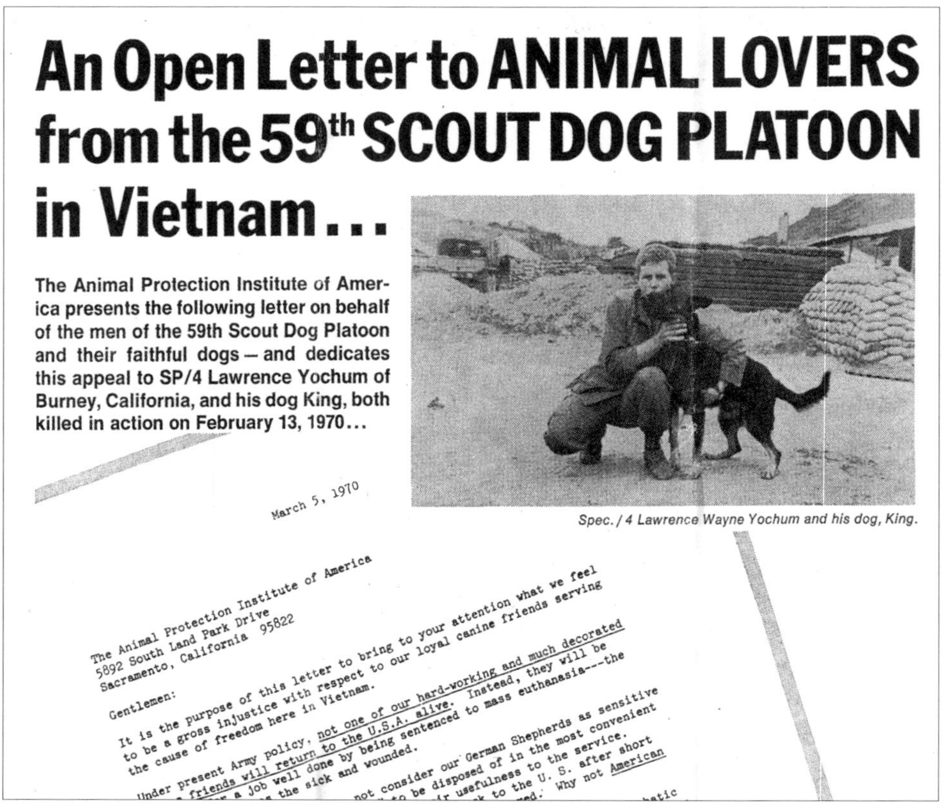

An Open Letter to ANIMAL LOVERS from the 59th SCOUT DOG PLATOON in Vietnam...

The Animal Protection Institute of America presents the following letter on behalf of the men of the 59th Scout Dog Platoon and their faithful dogs – and dedicates this appeal to SP/4 Lawrence Yochum of Burney, California, and his dog King, both killed in action on February 13, 1970...

Spec. / 4 Lawrence Wayne Yochum and his dog, King.

March 5, 1970

The Animal Protection Institute of America
5892 South Land Park Drive
Sacramento, California 95822

Gentlemen:

It is the purpose of this letter to bring to your attention what we feel to be a gross injustice with respect to our loyal canine friends serving the cause of freedom here in Vietnam.

Under present Army policy, not one of our hard-working and much decorated friends will return to the U.S.A. alive. Instead, they will be ... a job well done by being sentenced to mass euthanasia---the ... the sick and wounded.

... not consider our German Shepherds as sensitive ... to be disposed of in the most convenient ... usefulness to the service. ... to the U. S. after short ... Why not American ...

The Animal Protection Institute of California printed posters of the plight of the war dogs of Vietnam and attempted to raise funds for their return. The request fell on deaf ears as the organization could not persuade the military to have the war dogs of Vietnam returned to a civilian environment. *(Author's Collection)* "no" than it is to say "yes." Other handlers in Vietnam tried a different approach and contacted their Congressman or Senator. The 59th IPSD decided to take things public and went directly to the media and organizations involved in the welfare of animals. On 5 March 1970, the platoon sent a letter to the Animal Protection Institute of America, located in Sacramento, California. Their appeal was dedicated to SP/4 Lawrence Yochum, of Burney, California, and his dog, King (7A65), who were both killed-in-action on 13 February 1970. By writing this letter, all the handlers knew that there might be repercussions – but when you are walking point for a patrol in Vietnam, they also considered what could the military do that would be worse? The letter, stated here exactly as it appeared, was dated 5 March 1970:

> Gentlemen:
>
> It is the purpose of this letter to bring to your attention what we feel is a gross injustice with respect to our loyal canine friends serving the cause of freedom here in Vietnam.
>
> Under present Army policy, not one of our hard-working and much decorated canine friends will return to the U.S.A. alive. Instead, they will be rewarded for a job well done by being sentenced to mass euthanasia---the healthy as well as the sick and wounded.
>
> Unfortunately, the Army does not consider our German shepherds as sensitive friends—but merely as "property to be disposed of in the most convenient way possible once they have outlived their usefulness to the service." (Vietnamese mascot dogs are easily brought back to the U.S.A. after short periods of quarantine and a few shots are administered. Why not American canines???
>
> Furthermore, some of our dogs have contracted a disease call Idiopathic Hemorrhagic Syndrome or "bleeders disease." We believe the Army is not doing enough to find a cure for this disease. (Present Army policy states that even when a dog has this illness, it is perfectly all right to work him until he becomes too sick to function or drops dead.)
>
> We of the 59th Scout Dog Platoon feel very strongly that all of our dogs should be given a chance to live out their lives in peace and reap their much deserved rewards.
>
> We most sincerely seek your active support in this matter before it is too late!
>
> One member of our unit who perhaps felt most strongly in support of this cause was Pp/4 Lawrence Yochum who, along with his dog King, died in action on February 1, 1970.
>
> We believe it is our duty to uphold his and our beliefs.
>
> Sincerely,
>
> (signed)
> The Men of the 59th Scout Dog Platoon
>
> P.S. Contrary to popular belief, our Scout and Tracker Dogs have not been trained to attack or kill and could quite easily be converted into wonderful and useful pets. Furthermore, Sentry dogs could be used by civilian police forces back home. [37]

Although the war dogs were considered "low priority," the complaints stateside and from the handlers serving in-country managed to get the attention of the top dog,

General Creighton W. Abrams. The Animal Protection Institute and its president must have hit a few raw nerves with the Army about their Vietnam dog return policy and managed to solicit a response from the commanding general who stated:

> Dear Mr. Mouras,
>
> In response to your recent letter, I am sure that we share a mutual concern and admiration for the faithful service and performance of duty by the military dogs in the Republic of Vietnam. Every effort is made to provide the maximum care, treatment and most efficient utilization of these dogs in support of our Armed Forces. Through their efforts many Americans and Vietnamese lives have been saved.
>
> It is Department of the Army policy that government-owned military dogs will remain in the overseas theatre permanently under military control, and will not be released from service to private individuals or organizations. Upon reassignment of a handler, the disposition of the dog is based on mission requirements. Normally the military dog is retrained to serve another handler.
>
> I have referred your letter to the Department of Army for consideration.
>
> Sincerely,
>
> Creighton W. Abrams
> General, United States Army Commanding

Essentially, even amidst the pullout of American troops after a devastating war, Abrams wanted no part of this. Of course by this time, even with the pullout, Abrams would reiterate the need to retrain the dogs for another handler. But those American handlers he wrote about were already headed home. The only handlers they could be turned over to would be the ARVN. Creighton does not even mention the possible diseases brought back to the United States. Everything is left open when he states that "I have referred your letter to the Department of Army for consideration." In other words, the letter was sent to no one and Creighton just hoped that time and distance would make this problem go away.

Even though he was the head honcho in Vietnam, Abrams wanted to see "the dog problem" disappear. Mouras and the API organization even located a former army dog instructor who was willing to retrain the dogs at his kennel in Edwardsville, Kansas, over a three-week period. API stated the conversion to civilian life would be only $50 for each dog. [38]

For the Australian handlers, their best mate would not be going home either, but most of them shared a better future than the American dogs. The dog return policy for Australia mirrored that of the United States, with a slight difference. According to various reports, the Army was reluctant to carry the high cost of quarantining the dogs for an indefinite period of time. If this in fact was the case, then it would not explain what happened to tracker dog Julian.

Gary Polgase had handled Julian for a period of time until Gary was accidently killed on 13 April 1968. With the loss of her son and just photographs and memories of him, Polgase's mother petitioned the Army to have Julian returned to Australia.

She was rebuffed by the military based on the high cost of getting a dog back to Australia, the care needed during the quarantine period, and the medical costs involved. Apparently the situation was brought forth in a session of Parliament, but like most politicians worldwide, no action was taken. The family, along with friends and many military dog handlers, helped to raise funds that would not only pay for the quarantine costs for Julian but every tracker dog in Vietnam to be safely brought home. The Army still refused to pursue the issue and avoided discussion of returning any dogs home.

The Australian military quickly decided to issue an edict in 1968, that when a tracker dog was worn out or just too old to continue working, he would be kept in the battalion as a "reserve." Being in reserve simply meant out of combat and in a kennel environment. The dogs would be later passed on to Australian or European families living in Saigon. The Australian military could do this becasuse they had only a handful of dogs. The American dogs numbered in the hundreds and this was just not a viable option.

In 1971, all of the Australian tracker units stood down. Of the eleven Australian dogs that served in Vietnam, none were euthanized or KIA (although Cassius died of heat exhaustion in Vung Tau after a training run). Caesar was retired to the British Embassy in Saigon in July 1970. Marcian retired to the British Embassy, and Julian took up residence with the Air Attaché at the Australian Embassy. Justin and Milo were reportedly given to employees of the Chartered Bank in Saigon. Exactly what

Retired tracker dog Milo (D7N06) meets his new family. Identified left to right are: Mrs. Cochrane, 2nd Lieutenant Mick "Spud" Murphy, Mr. J.R. Cochrane, assistant manager of the Chartered Bank in Saigon, and Milo's former handler Private David Cree. *(Courtesy of AATWDA)*

happened to Janus, Julian, Juno, Marcus, and Trajan is not resolved. Tiber was retired in June 1970 when he was given to Mr. and Mrs. Gordon Selleck, from the Australian Embassy. Upon return to Australia in 1971, Tiber remained living in an Australian Embassy house and was still alive at the time of the fall of Saigon in 1975. [39]

At least a few people back home in the United States did not forget the dogs in Vietnam and persuaded Representative John E. Moss, a Democrat from the state of California, to file a bill for their return. It was a long shot to be sure. On 16 September 1970, the WWII Navy veteran introduced bill H.R. 19241 in the House of Representatives. Moss wanted to bring the disposition of the Vietnam working dogs onto the floor of the house for discussion and vote. The bill was intended to provide for the humane disposition of military dogs and stated:

> Be it enacted by the Senate and the House of Representatives of the United States of America in Congress assembled,
>
> That, when the Secretary of Defense has determined that any dog trained for military use and used by the United States armed services outside the United States is no longer suitable for military use by such services outside the United States, or that such dog has been used for a sufficient length of time, or that such dog is to be removed from use with such services for any other reason, and that such dog is in a reasonably healthy condition so as to present no health hazard to either the animal population or the human population residing within the United States, the secretary shall return such dog to the United States so that it may either be retrained for other military or law enforcement assignments within the United States or housed in permanent kennels owned by a suitable humane organization whose facilities permit them to care for such dog during the remainder of their life at no cost to the Government. Such suitable humane organization is not prohibited from retraining such military dog for use by civilian individuals for non-commercial purposes."

Retired tracker dog Tiber (D6N08) at home in Saigon with his new owner Mrs. Roslyn Selleck from the Australian Embassy. On Tiber's collar are his Vietnam service ribbons. *(Courtesy of AATWDA)*

Moss succinctly outlined why the dogs should be returned. He cited not only historical reference to the returning dogs after World War II, but what the dogs meant to those who served with them. As with so many bills sent forth to Congress, this one floundered in committee hearings and never reached the Senate floor. A month later, Representative John R. Rarick, a Democrat from Louisiana, re-introduced the bill as H.R. 19750. Rarick, a WWII veteran and former POW, carried some weight with the military, yet the bill was destined to go nowhere.

In his thesis presented to William Paterson University, David Jay Arts interviewed Congressman Rarick over the phone, and Arts stated:

> "I asked him why they would leave all those dogs in Vietnam. All they had done was to care for and protect Americans in a foreign and hostile land. The Congressman didn't hesitate. "Too expensive, they had a bunch of dogs on their hands and didn't know what to do with them." I asked him how he had found out about it. Rarick said that he was shown a list of things that we were going to leave in Vietnam, including tanks, guns, armaments of all kinds. Rarick explained that it was cheaper and less convenient to just leave everything there than to ship it back to the United States. "It didn't matter if the North Vietnamese got hold of tanks, for instance, the first time one broke down, it would be obsolete. They couldn't get parts for them." But American dogs were also on that list. The ones that weren't being euthanized were being given to the South Vietnamese. "The dogs were used to the companionship of Americans," the Congressman opined, "the Vietnamese didn't know how to use the dogs." Rarick said that his resolution was "asking that they [the dogs] be given asylum until people could adopt them. Not euthanized. And not left to the Vietnamese." [40]

According to Arts, Colonel William Clark speculated that the resolutions that both Moss and Rarick introduced were never moved forward because the military interjected with the belief that TCP could be introduced to dogs in the United States. According to Arts, Rarick said that had nothing to do with it. "They just didn't want to take the time and space to get them out." [41]

Rarick appears to be on target with his statement. If the military was concerned with introducing a disease to the American dog population, it could have taken appropriate measures to ensure that this wouldn't happen. The biggest step would have been to quarantine the dogs for a period of time. Rather than make a determined effort to bring home the dogs, the Department of Defense decided to use subterfuge and adopt an appeasement policy. Although the technique was never in any of their "Lessons Learned" papers that had been published, it seemed to have worked quite well in many situations throughout the course of the war. So it was that on 4 May 1971, the military issued a press release sounding a "…change in Department of Defense policy" regarding the disposition of the war dogs of Vietnam. The headline for the piece in the *New York Times* read, "Dogs Begin Return From Vietnam."

The military wanted everyone to know that the first fifty dogs were being sent home stateside to Lackland AFB. This was the appeasement policy to pacify the American public. Only "healthy" dogs would be returned to the United States and the Veterinary Corps was going to make the decision on what constituted a healthy dog. This meant that no quarantine camp for veteran dogs would need to be established back home.

What the American public did not know at the time was that dogs were already being euthanized or turned over to the South Vietnamese as part of the withdrawal and the on-going Vietnamization process. The Vietnamese Air Force started their own sentry dog program in 1970 and began to take in dogs from the USAF as the bases were turned over to them. The ARVN had staggering losses within their military dog program and on average lost 150 to 200 dogs each year, typically from malnutrition or disease. Yet even with these numbers they were reluctant to acquire more dogs. By October 1971, 200 dogs were turned over to the ARVN and just 115 had been returned to the United States.

Throughout the first few months of 1971, all operations of the Third Marine Amphibious Brigade wound down in rapid fashion. This also included the 270-day evaluation of the Marine mine/booby trap dog teams. During the evaluation there were 266 commitments that resulted in at least ninety-four detections and forty-nine alerts, along with fourteen misses. The program was deemed successful and one of the recommendations was that the Marine Corps adopt a mine/booby trap dog program for the future. Of course, with the continuing drawdown and no other immediate need for this type of detector dog, the future was quite bleak for advancing any type of dog program.

That being said, according to the report, "On many occasions, interviews with unit leaders regimental level or below disclosed that there was tremendous lack of confidence in the dog's overall ability." Yet the evaluation never states what these same commanders expected from the dogs or what was told could be expected from them. One has to ask the question, "In an area known to have mines and booby traps, would you rather have a mine/booby trap dog lead the patrol or a man?"

The evaluation broke no new ground, but did reinforce the known strengths and weaknesses of the dog teams that operated in Vietnam. One interesting aspect is how the dogs were graded (i.e., above average, average, or poor). Of the ten dogs rated poor, seven of them were gun shy. Another aspect is that of the six dogs KIA, all were rated above average or average. Unfortunately BSI, the company that trained the dogs, was no longer under contract, so the trainers could not be questioned about the results of the evaluation. Overall, the Marines did a commendable job in evaluating one of their own programs.

Nonetheless, the evaluation was flawed and would have been more productive if it were conducted by an independent agency. [42]

In the first week of May, the two Marine marijuana detector dogs were turned over to the Army at Long Binh. These dogs would still be needed to help process luggage accompanying the soldiers heading home. On 20 May, the remaining fifty USMC military working dogs were packed up on trucks and turned over to Vietnamese via the Army Quartermaster Advisor. About twenty of these dogs would have been the mine detector dogs trained by BSI. The Marine Corps was no longer in the war dog business. [43] Then again, the ARVN never used mine detecting dogs, and it seems absurd to hand over such well-trained animals.

During this same period, the Army Veterinary Corps was dramatically scaled back, leaving just the 4th at Long Binh and the 175th at Da Nang and about thirty-two veterinarians in-country. Their numbers were gradually reduced to twenty-one by the end of the year. The 25th IPSD, 37th, and 38th stood down in March, followed by the 39th, 43rd, 47th, 58th in July, the 59th in October, and the 42nd in December. Combat tracker teams also ceased operating during 1971, including the 67th, 75th, 76th, 77th, and 557th, leaving just the 62nd IPCT in Vietnam to support the 1st Cav.

In January 1972, the 175th Veterinary Detachment ceased to exist. Americans were leaving *en- masse,* but the war was far from over. On 30 March, three whole NVA divisions surged across the DMZ in an action unheard of since the 1968 Tet offensive. Nixon responded with an iron fist, as waves of B-52s pummeled the north with fierce bombing and the mining of Haiphong Harbor.

By the end of spring, just nine Army veterinarians were available in South Vietnam. The 48th IPSD was deactivated on 30 March, followed by the 34th IPSD on 20 August. These two scout dog platoons had the longest tours in Vietnam. The last American ground troops departed in August, leaving about 43,000 Air Force personnel behind. In Da Nang the 366th USAF Dispensary closed down. Its veterinary technician, E4 Rick Mullins, transferred to Takhli, Thailand, and the dispensary veterinarian, Lt.Col. Shilling, was re-assigned to Saigon. The 3rd USAF Dispensary remained in operation at Bien Hoa as Air Force dogs were processed for re-assignment in Thailand, euthanized for medical reasons, or transferred to South Vietnamese forces.

In November, Long Binh was turned over to the ARVN and U.S. forces consolidated their remaining people in and around Saigon. On 12 June, the

With the on-going withdrawal, signs such as this one no longer greeted any Americans. *(Courtesy of Robert A. Kollar)*

Joe Ertel (34th IPSD) takes a break with his scout dog Casey (421M). The bonds formed between men and their dogs forged during the war would last a lifetime. *(Courtesy of Joseph Ertel)*

bribes given to the ARVN were in place and they finally agreed to take the remaining dogs from the USAF and Army. This final group comprised 104 sentry dogs, fifteen patrol dogs, eight trackers, and four scout dogs. The 212th Military Police Company (Sentry Dog) continued on, without the benefit of dogs, until 8 November. By the end of the year just one veterinarian remained in-country. Vet services by this time were only interested in inspecting food, as all the dogs had been turned over to the ARVN, euthanized, or returned to the United States.

Close to 1,000 dogs were transferred by the Americans to the South Vietnamese. Among them were the black Labrador retriever tracker dogs, although the ARVN had no tracker program and all black dogs were considered bad luck. Nor did they have anyone trained for tunnel dogs. The same held true for mine dogs trained by BSI. Whatever became of all these dogs and the ones they already possessed is not known, even to this day.

Saigon fell on 30 April 1975. And although the military dismissed mass-euthanasia of the dogs in Vietnam because of the potential public outcry, it was an event still to take place, quietly and with no media coverage. It was a time when many Americans just wanted to forget what the country had been through, even if it was for just a brief period. The story about these dogs never made it to the American media; it was done swiftly and secretly in Thailand. The Air Force bases in Thailand were downsizing during 1975 and 1976. Thai Guards now patrolled the bases and controlled most of the kennels, but more than sixty military working dogs still remained without handlers.

At the time, Major F.T. Satalowich, DVM, was assigned to the 11th USAF Hospital at U-Tapao and was shocked when he received a directive from the Commander in Chief Pacific Air Forces (CINCPACAF), Hickam AFB, to destroy all the remaining dogs that were TCP (canine ehrlichiosis) suspect or past the age of peak performance. [44]

Satalowich responded that the dogs at U-Tapao were all TCP negative. He even provided serological data from blood drawn on 6 November 1975, 6 February

1976, and 6 April 1976 to prove his point. CINCPACAF dismissed these results and considered all dogs within Southeast Asia to be exposed and infected. [45] On the face of it, the military wanted to pull out quickly and cheaply. Eventually CINCPACAF agreed with Major Satalowich, but stated that Lackland had already made its decision and to proceed with the triage and euthanasia. This also flies in the face of the work done by Army veterinarians and the research conducted at Walter Reed years earlier. TCP could be controlled with antibiotics (Tetracycline), and the disease was already present in dogs in the United States. Clearly Lackland was aware of this information but refused to consider using it.

It was an unpleasant task for Dr. Satalowich and the personnel that worked with him, but a necessity based on military orders. In the end, fifty-eight dogs were destroyed, and seven were sent to Kadena AB in Japan. Two years later a report was issued by the Air Force about how TCP should be handled in the future for military working dogs. The report did not mention the disposition of the dogs destroyed in Thailand, but brought forward just how widespread the disease truly was:

> "It is now recognized that canine ehrlichiosis exists endemically in Thailand. The incidence of canine ehrlichiosis in military working dogs at Kadena AB, Okinawa, Japan and at Clark AB, Republic of the Philippines, suggests that the disease is probably endemic to these countries also. There exists the possibility that canine ehrlichiosis might be encountered at practically any location in Asia which is suitable for maintenance of a population of the vector tick." [46]

Both Clark and Kadena were major portals for dogs traveling to Vietnam and Thailand, and South Korea as well. The same transition points were used for dogs being returned to the United States. What is shown in this report, and others before it, is that the problem did not reside within the dogs themselves, but with the agent tick that carried the disease. Walter Reed also determined exactly what TCP truly was back in 1969. It was also determined at this time that Tetracycline could be used not only as a treatment, but a preventative as well. From 1968 to 1976, about 550 dogs served in Thailand, but just four made it back home to Lackland. These were Coffee (903M), Lucky (9M18), Major (053M), and Sam (983M).

It is easy to look back on the mistakes of the past and what might possibly have been done and to cast blame. Education, civilian and veteran involvement, and leaping strides in veterinary care have ensured that what took place with the war dogs of Vietnam and Thailand will not occur again. Public faith in the military and our government should remain rock solid, but a wary eye should be cast upon those who might misuse that trust and dismiss our support as complacency.

It's difficult to say exactly when the Vietnam War was over for the United States; that would be like asking, "When did it really start?" It doesn't always occur with signatures on a piece of paper and a date on a calendar. For some folks it was when the American POWs were returned or when the final ceasefire was signed. A returning soldier, coming home in one piece, may have considered it a done deal as soon as he stepped off the airplane onto American soil, even if it was 1967. President Nixon did disentangle us from the affair in 1973, but two years of fighting was still

Left: Wherever war dogs worked in Vietnam, there was a graveyard for the fallen. This is the entrance to the cemetery at Phan Rang. *(Courtesy of Craig Lord)* **Right:** The dog cemetery of the 48th IPSD. *(Courtesy of Bob Railey)*

The 12th SPS cemetery at Cam Rahn Bay. *(Courtesy of Larry Chilcoat & Geisha A871 USAF)*

in the cards for a lot of people. For others it was in 1975, with images of helicopters landing on the roof of the U.S. embassy as frantic crowds stormed the gates in a remote chance to be airlifted out. Or perhaps it was a television shot of those same helicopters being pushed over the sides of aircraft carriers to make more room for other ones to land after they left Saigon. In many cases, particularly for Vietnam veterans and those who lost someone close, the war was never truly over. Gone, yes, but never forgotten, and for many of us never truly understood.

So Long, Goodbye, It's Our Time to Go Home

History and the actions of people as they move through time are like a meandering river with eddies, rapids, curves, and switchbacks. Make one change upstream, say adding a dam, and numerous changes can occur downstream—some inconsequential and others with greater ramifications. One change here, a word to someone else there, and who knows what events may have occurred or what type of outcome might have taken place. The war that took place in Vietnam and our country's involvement is like that.

Some would say, "How can you talk about dogs, when countless men and women lost their lives?" And I would say, "How can you not talk about them?" They are attached to us with a bond that transcends humankind. They could care less about how much money we make, what color we are, the religion we worship, or what we are fighting for. They come to be with us with no baggage attached. They do not start the wars we fight in, but will participate alongside us as willing combatants. They are there for us; without us, who would be there for them? For most handlers, they were attached to their dog in more ways than just the short length of a leather leash.

For most handlers, rotating out of Vietnam and leaving the dog you worked with was a gut-wrenching experience. It didn't matter how many firefights you had been in or how many bodies you saw during the course of your duty, it was never easy. That very animal you are leaving behind may have saved your life on at least one occasion, and for many, several times over. When the days peeled away from your DEROS calendar and it was your time to leave, your dog probably understood that as well. Most men had to just walk away and make sure that they didn't look back. It was like that for Peter Haran, from the Australian 2RAR trackers, who worked with tracker dog Caesar. Haran would later say:

> "In the last day, I went up and I actually spoke to him [Caesar] through the cage. I said, "This is the way they run the war - I'm going, you're staying. I don't want you to forget me 'cause I won't ever forget you." And I turned and I walked away - he had his bowl in his mouth, expecting food - and I heard the bowl hit the concrete. And as that happened, I felt this ton of lead just fall straight through me from the top to the bottom." [47]

Many dogs were quite happy working in Vietnam, since this was the only life they knew. Countless handlers did not feel that way, since they all knew about the "world" that waited for them when they left. They knew they would be leaving, but they still loved the dogs they worked with and would eventually leave behind. Did war dogs ever think of "home" in the same way humans did? Pete Peters, a scout dog handler with the 38th IPSD (the sister platoon that trained with the 39th at Ft. Benning), believed that they did. He knew the unique bond between a handler and his dog—a bond that transcends time and events. The handler *wanted* his dog to know about home, his home, even if that dog only lived in the moment. If the handler thought otherwise, then his dog would be just a piece of equipment like anything else used and discarded in this brutal and ugly war. The attachment between human and canine often rises above common sense and expresses the dignity and freedom of a very special relationship.

Thousands of dogs served in Vietnam, but Budda was the longest working scout dog on record. He arrived in-country in 1966 assigned to the 39th scout dog platoon. He survived everything thrown at him. One morning in 1969, he alerted to two punji pits and a booby trap, and just hours later he took a spear in the neck from another one. He handled it all without complaint and this included the military's unwillingness to make things right and bring home all the dogs of war when our time in Vietnam ended. [48]

In a short story, "If Only I Could Talk," Peters provides us with Budda's thoughts on that fateful day as though the dog was speaking to all of us in a way that we would want every dog to talk with us. It doesn't matter if it was a war dog in Vietnam or a mutt sitting alone stateside at night in a rescue kennel, waiting for someone—anyone—to come for him. It is the reason why decades later, a grown man keeps a faded picture of a dog in his wallet and remembers. It is the reason tears are brought to his eyes when talking about an animal that perished decades ago. And if Peters could write this, so many years after leaving Vietnam, with so much water passed under the bridge, is there any doubt this is how Budda felt?

Budda (4A82) as he appeared in 1971 at Camp English. *(Courtesy of Johnny Mayo)*

> "Then one day in July of 1971 I noticed a different mood around the kennels. Many of the other dogs were being put in their crates and loaded onto a truck. I eagerly followed because I was tired of Camp English. Since most of the handlers had left, we might even being going

The foot prints of a military dog team. Their imprint was not only made in the soil of Vietnam but upon the hearts and minds of many people during the war and as a life long memory. *(Courtesy of Gary Zemel)*

home. That would be great. We deserved a break after all we have done. It wasn't a very long trip. We were taken to a nearby air base and there were many other dogs from all over the country. There were scouts, trackers, and sentry dogs all together here. I guess we really are being sent back home! Maybe they will ship me to Brownie. I wonder if he thinks of me as often as I thought of him. Does he remember what we went through together? I am so excited that I can hardly stand still.

In the veterinary clinic I can't understand why everyone is crying. Just give me the DEROS shots and get me on the plane and I'll finally be getting out of here. I can hardly wait! In all my excitement I barely feel the needle. I was used to them anyway. It feels just like the tranquilizer shot we got before the plane ride over here back in July of '66. I feel a little sleepy all of a sudden. I think I'll lie down and rest right here. It seems to be getting darker. Will Brownie remember me? I feel numb. I think I'll rest a while and think of what it like to be home. I'm tired."

I – ZZZ ZZZ Z Z Z Z Z Z..."[49]

5

In Our Hearts, We Did Bring Them Home

"Within the soul of each Vietnam veteran
there is probably something that says
"Bad war, good soldier."
Only now are Americans beginning
to separate the war from the warrior."

Max Cleland,
former head of US Veterans Administration
at the dedication of the Vietnam Veterans Memorial, Washington D.C.[1]

For many people across the United States, Vietnam was a 10,000 day war that had no definitive beginning and no satisfying conclusion. A million or more tales can be weaved from the fabric of the people that were involved in the war. Decades later, there would always be more stories begging to be told and times-gone-by to be recorded and, on occasion, accounts to be corrected. The activities of military dog teams during this era is just one aspect of the war that needs to be examined. The K-9 operations should not be placed higher or lower within the effort afforded and compared to other soldiers that have served their time there. The bond between men and dogs is another piece in the jigsaw puzzle of life that needs to be looked at and placed in its appropriate spot. And if that puzzle is finally finished and all the pieces assembled in proper order, perhaps at that time a sense of accomplishment and purpose can be attained, or at the very least a compelling reason for our involvement. When we look at history and need to recognize that it is more than just a chronological record of past events. Actions that have taken place need to be analyzed and placed in their proper perspective.

History is a good teacher and we can often look to the past for answers that will help us with our future. Many of the problems that we encounter in the present day and the troubles that will come that shape our lives, have already been dealt with long ago. From a military standpoint, scores of problems currently facing our country have their roots in history. This is not to say that the past holds all the answers, but it does contain a treasure house of information that can help in a variety of issues: such as the menace of terrorism, conflict in the Middle East, a potential nuclear threat, or a civil uprising somewhere in the world. The idea is not to be a slave of history, but to use it as another tool that helps us go through life on this planet.

The Vietnam Dog Handler Association

The Vietnam War had reached a conclusion, in part, with the fall of Saigon in 1975 and the reunification of the country. It was seven years later, in 1982, when the Vietnam Veterans Memorial was being dedicated, that John Langley first had an idea of contacting former military K-9 handlers. Langley had worked alongside Vogie (A927) with the 377th SPS at Tan Son Nhut Air Base. He began thinking about forming an association of veterans with a membership built around former dog handlers who had served in Vietnam. In the next few years, he talked with a few other people about it, but nothing substantial took place until 1993. Langley then met another Air Force handler, Tom Mitchell, through an innovative service called "Prodigy" that was part of a new communication system called the Internet.

Mitchell was with the 12th SPS at Cam Ranh Bay and worked with Buck (323E). He had also had an inner urge to do something and started reaching out to find other handlers. Like Langley, he began using the new Internet tool as well. He made contact with Tom Sykes (48th IPSD), Craig Lord (35th SPS) and Steve Janke (483rd SPS). In May, Tom heard about a man in Florida looking to start an association of dog handlers, and finally made contact with Langley on 1 June 1993. The two connected and decided to work together, pool their resources, and contact the handlers from the meager list of names they had acquired. This new group was to be nothing formal, just a fraternal

John Langley (377th SPS) and Vogie (A927) at Tan Son Nhut Air Base, Vietnam. Langley was instrumental with getting the VDHA off the ground. *(Courtesy of John Langley)*

organization of former dog men, with Langley handling the membership and Mitchell writing a newsletter.

Later in 1993, they conversed with Dr. Howard Hayes, an investigator at the National Institutes of Health, who was working on research involving the handlers and dogs in Vietnam. Hayes was looking for a link between testicular cancers in the Vietnam military dogs and the use of the herbicide called Agent Orange. If a connection could be found, then the research could also be applied to veterans who acquired the same cancer. Unlike the dogs of Vietnam, testicular cancer in humans surfaced only years later in their life. Hayes also had vital information gathered about the final disposition of many of the dogs that served in Vietnam and Thailand.

In October of that same year, the pair talked with Larry Majeski from the 212th MP Sentry Dog Company. Majeski provided the names and addresses of over 400 dog handlers and most of them had served in Vietnam. It was at this time the pair decided to name the new organization the Vietnam Dog Handler Association (VDHA), even though the organization would be open to any military dog handler, past or present. The group also welcomed civilians and offered an associate membership to broaden their appeal to an even greater degree. The pair kept things informal and began to put together a small newsletter that was mailed out on a quarterly basis.

In May of 1994, over 700 people received the four page newsletter dubbed "DogMan." The newsletter format changed in October, when Ray Carpenter, a 37th SPS Phu Cat handler who worked with Thunder (0A76), volunteered his services. Ray increased the size of the newsletter to 9.5" x 13" and began to add photos to accompany the articles. As information began to flow, the first list of fifty-five dog handlers who were KIA in Vietnam was compiled and published.

A month later, 112 people attended the first reunion in Washington, D.C. It was during a ceremony at the Vietnam Veterans Memorial that a dog was first allowed onto the grounds at the memorial site. Following the reunion, the group formally organized, and in February 1996 the VDHA became a nonprofit organization as recognized by the IRS. Up to this point, Langley and Mitchell had paid for all out-of-pocket expenses, but the organization had grown beyond their wildest expectations. An annual fee of twenty dollars was established and on 21 September 1996 the organization expanded to 491 members. The VDHA was able to set their roots to continue operating and expand the association.

The Internet helped pave the way to locate more dog handlers from all over the country. Unlike other veteran organizations, dog handlers came from every service branch and getting the word out about this new organization took time and patience. Just a year later the first documentary about military dogs in Vietnam was aired as part of a segment on PBS titled "Extraordinary Dogs." The piece featured scout dog handler Bob Himrod, who had worked with Cracker (60X1) while with the 49th IPSD. Besides a handful of news stories that had appeared on television during the war, this was the first time in recent history that information about the war dogs of Vietnam would garner a national audience.

In 1997, the VDHA surged ahead and began thinking of a national monument to honor all the dogs that served in the military. Ideas began to take place and

One of the missions of the VDHA is to educate the American public on the history of military working dog teams. Children in particular can relate to military animals and learn a segment of history often overlooked by military authors and historians. *(Author's Collection)*

it also seemed to be an appropriate time to pitch the idea of a commemorative stamp to the United States Postal Service. For many members, it was thought to be a slam dunk proposition, since commemorative stamps honoring Elvis Presley, Marilyn Monroe, and Bugs Bunny had already been issued. Surely a stamp honoring the thousands of dogs that served this country would be a no-brainer. A letter was sent to the Citizens' Stamp Advisory Committee (CSAC), the civilian group that makes recommendations for commemorative stamps to be issued by the Postal Service. Within a month the VDHA received a rejection form letter.

Undeterred, the VDHA formed a K-9 Commemorative Stamp Committee and reached out to the American public for support. Petitions were filled out from all parts of the country and over 80,000 signatures were forwarded to the CSAC only to receive another form letter of rejection. VDHA members and American citizens all over the country pressed ahead and collected additional signatures.

With the second drive, over 100,000 signatures were gathered and sent to the CSAC. The stamp was also endorsed by Senators Max Cleland, Joe Lieberman, Spencer Abraham, among others, along with such notable organizations as the American Legion, Veterans of Foreign Wars, and the American Kennel Club. The signatures and endorsements were all forwarded to Dr. Virginia Noelke, who headed the CSAC at the time. On 22 September 2000, Terrence W. McCaffrey, Manager, Stamp Development, forwarded a letter to the VDHA and stated in part:

> "You will be pleased to learn that the nomination of war dogs is before the Citizens' Stamp Advisory Committee and remains under consideration. The committee is responsible for reviewing stamp proposals and making subject and design recommendations to the postmaster general."

It was the last time anyone from the VDHA heard from the postal service regarding issuing a commemorative stamp for military working dogs. In the meantime, Dick Tracy got his, along with Betty Boop, and W.E.B. Dubois, a communist who renounced his United States citizenship, received one. Dubois is always remembered as saying that Harry Truman, "...ranks with Adolph Hitler as one of the greatest killers of our day." The thousands of dogs that served America faithfully and saved an uncounted number of lives over the decades and continue to do so, still await recognition from the United States Postal Service.

Although a commemorative stamp was not issued, the effort to obtain one would eventually be rewarded in many different ways. The information spread to thousands of people who knew nothing about the dogs in Vietnam or during any other conflict that they participated in. This awareness would lead to a number of memorials proposed across the country and helped to inform a vast number of people of the contributions that military dogs have made. Numerous efforts were conducted on the local and state level to recognize these accomplishments. And although a stamp was never issued, a commemorative envelope, called a "cachet," was introduced at a fund-raising event in Hartford, Con-

Robert Kollar (58th IPSD) and his scout dog Rebel (M421) at Camp Evans in 1969. With no commemorative stamp, Kollar took advantage of a new USPS service and had this image printed on a set of first class stamps. *(Courtesy of Robert Kollar)*

Bryan Colletti (left) and Robert Kollar hold a poster of a limited-edition envelope issued by the Manchester, CT Post Office. Pictured is Charlie Cargo (48th IPSD) and Wolf (66M0). *(Author's Collection)*

Prior to the Vietnam War dog cache, another one appeared in New York in 1966. This one featured a Marine handler and his Doberman and was dedicated to the dogs that served in WWII. *(Author's Collection)*

necticut, on 30 January 2000. The limited edition envelope was made available by the Manchester, Connecticut, Post Office through the efforts of VDHA supporter Bryan Colletti and Postmaster Ron Boyne. It did not reach a national audience, but still signified a small effort by the postal service on the local level.

MYTHS, LEGENDS, AND HOPES

As with all wars, Vietnam held for itself its unique share of tall tales, fables, and mysteries. Some were conjured during the war years and quickly died with the withdrawal of troops from South Vietnam. Other stories began with a kernel of truth, which was passed along from one combat veteran to a newbie and then, as the years sped by, took on a life of its own. Other tales, malicious and false, would surface in the United States during a period immediately after the war when people expressed denial, then for some reason remorse, that we were ever really involved in Southeast Asia. This era of national guilt would eventually be replaced mostly by truth, wisdom, compassion, and understanding.

During the 1960s, before Tet, when it looked like we could win in Vietnam, quite a few handlers actually believed they might be able to bring their dogs home with them. Of course many others also hypothesized that the war would be over soon. Neither course of events would take place, as history has shown. For many handlers there remained the tantalizing thought of smuggling your dog out of Vietnam. They may have been dreams, but some men thought their dog could be shipped back to the folks at home in the states and live out his remaining years on a quiet farm. Wishing and actually accomplishing the task are two different things. If drugs could be smuggled out, or an AK-47, it made some sense that a dog wouldn't pose too much of a problem. Grease the right hands with some American dollars and maybe your dog could make it back to San Francisco or Los Angeles on some freighter out of Vung Tau or a military flight from Tan Son Nhut.

Several rumors have circulated for years after the end of the Vietnam War that a couple of dogs may have actually been slipped out of Vietnam through the palming of American money and creative paperwork in administrative circles. One story circulated about a sentry dog that was sent home to Chicago. With no name, year, unit, or handler to investigate or locate, the case of the sentry dog remains a fable, until someone can step forward and prove otherwise. In a story that appeared in a 1966 Pacific Edition of *Stars and Stripes,* a reporter stated, "There have been cases, it seems, when handlers who have grown extremely fond of their four-footed friends and have faked death certificates and gone to all sorts of trouble to smuggle their dogs back home with them."

Years later, another tale circulated about a scout dog that found a home on a farm in Iowa. The story was given credence by a piece published in the *Reader's Digest* magazine in 1996. In his *Reader's Digest* story, author Joe Kirkup tells about his encounter with a scout dog named "Bo" and his handler.[2] Kirkup was a grunt with an infantry unit that the dog team was attached to. While being processed out of Vietnam on 19 September 1967, Kirkup encountered another soldier and the conversation surrounded a scout dog named Bo. The soldier stated that he got his company commander to fill out a death certificate and the dog was sent back to his parents in Iowa.

Cowan and Kane on patrol in Burma during WWII. The pair actually enlisted together, something unheard of today. Unlike Vietnam, at the conclusion of WWII, most military dogs were retrained and returned to civilian life. *(National Archives)*

Incredibly, the dates and events recounted seem to relate to a scout dog that served the 44th IPSD. His name was Beau (07X5) and in the spring of 1967 he was a scout dog with the 44th IPSD and paired with SP4 Michael R. Phillips as his handler. After being in-country for five months, Beau had tasted the bitterness of war and savored the respect afforded to an accomplished war dog. During one encounter while on patrol, the dog alerted the platoon to an ambush and took an AK-47 round in his foreleg as payment.

Several months later, in May, Phillips and Beau participated in Operation Junction City. Beau would alert again, but this time not to enemy personnel but to incoming artillery rounds. A dozen shells exploded nearby in quick succession as both Beau and Phillips were sprawled out in the mud. A piece of shrapnel pierced Beau's backbone and continued on to nail Phillips's right arm.

Both Phillips and Beau were evacuated to Saigon on a medevac chopper. Phillips was treated for a minor wound while Beau underwent major surgery. So serious was the wound that the veterinarians did not expect the dog to survive, and they went ahead and made out a death certificate, even though the dog was still alive. Forty days later, Beau returned to active duty and, according to one report, the "death certificate was torn up."

The next several weeks were quite easy for the 44th IPSD, all things considered. About 200 patrols were conducted and there was no contact with the enemy. No further mention is made of Beau and a dog listed as MIA in June turned out to be Ringo, who showed up at the base camp ten days later. If a dog named Bo or Beau did make it home, it remains a mystery.[3]

During the Vietnam War, students at colleges and universities all over the land spawned a host of demonstrations, sit-ins, draft card burnings, all in some fashion to protest U.S. involvement in Vietnam. They not only targeted those who prosecuted the war from the comfy environs in Washington, D.C., but also those who had to participate. In some cases this extended to the families of the servicemen, who would receive a fake Western Union telegram on the order of, "…we regret to inform you that your son --- was killed…"

When the war was over, and there was nothing more to protest, it would be up to ivory tower elitists to ensure that the Vietnam War be given proper treatment within the literary world. Sorry to say, but Vietnam vets cannot accept exclusive rights to history altered by revisionists, as many other examples are awash in the literary landscape of the so-called experts from academia. For instance, "facts" would be brought out that President Franklin Roosevelt knew ahead of time that Pearl Harbor would be attacked. Another favorite among revisionists is that President Truman's authorization to drop atomic bombs on Japan was a racist act and not a military necessity.

One problem that has plagued Vietnam veterans over the years has been people posing as military veterans. In many cases, they never served in the military; in some cases they were veterans who inflated their resumes with tales of heroic deeds. When one of these impostors is quizzed, the classic response is, "It is classified and I can't talk about it," or "I just like to forget the whole thing." Several excellent books have been published that deal with "phony warriors," and a law has been passed making it a criminal offense to falsely portray oneself as a Vietnam veteran.

No doubt some wartime experiences can become embellished over the years. From the perspective of a dog handler, none could compare to that of a professed

Vietnam dog handler named Dave Baker, whose "testimony" was published in a book purported to be about "the sixties experience."[4]

Baker's fable is intriguing for what he doesn't say. Although he states he was in the Army, we never learn his rank, dates of service, location in-country, and whether he was a sentry or scout dog handler. At no time during this account of his experiences is his dog's name mentioned. Yet, he states how "they" whipped their dogs with barbed wire to make them more aggressive. Every legitimate handler knows this is an outright lie and cringes at the thought. Some of Baker's exploits would challenge even the best fabricated stories recounted at a bar after quite a few drinks. He recalls the time he unleashed his dog with no name, to attack a Viet Cong guerilla coming out of a tunnel. Baker says, "As soon as he stuck his head up, my dog saw him, grabbed him by the throat, ripped him right up. When I got to them, the dog had taken his head off, torn his arms off…"[5] Of course Baker was there during Tet, took a mortar round and survived, spent three days alone in the jungle eating dirt, saw his dog with no name nip off the head of a civilian at another unnamed village, and so on.

Apparently the husband and wife college professors who edited the book and recorded this so-called "testimony" took it all in, hook, line and sinker. In the preface the editors note, "Baker's testimony is an account common to many soldiers who went to Vietnam…" Unfortunately the editors never vetted this

Craig Lord (35th SPS) and his dog Winston (A170) at Phan Rang. Winston particularly liked Lord's beans and weenies c-rations. No good handler ever allowed his dog to be abused. It was not only counterproductive, but broke the trusted bond of a military working dog team. *(Courtesy of Craig Lord 35th SPS and K9 Winston)*

so-called dog handler or any of his amazing experiences. As recounted in these pages, Baker's testimony is purely fiction, an affront to every dog handler, and is not representative of those who served with honor in Vietnam.[6]

The Road to Recognition Begins

While the man Dave Baker weaved fairy tales to a couple of enthralled college professors, bona fide dog handlers reached out to the public to educate them about the true history of military working dogs and established long-overdue recognition for their accomplishments. Memorial projects often involve a lot time, people, the occasional political squabble, and money, but not always. Gordon Greene, from Lincoln, Nebraska, was a Marine veteran of the Korean War. In 1943 he was 10 years old and donated his dog, Buster, to the United States Army. A year later he learned that Buster was KIA. Even at that young age, Greene knew he should do something to honor the memory of Buster and all the dogs that served. It took him fifty years to accomplish the task, but that dream came to fulfillment.[7]

The war dog memorial Greene envisioned took shape in 1993 in Nebraska. The Lincoln Parks Commission decided to set aside a large section of Antelope Park as a "War Memorial Garden," to honor veterans from each service branch in each of the wars that took place in the twentieth century. Greene pitched the idea of a K-9 memorial, and the commission accepted the proposal with the provision that he provide half of the expense.

Handlers from the World War II China-Burma-India War Dog Detachment helped raise the necessary funds. A beautiful black granite stone was dedicated on 4 June 1994, with K-9 units from Offut AFB, the Lincoln Police, and the Nebraska State Police in attendance to share in the celebration.

Memorial bricks inscribed with the dog's name, tattoo number, and the war in which they served have been placed in front of the memorial. While other veteran memorials in Antelope Park generally face each other, the K-9 memorial faces outward, toward a small knoll. This is as a reflection of the outpost and perimeter work done by many military dogs, in every war, and signifies that the dogs will always be on guard, for as long as they are needed. Gordon Greene's vision for a memorial was not the first in the United States to recognize military dogs, and it certainly was not the last.

There is one monument that preceded all others, and when it was built, those involved truly believed it would be the last tribute of its type. It was erected in 1923, when World War I was known as "The Great War." For a very short period of time, folks thought of it as "the war to end all wars."

The memorial is located at America's first pet cemetery in Hartsdale, New York, established in 1896 by Dr. Samuel Johnson, a local and well respected veterinarian. A former apple orchard is now the eternal home for over 100,000 pets, including dogs, cats, birds, horses, a lion, and other exotic animals. The cemetery's growth parallels man's relationship with animals in the modern era. By 1918, over 2,000 animals were interned there. Plot owners and an enlightened public pay tribute to Red Cross dogs that served during the First World War.

Gordon Greene's tribute to the K-9 Corps is displayed on the grounds of the monument company that created it. The three dogs represent the predominant breeds that served during WWII. *(Author's Collection)*

The original proposal was sketched as a tall obelisk, rising from a broad square base and supported by two dogs on alert. For many involved it, seemed a bit far-reaching and a design by Robert Catterson was chosen instead. Catterson had been involved with the building of the Grand Central Station in New York City and owned his own granite quarry in Vermont.

Like other monuments on public display, observers see each one in a different perspective. The War Dog Memorial shows everything, but only the educated recognize the clues today. The shepherd is wearing a Red Cross blanket and there is a canteen and helmet by his feet. These are significant to each other and should be recognized by the casual observer. Red Cross dogs usually carried water or spirits in a canteen for the relief of those people they found. If the man was found conscious, he could refresh himself. Upon finding a wounded man, many dogs were trained to take away an article of clothing, usually the helmet, to signify they had found someone. The dog returned with the artifact and the handler followed the dog back to try to retrieve the wounded soldier. According to written accounts and legend, many Red Cross dogs could discriminate between the living and the dead, and there was no shortage of either in "no man's land."

On Veterans Day, 11 November 2000, John Burnam, a Vietnam scout dog handler and former president of the VDHA, stood in front of the same statue as a wreath was laid. "It is a powerful feeling standing in front of that memorial. I could almost feel and sense the spirits and the energy of the many, many war dogs we left behind in Vietnam," he later stated. The significance and power a memorial can hold for someone with ties to the history it encompasses is powerful.

The War Dog Memorial in Hartsdale, New York was the first of its kind in the country. The memorial honors the military dogs that served in WW I, even though most of them belonged to our allies. *(Author's Collection)*

Education and recognition of America's war dogs continued to spread across the country. A big boost to the promotion of military dogs and their rich heritage took place on 5 May 1996, when the Dog Museum in St. Louis, Missouri, opened a four-month tribute, "Dogs of War." Museum curator Barbara Jedda helped orchestrate this incredible display of photographs, personal stories, and memorabilia honoring dog teams that served the U. S. from World War I through Desert Storm. Several hundred people participated in the exhibition with contributions; not all of them were monetary. Part of a letter written by SGT William C. Brown (40th IPSD) appeared on the opening pages of the museum's program about his scout dog, Rover (6X01):

> "...he was more than a best friend and companion to me, he was part of me, which I miss very much. Words cannot describe him because I slept, ate, and played with him. I cried when he hurt, he protected me, and I protected him."[8]

The Dog Museum helped spread the word about military dogs while the VDHA was still casting about for an appropriate memorial and suitable recognition for the war dogs. Talks evolved into possibly placing a "Living Memorial" at Arlington National Cemetery, which constitutes the planting of a tree on the cemetery grounds along with a small plaque. Veteran's organizations at the state and federal level are permitted to do this after the appropriate application has been made. Apparently, according to the Superintendent of Arlington at the time, John C. Metzler, a law was passed in 1986 that prevented small individual units from having monuments or living memorials in the Washington, D.C. area.

Although the VDHA represented 10,000 Vietnam handlers and 4,000 dogs, it was still considered a small representative of the forces that served there. To get a tree and plaque installed at Arlington would literally "take an act of Congress." The VDHA membership did not want to pursue the issue at this time, especially with Congress, and possibly risk being immediately turned down for a more meaningful memorial in the future. The idea of a small, albeit significant, K-9 memorial in such a sacred place as Arlington National Cemetery soon faded away.

Still, the VDHA wanted to see a memorial somewhere near the Vietnam Memorial in Washington, D.C. The organization teamed up with Nature's Recipe, a respected pet food manufacturer and the company's CEO, Jeffrey Bennett. What transpired yielded the biggest boost for pubic recognition and education about the American war dogs. The Discovery Channel on television produced a one-hour, semi-documentary titled "War Dogs – The Untold Story of Dogs in Combat." On 10 February 1999, a private airing of "War Dogs" took place at the Leonard H. Goldenson Theatre, in North Hollywood, California. Five days later it premiered publicly on the Discovery Channel. With the documentary came the planned dedication of the first Nature's Recipe war dog memorial at Riverside National Cemetery, in Riverside, California, on 11 November 1999.

Riverside is the third-largest veteran's cemetery in the United States. With over 1.5 million veterans interred there, it was hoped to be the linchpin for securing a monument site in Washington, D.C. the following year. At the time, few people realized that the proverbial train carrying the war dog memorial and picking up a good head of steam was about to come flying off the tracks.

The sculpture Nature's Recipe chose was designed and created by A. Thomas Schomberg. The bronze sculpture of a handler emerges from a large polished granite wall with a dog on a leash. No weapon is present and the dog is definitely German shepherd in appearance, but is meant to represent all the breeds that served. With a Vietnam era flak jacket and helmet, the dog team epitomizes all that came before them and those who will follow. Over sixteen feet in height, the statue weighs in excess

John Burnam (left) and Charlie Cargo were both scout dogs handlers in Vietnam who worked as technical advisors on the Discovery Channel documentary "War Dogs – The Untold Story of Dogs in Combat." *(Courtesy of John Burnam)*

of 9,000 pounds. At the top is a valance that allows the sun to shine through and cast shadows throughout the day. The base is inscribed: "They protected us on the field of battle; they watch over our eternal rest – we are grateful." Schomberg stated:

> "The war dog memorial, as I created it, is meant to illustrate first, the bond between humans and their canine friends. Second, this bond is applied to a military activity and finally, and most importantly, the sacrifice that these two figures have made under combat circumstances. We all owe a debt of gratitude to the men and women who have served and are serving to protect our rights of freedom. The assistance of "man's best friend" has played a major and unforgettable role in this pursuit."[9]

Tom Mitchell finished his term as President in October 1999, during that pivotal year. Yet he did not see the memorial dedicated at Riverside National Cemetery nor would he travel to Washington, D.C., for a second memorial dedication. The two locations where the VDHA wanted the memorials placed would not come to fruition and alternate sites were developed.

Even though Bennett, president of Nature's Recipe Pet Foods, sponsored both the War Dogs documentary and the two memorials, the VDHA was still deeply involved. The VDHA was an integral part in establishing the war dog memorials, but was not involved in the legal or financial concerns of the enterprise. Corporate wheels were turning. The parent company of Nature's Recipe, Heinz Pet Products, administered a corporate restructuring that closed Nature's recipe's office in California, although Bennett continued on as CEO.[10]

In March 1999, the War Dog Memorial Fund, Inc. was established as a 501(c)(3) independent entity, not to be associated with Heinz or Nature's Recipe. The separation of power and funds associated with haunted and confused the VDHA membership for years to come. Bennett's original contribution of $300,000 would be supplemented by $250,000 from the dog food promotion, another $250,000 by Heinz, and approximately $200,000 from private donations. Yet in October of 1999, the NCA had issued a second denial about erecting a war dog monument at Riverside National cemetery or any national cemetery.[11] Effectively, there were two statues designed and built, but no place to put them.

The Schomberg sculpture is both elegant and simple. It combines the two key elements of a dog team in an extraordinary way. Although the soldier is in Vietnam-era equipment the purpose was to include all handlers throughout United States history, past, present, and future. *(Photo courtesy of Robert Saracino)*

The rejection of the memorial at Riverside Cemetery was received by the VDHA in a letter, on 17 June 2000, issued by a government official of the Veterans Administration Secretary Togo West, on behalf of the National Cemetery Administration (NCA). The NCA stated that the memorial would not be approved because: 1) The dogs were "incidental" to military operations, and 2) would be inappropriate to put such a memorial in a place where people receive their final honors. These statements display narrow mindedness of the government bureaucracy and their ignorance of the contributions of our military working dogs throughout history. In response to the denial of the NCA, Brigadier General Stan Brown USAF (ret.) and Chairman of the Riverside National Cemetery sent an appeal to VA Secretary Togo West that stated in part:

> "If asked, those saved, their comrades, friends and families would not agree that these dogs were "incidental." In fact, one could easily contend that the fitting place for such a memorial is a national cemetery. No one is suggesting that any dogs be interred at any national cemetery. Mr. Secretary, while we understand the NCA's response we cannot agree on the logic. These animals did the work that otherwise would not have been done by Americans that would now be interred in 'fields of honor'."

What is incredible is that the proposed memorial site was not part of the cemetery proper. The monument, with its production and perpetual care costs in excess of a million dollars, was intended to be placed along the Memorial Walk and situated across from the cemetery. The intention was to form an "eternal watch" over the veterans interred within the cemetery. While General Brown issued his appeal, Bennett issued a separate plea and considered using land across from the cemetery entrance that would be donated by the county. What was to be another "slam dunk" undertaking at the onset turned out to be a major disappointment for everyone involved. If this was the response from a National Cemetery in California, the realization of a memorial in Washington, D.C., began to look bleak.

While the two statues sponsored by Nature's Recipe took on a national significance, there were other projects taking shape across the country. Based

The expression of the German shepherd is not one of an alert but that of fierce determination of loyalty, trust, and a willingness to succeed. *(Courtesy of Robert Saracino)*

The words inscribed on the base of the memorial reinforce the job given to a dog and the thoughts of his handler. *(Courtesy of Robert Saracino)*

on the number of projects proposed, many efforts can be attributed to members of the VDHA and the work of hundreds of people who believed that the dogs needed to be recognized. Continuing efforts of the VDHA to educate the public took on a steamroller effect as both veterans and citizens from all walks of life expressed great interest in recognizing the accomplishments of military working dogs.

After denial for the monument at Riverside National Cemetery, the group refocused and sought a different location. Near the cemetery, just a half-mile away, was March Field Museum, an excellent location for both accessibility and exposure. The museum's director, Steve Clark, stated, "The War Dog Memorial will be a great addition to our collection. We're honored to have received this meaningful representation of military history. We are certain it will generate a lot of visitors and interest; it already has."

With a half-million visitors expected for its annual air show, the memorial would garner plenty of attention and a new dedication date was scheduled for 21 February 2000. On a rainy Monday morning, more than 2,000 people attended the dedication ceremony. Over 100 handlers stood in line and patted the bronze replica of the dog, while saying a few words; many left flowers. It was a successful event and those involved looked forward to the dedication of the second monument, scheduled to take place at Fort Benning, Georgia, in the near future.

Since the dedication of the memorial at March Air Base, Bennett and other members of the War Dog Memorial Fund worked with the Army to establish the second memorial at Fort Benning. In September 2000, the paperwork was done, the handshakes were made, and the Army agreed to place the monument opposite the National Infantry Museum overlooking Sacrifice Field. The dedication was scheduled just one week prior to the biennial VDHA reunion. Many members who could not possibly attend both events were upset. VDHA president Randy Kimler stated, "As a result, we [the VDHA] did not have the final say on when the memorial would be dedicated. The sponsoring organizations, the Army, and the Memorial Fund, scheduled the time and date. While I had hoped to have it farther away from the date of the reunion and allow more time for people to make plans to attend, we must be grateful that it is actually happening at all."[12]

Among memorials and events planned surrounding the Vietnam War dogs and handlers, is one group that planned their final reunion. Age had finally caught up with the World War II handlers, as the CBI War Dog Detachment prepared for their final gathering. These pioneers were among the first soldiers in the American military to work alongside war dogs on the front lines. Their final reunion took place at Fort Robinson, Nebraska, on 20 June 2000. Fort Robinson was one of the original training and acquisition sites for many war dogs during World War II. The CBI handlers have yielded to time and passed their experiences along to those who fought in Vietnam. As one generation moved aside, the Vietnam handlers have passed the baton of their experiences to the dog handlers who have served in Iraq and Afghanistan. These were entirely different wars and circumstances, over decades of time, but with the common core of soldier and dog working together.

On 11 November 2000, a war dog team monument was dedicated in Port Neches, Texas. Sculpted by artist Doug Clark over a three month period, the monument is the centerpiece for eleven-acre Golden Triangle Veterans Memorial Park. The memorial is located close to the Louisiana state line, about twenty miles north of the Gulf of Mexico.

The project emerged from the members of the Wayne P. East VFW Post 4820. Randy Kimler, a scout dog handler and past president of the VDHA, was a member and became instrumental in seeing the bronze sculpture erected. According to the *Port Arthur News*, an article

Port Neches, Texas celebrated their dedication of a war dog memorial in November 2000. This is another example of the impact VDHA members had on the public and a tribute to United States citizens that recognition for the accomplishments of war dogs teams was long overdue. *(Photo courtesy of Randy Kimler)*

about American war dogs written by Kimler began the idea for the statue. One of a series of monuments to be erected across the United States, it was the result of veteran and civilian actionworking together.

For Australians who served in Vietnam, their post-war experience mirrored that of many Americans (i.e., forget about it, get on with life, it's in the past.). Many years passed before people began to recognize that the fight in Vietnam was filled with honorable intentions. Only a small number of people knew of the eleven Australian tracker dogs that served in Vietnam. Peter Haran's book, *Trackers: The Untold Story of the Australian Dogs of War,* published in 2000, became the catalyst to bringing together veterans and enlightening the public about this little known part of their own military history. Anne Dunkeley, historian for the Australian Defence Force Trackers & War Dogs Association (ADFTWDA), stated:

> "When Peter wrote *Trackers,* it obviously stirred up a lot of old memories as well as inspired many others. I myself stumbled across Peter's book by accident and after reading it, was interested to learn more about the Vietnam tracker dogs. However, upon searching [for information] found there was little documentation. Consequently this led me to meet Bob [Bettany] and offer to assist him in compiling [tracker] history as I thought it would be such a shame if much of this just slipped through the cracks."[13]

Vietnam veteran Ian Atkinson and the Vietnam Veterans Association of Australia launched the initial effort and secured the first war dog memorial in Australia. It is classified as the first National War Dog Memorial, located at the Bluff, Alexandra Headland, on Queensland's Sunshine Coast. Overlooking the Pacific Ocean, about an hour's drive north of Brisbane, the memorial, created from sandstone by Vietnam veteran and stonemason Dick Meisenhelter, was dedicated on 7 April 2001. This "interactive" monument allows people to water their dogs from a trough at its base. The inscription reads:

WAR DOG MEMORIAL
DEDICATED TO THE AUSTRALIAN TRACKER DOGS
THAT SERVED IN VIETNAM
1967-1971.
THEY DID NOT RETURN FROM THE WAR
CAESAR, CASSIUS*, JANUS, JULIAN, JUNO, JUSTIN, MARCIAN,
MARCUS, MILO, TIBER, TRAJAN

*Died on active service

Down jungle tracks, through shot and shell
Ears pricked high, keen sense of smell
Our tracker dogs with care and poise
Alert to ambush, foreign noise
Never whimper, whine nor bark

Their service honoured with the plaque
No medals pinned to hairy chest
They stayed behind, they were the best.

ALL GAVE SOMETHING, SOME GAVE ALL
THOSE WHO KNEW YOU, WILL NEVER FORGET YOU

Since the Australian memorial was dedicated, additional plaques have been added to the National War Dog Memorial to recognize the service of dogs that served in Bougainville, Borneo, East Timor, Malaya, Singapore, Somalia, and the Solomon Islands.

Just two years later, a second monument was dedicated in Goolwa, the historic port on the River Murray, in South Australia, on 26 April 2003. The face of the memorial has a picture of Russell "Mooka" McDonald and his tracker dog, Trajan, etched in stone. An ideal location, it proved to be a popular site for dog walkers. The design includes a water fountain and a paw-print carved in black marble at the base. Inscribed alongside the drinking bowl, are the words: "Have a drink on me."

A third Australian memorial was erected at Lowestoft Bay, Berriedale, in Tasmania, an Australian island about 150 miles off the eastern side of the continent. The memorial was dedicated on 11 March 2006 by the Governor of Tasmania, the Honourable William Cox AC RFD ED. An expansive monument, it features several totems listing the names of dogs that served with the armed forces since

On the other side of the world, Australia established their first monument in April 2001 to commemorate their military dogs. *(AATWDA)*

Two years after establishing their first war dog memorial, Australians dedicated a second monument in Goolwa, along the southern coast of the continent. *(AATWDA)*

WWI. A circular seating arrangement, called a "contemplation area," overlooks the bay, with paving leading up to the tribute commemorating friends, both two-legged and four-legged.

In the United States, memorials and plaques have been erected in many parts of the country including New York, Nevada, Illinois, Florida, New Jersey, Alabama, Minnesota, Pennsylvania, and Kentucky. For years the VDHA envisioned a national monument erected on the mall in Washington, D.C. With the World War II memorial and other tributes recently dedicated, space has been at a premium and the government has all but buried any possibility of building a military K-9 tribute in that setting.

However, a national tribute is still in the works and may soon become a reality. Originally called the National War Dog Committee and working under the VDHA umbrella, the group formally separated from the association in 2006. The committee was abolished and became a nonprofit organization called The National War Dog Monument, Inc. (NWDM) to continue with the quest of a federally recognized national K-9 memorial.

In February 2008, President George W. Bush signed H.R. 4986, which contains a section titles "Establishment of National Military Working Dogs Team Monument on Suitable Military Installation." The bill recognizes the NWDM as the representative organization for the effort and also stipulates Fort Belvoir, Virginia as a possible site. NWDM officers are pursuing the effort and exploring all possible sites available.

The artist selected, Renee Headings, envisions a bronze sculpture with a handler and the three primary dogs used by the military since World War II: the Ger-

man shepherd, Labrador retriever, and Doberman pinscher. Reliefs and other artifacts will represent different services and eras in which military dog teams worked in.[14]

The memorials erected in both the United States and Australia illustrates the bond that the handlers had and still maintain with their four-legged warriors. Bob Bettany, the secretary for the Australian Tracker Association believed the monuments were part of a long overdue payment to the dogs and said, "All of this I guess stirred up our guilt for not fighting harder at the time to bring them home." Although the handlers clearly should not be faulted at all for what finally happened to the war dogs of Vietnam. In their hearts, they did bring them home. The memorials and tributes, along with continually educating the public, meant that they truly did bring them back – not physically, but perhaps in better and more permanent ways that keep their spirits alive, decades after they were gone.

Although the Australians worked with just eleven dogs in Vietnam, a third memorial was established on the island of Tasmania. The three memorials honoring the country's war dogs is a testament to the spirit and dedication of the Australian citizens in recognizing their four-footed comrades. *(AATWDA)*

Among the people that the Discovery Channel documentary touched was a high school girl, Jennifer Pfannuche, from Streamwood, Illinois. She told her father, the commander of VFW Post 5151, that it would be nice if a memorial was built to honor the K-9s that served. The rest, as they say, is history. Volunteers banded together to raise funds and sculptor Anthony Quickle was commissioned to create the monument.

The city of Streamwood embraced the project, and a number of fund raising events ensued, culminating with the dedication on the Memorial Day weekend 2001. On hand for the event were forty K-9 teams from nearby Chicago and other surrounding towns. The quiet was broken by a twenty-one gun saluted followed by the barking of just about every dog in attendance. It was truly a fitting tribute.

On hand for the dedication was 93-year-old, USCG Lt. Commander Willie Necker, a legendary trainer of military dogs during World War II. Necker was one of the pioneers, an instrumental figure in developing the military working dogs during the early years of the program. He spoke of his pride of being a K-9 handler and seeing the recognition the MWDs have so longed deserved. Lt. Commander Necker placed three red carnations at the memorial's base where a poem, written by Carolyn Pentecost was etched into the marble base. The poems reads:

In Loving Memory

You were there to watch for the enemy
You were there to lead us.
You were there to love and comfort us.
You were there to die for us, and you did.
You were our friend, our comrade, our family
But most of all, your were there to serve.
With courage, dignity, and pride.
Always, you will remain in our hearts
As a lasting tribute to unconditional love
And service to your country.
War Dogs, we salute you!

Even with a pending rainstorm, over 1200 veterans and local citizens attended the dedication of the latest war dog memorial in Streamwood, Illinois. It started as a desire by a local high school girl to honor the nation's military dogs and evolved into a project that drew in hundreds of people to see it become a reality. *(Author's collection)*

The War Dog Memorial located in Bristol Township, Pennsylvania. *(Photo courtesy of Jesse E. Hill)*

Throughout the United States, as the years rolled along, there continued to be a public enlightenment to the contributions that military working dog teams have made and continue to make on behalf of our citizens. It might be a modest plaque or a full blown sculpture that represents the unsung heroes of our nation's history. In some cases it embodies the commitment of fire, police, and rescue personnel. This is the case of a K-9 monument erected in Bristol Township, Pennsylania. It is a dedication in a memorial garden adjacent to the Vietnam Veterans Memorial and a monument representing Bristol Township's police, fire, and emergency personnel.

It is another indication that the time has finally come to honor these heroes. Dedicated on 16 September 2006, it took six years and $100,000 to accomplish the task. It is a stunning bronze memorial that depicts a six-foot, 4-inch soldier in a flak jacket alongside a German shepherd at the moment of an alert. Sculpted by local artist Joe Pavone, it is another fine example of an artistic tribute that begs those that see it to explore this unique history even more.

Most of these memorials depict war dog teams from the Vietnam era. Not to be forgotten are the dog teams from World War II that set in place the building blocks for all future endeavors. William

California artist Susan Bahary was commissioned to sculpt the Marine dog memorial "Always Faithful". The memorial was featured on CNN and unveiled at the Pentagon in 1994. *(Photo courtesy of Susan Bahary)*

W. Putney, D.V.M. was a first lieutenant and commanded the 3rd Marine War Dog platoon during World War II. He never forgot the effort made by the men and dogs under his command during the invasion of Guam.

The Marines had honored their war dog dead on the island. But as years passed the cemetery was forgotten and the site became overgrown with vegetation and had fallen into disarray and damage by vandalism. In 1994, Dr. Putney worked with the United States government and had the cemetery moved and rededicated within a national park. He went even further and had two memorials commissioned to honor the dogs that had served their country. The twin memorials reside at both the U.S. Naval Base at Orote Point, Guam and at the University of Tennessee. For Dr. Putney, as with so many other handlers, time and distance prove no obstacle for remembering those that you lived and worked with.

Finally a Chance to Retire with Dignity

Several decades have passed since the close of Vietnam and the dogs that served there are long gone and a distant memory for many men. During the war, attempts to have them repatriated to handlers or responsible civilians fell on deaf ears. Even though Vietnam was over, the use of dogs within the military did not end. The average life of a military working dog today is just eight years, much shorter than the same dog in a civilian environment. Nor did their final disposition change after Vietnam when they could no longer work well. It was still Department of Defense (DoD) policy to euthanize dogs that were no longer effective or proficient in a military environment. This had been the standard procedure of the DoD since 1949, with just a couple of minor exceptions. Then fifty-one years later, along came Robby (W005), a Belgian Malinois that would forever change this policy and provide a second chance for dogs considered by the government to be "surplus."

Robby was eleven years old, tired, and hurting badly. He was diagnosed with elbow dysplasia at the age of two, and about two years later he occasionally exhibited acute pain from progressive arthritis and a protruding disc in his spine. During a public exhibition in the autumn of 2000, Robby ran on an attack command from his handler, Lance Corporal Shawn Manthey. He picked up speed and a few seconds later yelped and collapsed to the ground in pain. It was a watershed moment, for in the audience to view this scene was House Representative Roscoe Bartlett (R-MD).

Air Force veterinarians planned to have Robby returned to Lackland for additional medical evaluation. Manthey knew it was the end of the line for the dog; what else was the military going to do with a gimpy working dog other than put him down? Knowing what lay in store, he asked for permission to adopt him and was soundly rejected. But timing can be everything. The Discovery Channel had previously aired *War Dogs: America's Forgotten Heroes,* and with the dedication of two bi-coastal monuments, public awareness about military working dogs had escalated enormously within a short period of time. The Internet hummed with traffic and a "Save Robby Campaign" evolved. Thousands of people were drawn in, but at the core of the effort were Dr. William Putney, Mary Thurston, Tim Johnson, and Representative Roscoe Bartlett.

Dr. Putney was not only a noted veterinarian, but also the Commanding Officer of the Marine 3rd War Dog Platoon during World War II and participated in the invasion of Guam. He received the Purple Heart and Silver Star and was instrumental in "retraining" hundreds of Marine military dogs and ensured that they were handed over to responsible civilians. Dr. Putney was a well respected figure within the military ranks, and both compassionate and pragmatic.

Johnson was a medic in Vietnam and became chairman of the loose-knit organization and helped organize Internet chats and soliciting various national organizations for support. Johnson stated, "It was apparent to me that there needed to be a central source of information on this issue in order to keep folks informed and involved."[15]

Also involved in the effort was Texas anthropologist and author, Mary Thurston. Thurston wrote *The Lost History of the Canine Race* and was a founding member of the Animal Trustees of Austin. She wrote numerous articles about Robby and the efforts to establish the nation's first war dog retirement law. For years she was an ardent opponent of the armed forces policy of euthanasia for military working dogs.

The two-prong national effort, both to save Robby and establish a MWD retirement law, would eventually pay off. Although the bill moved along quickly, Robby's medical condition had worsened to the point where euthanasia was the most humane response. Even Dr. Putney agreed with that decision after reviewing the medical records and informed Representative Bartlett, stating, "His condition had deteriorated too far. It wouldn't be fair to prolong his life."[16]

On 10 October 2000, H.R. 5314 had thirty-eight co-sponsors when it made it to the floor of the House. The bill was considered in quick order by those present and passed. Two weeks later, it was amended by the Senate and the House concurred on 26 October. President Clinton signed the bill into law on 6 November 2000, as it officially became "Public Law 106-446." Under the new law, the commander of the dog's last duty unit will, in consultation with the unit veterinarian, decide whether the dog is suitable for adoption. Dogs found suitable will be available for adoption by law enforcement agencies, former handlers and trainers, or other persons determined "capable of humanely caring for these dogs." The law also requires anyone receiving a retired military dog to agree not to hold the government responsible for injury, damage, or other damages resulting from ownership of the dog. Dogs not adopted or euthanized for medical reasons will be sent to Lackland Air Force Base in San Antonio, Texas, for use in training new dog handlers.

Essentially the new retirement law for military dogs mirrored House bills introduced by Congressmen Rarick and Moss thirty years earlier. It appeared that the difference this time would be the incredible civilian involvement made possible through the various media outlets and the Internet that helped move the bill along. However, the new law is not perfect, since it promotes retirement as an "option" to euthanasia and does not dictate that retirement be the primary determination. What is not understandable is that the DoD fought tooth and nail against the new law, citing in a letter that it would be costly, provide a hardship for military personnel, and poise a liability issue since the dogs were considered dangerous.

Johnston was incredulous and asked, "Well which is it? In one breath the military is bragging about the precision training of their dogs and how they respond only on command. And in the next breath they're trying to paint the animals as psychotic killers. If they're so proud of their so-called retirement program at LAFB, why are they objecting at all?"[17]

The "retirement" Johnston referred to appears in a DoD press release issued in August 2000. "Within the DoD, military working dogs are not euthanized solely because of age. Instead they are retired to the 341st MWD Training Squadron here at Lackland, where they live out the rest of their lives in a quality environment." Dr. Putney wholly disputed the claim and stated, "They're trying to play word games. No matter what they want to call it, this is a far cry from what most of us think of as retirement."

In any event, the military lost this battle, but few people can understand why the DoD would draw a line in the sand regarding the retirement of military dogs to begin with. The training for MWDs is basically the same as any civilian police agency dog. Yet the police dogs are given a retirement party and assume a peaceful existence when their working life is finished, usually at the home of his handler. The fact that the DoD can retain any dog that is physically able to do "any" work, could mean that they have absolutely no quality of life available to them once they are released to a civilian for retirement.

The DoD maintains more than 1,700 dogs world-wide in what is now called "force-protection support in security and contraband (narcotic and explosive) detection." Prior to establishment of the retirement law, about 200 MWDs were either euthanized or died each year. In one study, the leading cause for euthanasia was "degenerative joint disease of the appendicular skeleton" affecting about 20% of the dogs with a mean age of 10 years.[18]

Of course, not every potential MWD eligible for retirement is old or infirm. Baro (D134) was a purebred German shepherd and just two years old when his right forepaw was severely injured in an accident. Based on the future premise that Baro would not be able to work as a bomb detection dog, the Air Force deemed him excess and scheduled him to be euthanized. Fortunately for Baro, the retirement law was in place and there was someone waiting for him.

Alan Driscoll was a handler with the 377th SPS at Tan Son Nhut in Vietnam and worked with Dutchess (A649) in 1966 and 1967. They were a team like so many others that worked the perimeter of an air base after sundown, sometimes referred to as "nightwalkers." The pair was on duty one night in December 1966 when two dogs were killed and another (Nemo) was wounded in the first major Viet Cong ground attack on the air base. Driscoll would later move on, leaving the Air Force and distinguishing himself as a Captain in the U.S. Merchant Marine. Several years later, while many people look forward to retirement, he became involved with counter-terrorism training.

Dutchess never left Vietnam, but Driscoll never forgot her, and this prompted him to acquire a dog from the military. After a flurry of paperwork, he became the first civilian under the newly established retirement law to acquire a military working dog. Years later, Baro is quite healthy, although if you look closely you might detect a slight limp, but in no way has it slowed him down. Prior to enactment of the retirement law, he would have been euthanized with absolutely no chance of survival.

Captain Alan Driscoll and Baro (D134). Baro was among one of the first dogs retired by the military post Vietnam. *(Photo courtesy of Bonnie Driscoll)*

According to Driscoll, "A lot of us [Vietnam veteran dog handlers] were very upset with what happened with the dogs. We all complained about it; now we have a chance to do something about it and help change things."[19] And change comes with education and citizen awareness. The VDHA kept pushing to have each state issue a proclamation honoring the nation's war dogs and their handlers, and endorsing a national monument in their honor. Driscoll and Baro helped out by getting Massachusetts to issue such a proclamation on 23 June 2004.

Even with the MWD retirement law on the books, many civilians remain unaware of the possibility of acquiring a K-9 veteran. There is no mechanism in place for the government to advertise this program and the law does not address euthanizing MWDs as a military necessity or just a case of expediency. A case in point is Benny (B163), a German shepherd adopted by Debbie and Mike Kandoll of Pikeville, North Carolina. Benny was declared excess in October 2007 and his euthanasia was scheduled for December 2007 or the following month. After completing all the paperwork and questions, the couple eventually picked him up at Langley AFB on 4 January 2008.

According to Debbie Kandoll, "Almost any aged dog is going to be suffering from degenerative joint disease (DJD), which is "justification" for MWD euthanasia. For example, my Benny has DJD in his hips, enough to prevent him from searching "high" for drugs during long periods of time. However, with Glucosamine supplements, a softer bed instead of concrete, and a regulated ambient temperature in the winter, he shows no signs of problems. He probably has a good five [to] eight more years, barring any unforeseen internal happening."[20]

Because a law was passed making military dogs available to civilians doesn't necessarily mean the public has immediate access to information. As of this writing, there is no one-stop shopping or easy access to information about obtaining a retired K-9 veteran. Debbie Kandoll found that out before she was introduced to Benny and might have given up had she not been persistent. She found all Internet searches led to Lackland AFB and later found out that their website was taken down. According to Kandoll, "I made over 50 calls…at least thirty of them wrong numbers given by well-meaning but uniformed base operators! I was drowning in red tape and lack of contact information." She finally located a dog at Langley AFB. "I finally made my twentieth "correct" call to the Langley AF MWD facility. I asked whether they had a retiring MWD available for adoption, and MSgt Jack Davis, Kennel Master, answered with a smile in his voice, "Yes! I do! He's a big goofball without a mean bone in his body.""[21]

Kandoll and her husband finally secured their dog. While driving home after picking him up, she read his medical record with the last entry written on 29 November 2007, that stated, "Scheduled for euthanasia and necropsy in December 2007 or January 2008." Kandoll realized the date of the entry was the same day she had called Langley. If she had not been persistent, Benny would have received his death sentence and this made her begin to wonder how many other dogs shared the same possible fate.

Her husband, an Air Force Security Forces Officer, suggested she launch a website about what it takes to adopt an MWD. She dismissed it out-of-hand as "too much work." But after two weeks at home with Benny she knew it was the right thing to do, something that needed to be done, and changed her mind. The website she launched demystifies the adoption process and provides valuable information and phone numbers from all over the country that have MWDs available for adoption. Kandoll kept telling herself how many dogs have died because

Benny (B163) was scheduled to be euthanized by the military. Under the military dog retirement law he became part of the Kandoll family in Pikeville, North Carolina and has been a roving ambassador for MWDs and therapy dogs. *(Courtesy of Debbie Kandoll)*

of lack of information for civilians and the red tape involved in the process. She also reminds herself of a previous adoption application she mailed several years earlier – a request for an MWD that never received a response.[22]

Media War Dogs

Another good indicator of the recognition for war dogs and their handlers is how often they have appeared in film or other media since World War II, Korea, and Vietnam. Small stories have sprung up in newspapers and magazines across the country, and in recent years war dogs and their handlers have appeared often on television. During World War II, and immediately thereafter, many newspaper stories and newsreel footage emerged about Dogs For Defense, Chips the war dog, and other tales of handlers and their dogs. The stories died out when the war dog program evaporated and the military working dog program went dormant.

One comic book did emerge, and for just a brief moment in 1952, during the Korean War, military dogs took center stage when Avon Periodicals published "War-Dogs of the U.S. Army" as a single issue. These were not your typical military working dogs, as they parachuted behind lines, attacked machine gun nests, and captured enemy documents. What a hoot in a day before political correctness, to have Chinese communists yell out, "We must stop those Melican dogs!" In retrospect, the activities of military working dogs must have left some type of impact to have a publisher produce a comic book devoted to them, even if it was just pulp fiction.

Journalists picked up on the war dog commitment in Vietnam just a few years later, when correspondent Dan Rather ran one television news story about the dogs being trained for the ARVN. As in World War II, a number of newspaper articles and some special Sunday supplements were published about the dog teams of Vietnam. For the most part, people across America had no idea about our military dog program.

Then, in September 1974, after the Americans had left Vietnam and before Saigon fell to the NVA, the NBC television network launched a weekly Saturday morning program called, "Run, Joe, Run." Joe was a military working dog and a veteran of Vietnam. In the storyline, established for kids, Joe was falsely accused of attacking his handler, Sgt. Corey, and the military ordered him to be put down. He managed to escape and the Army posted a bounty for him in a classic "dead or alive" scenario. The series followed the same basic plot as the 1960s TV

The only comic known to have depicted war dogs debuted in 1952 as a single issue. *(Author's Collection)*

series the "Fugitive," starring David Jansen, but with a touch of Lassie tossed in for good measure. Joe was a canine Dr. Richard Kimball running away from authorities while helping people along the way.

Joe would have flashbacks to his military training that always helped him out in dangerous situations. Sgt. Corey tried to find him before the Army officials did, and although he came close, the announcer at the end of the program would always say, "But all Joe could do is keep running." The program ran for two years and twenty-six episodes.[23]

"Run, Joe, Run" appeared Saturday mornings as a television series for two seasons on NBC. One episode appeared as a slide program popular at the time. *(Author's Collection)*

A long time passed before a military dog would appear again in the movies or on television. Glimpses of war dogs can be found in several major movies. Look quickly in Clint Eastwood's "Flags of our Fathers" and you'll spot a couple of Dobermans with Marine handlers. The same with the ending of the movie "Platoon," and you'll notice a German shepherd scout dog with a rope for a leash.

Numerous television news accounts across the country have been broadcast and most of these appeared (by no coincidence) with the formation of the VDHA in 1996. Whether it was a parade or a memorial dedication, a local news crew was there to capture the moment. Other documentaries have appeared on the History Channel, PBS (Extraordinary Dogs), and the BBC.

Several notable books and memoirs have also been published in recent years. Captain William W. Putney, D.V.M., who singlehandedly managed the restoration of the war dog cemetery on Guam, penned a book about the Marine dogs of WWII. *Always Faithful – A Memoir of the Marine Dogs of WWII,* was published in 2001.

A year earlier, *Trackers: The Untold Story of the Australian Dogs of War*, by Peter Haran, appeared. Other books followed, such as *Dog Tags of Courage,* by John C. Burnam, recounting his experiences as a scout dog handler in Vietnam, and Toni Gardner's *Walking Where The Dog Walks*, as she chronicled members of the 47th IPSD in 1968-69.

Two authors approached the subject of military working dogs as a subject for young readers, from different angles. Nancy West took the story of Chips, K-9 hero of World War II and wove a fictional account (*Chips: The War Dog*) based on his true-life adventures. The book is suggested for ages nine and up, and gives a great opportunity for younger readers to look at a different aspect of history. In a message to the readers at the start of the book, West writes, "It was a time when the world desperately needed heroes to fight for freedom and justice. Chips was one of those heroes."

Two years later, West approached the daunting subject of war, land mines, and how to bring this subject to very early readers without talking down to them and patronizing young children. She hit a home run with *Kali Leads the Way*. This is the story of Kali, a black Labrador retriever, who started work as a humanitarian mine detection dog in Cambodia. The dog brings a family through unfamiliar and dangerous terrain so that a young boy can seek hospital care. With great skill and superb illustrations, West has broached a subject and presented a book that is of interest to readers of any age.

"Kali Leads the Way" by Nancy West is an early reader book that tackles the subject and the ongoing problem of abandoned mines and ordnance in different parts of the world. *(Author's Collection)*

Johnny Mayo tackled the subject of war dogs based on his own experiences in Vietnam. After being drafted in 1969, Mayo volunteered as a scout dog handler and was attached to the 39th IPSD where he worked with Kelly (819A). Mayo's book, *Buck's Heroes,* is the factual story of war dogs in Vietnam, but as

In Mayo's book, Buck learns the history of the war dogs of Vietnam from the ghosts of two scouts, Kelly and Tiger, during a visit to the Vietnam Memorial in Washington, D.C. *(Courtesy of Johnny Mayo)*

seen through the eyes of his beloved family dog, a husky named Buck. The book is fascinating and informative, and is enhanced by photographs and wonderful illustrations by the artist, Tonia Maynell.

Both West and Mayo have succeeded in approaching younger readers with a very difficult subject. Of course, the dogs become the conduit, as most young readers can respond as well as enjoy a story that has dogs involved. The mark made by these books is that they can be enjoyed by both the young and the old.

Then and Now

The scout and tracker dog programs were terminated shortly after the conclusion of the Vietnam War. That is not to say that the requirements for having dogs trained for these specialties has ended, only that the military has considered them superfluous to their current objectives. Since the 1970s, the primary focus has been to train dogs in a dual capacity: as explosive or narcotic detectors and as patrol canines to protect their handlers with the ability to attack on command.

Before 11 September 2001, the Air Force trained approximately 200 working dogs each year. That number is now more than 500 trained annually, with over 2,000 dogs deployed worldwide. In Afghanistan and Iraq, the

The New Jersey Way Dog Memorial is surrounded by handlers during its dedication in 2006. *(Courtesy of United States War Dogs Association)*

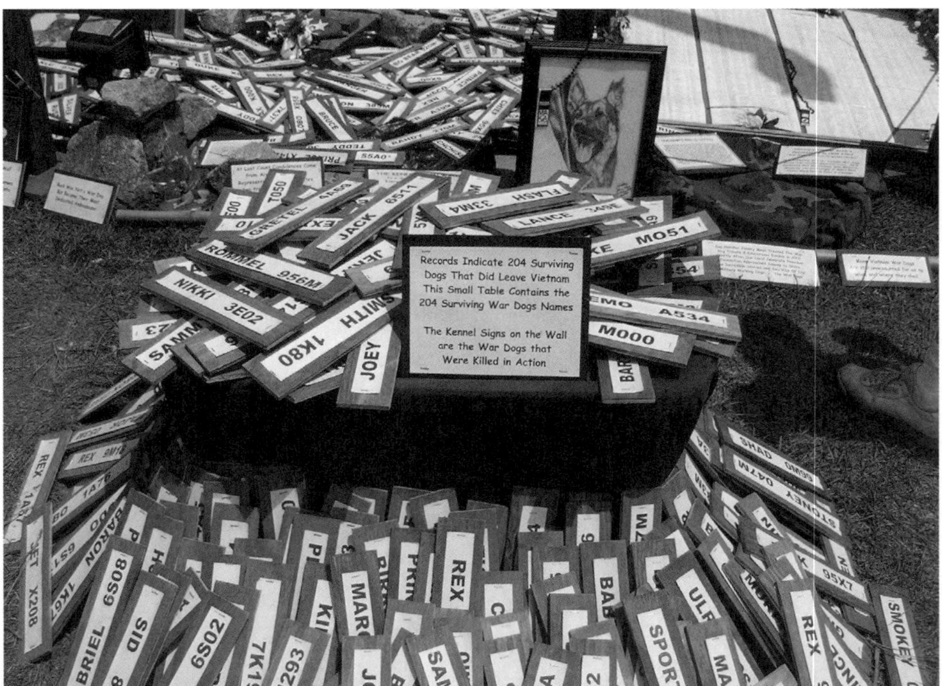
Records Indicate 204 Surviving
Dogs That Did Leave Vietnam
This Small Table Contains the
204 Surviving War Dogs Names
The Kennel Signs on the Wall
are the War Dogs that
Were Killed in Action

American military maintains more than 200 dogs, although exact numbers are not available due to security concerns. The jobs they perform are varied, but principally they work as patrol security or for the detection of explosive material. The military has also sought to re-establish the tracker dog program. They not only want to find out where the improvised explosive device (IED) is located, but who planted it.

The number of military working dog teams deployed today is a fraction of those that saw service in Vietnam. Their mission today is just as important as it was then. More civilians are also involved in supporting the dog teams in military combat areas since World War II.

Organizations such as the Space Coast War Dog Association (SCWDA) have packaged and mailed hundred of pounds of essential items requested by dog teams in Iraq and Afghanistan. President Sheri Wells has headed the nonprofit organization since its inception, and the group hosts a web site that can keep members apprised of dog units that have been sponsored. Donations are also encouraged to acquire critical material often overlooked by the military.

One important item that has been delivered to K-9 forces overseas by the SCWDA is cooling vests to help the dogs cope with extreme temperatures, often exceeding 120 degrees Fahrenheit in combat locations throughout the Middle East. Although similar items have been around for some time, it was not until 2004 that a safe and nontoxic vest emerged. Glacier Tek company, located in Melbourne, Florida, was founded by military veterans Steve Wuest and Ray Booska. They have developed a patent-pending technology called Revolutionary Phase Change (RPCM™) in their ChillyDog vests. Unlike ice and frozen gels that can get too cold, the RCPM uses a bio-based material that helps to regulate a dog's body temperature safely and efficiently.

Other organizations, such as the VDHA, Thailand Dog Handlers Association, and the Military Working Dog Foundation, among many others, continue to support dog teams in service to our country as they work overseas. It is an incredible show of support for both the handlers and dogs who continue to labor on our behalf in an often dangerous and undesirable environment.

Although technological prowess continues to evolve, there seems to be no immediate or long-term replacement for the assets of a well-trained military working dog. More dog teams saw combat service in Vietnam than in all the preceeding history of the United States, and this is an achievement that may not occur again. Dogs do have a place in today's military environment and in the foreseeable future, but even today we still explore and learn what our four-footed companion is capable of. If science were to create an electronic or mechanical device that could replace the dog, would we embrace that technology?

Opposite: Part of Johnny Mayo's travelling war dog display depicts the K-9 losses encountered in Vietnam. Each placard has a dog's name and tattoo identification. Those on the wall are the dogs KIA and on the ground are all that were lost or left behind during the war. A small table in front depicts the few that were able to return home. *(Courtesy of Johnny Mayo)*

Bagram Airfield, Afghanistan. 1st Sgt. Dean Bissey hooks the hoist harness to Staff Sgt. Michael Hile and his military working dog "Rronnie" (spelled with two "Rs"). *(Department of Defense)* Once secured, Hile and Rronnie are hoisted together to the awaiting helicopter. *(Department of Defense)*

A dog gives something not always felt or visualized, that a machine or electronic instrument could ever do. It has innate ability to communicate with another living creature and often in an environment unfamiliar or potentially dangerous to us. This is not displayed only in the military, it is there on a daily basis throughout the world. You hear about it every time a K-9 search-and-rescue team seeks a lost child. It is on a city street every day when a blind person puts his well being into the belief that a dog will follow the right path. It is present when someone subject to seizures can rely on their dog to forewarn them of the event, or when a hearing-assistance dog alerts his master that a smoke detector has activated.

The partnership of two living beings should not be trivialized or cast off as an emotional event of the moment. It is a bond that transcends time and a commitment that goes beyond the living. In 2007, CPL Kory Wiens and his Labrador retriever dog, Cooper, were killed by an improvised explosive device (IED) in Iraq. They were the first military dog team to lose their lives together since the Vietnam War. As was fitting, the pair were buried side-by-side in Wiens' hometown, Dallas, Oregon. Like many before them, they celebrated life together, worked together, and remain together for eternity. Their example reinforces the belief that human ties with the canine world are as strong as they ever have been. It also calls to mind the following passage, by an unknown author, that highlights a bond that transcends time:

Opposite: Johnny Mayo and Buck share a quiet moment together. The road travelled by military dog teams is often more than distance and time, but often a journey of the heart and soul. *(Courtesy of Johnny Mayo)*

My eyes are your eyes,
To watch and protect yours.

My ears are your ears ,
To hear and detect evil minds in the dark.

My nose is your nose,
To scent the invader of your domain.

And so you may live, my life is also yours.

HANDLERS KIA

Last Name	First Name	Branch	Unit I
Ahern	Robert Paul	Army	37th Infantry Platoon Scout Dogs (Phouc Vinh & Bien Hoa)
Alcorn Jr.	Dale Robert	Army	60th Mine and Booby Trap
Amick	Richard Michael	Army	57th Infantry Platoon Scout Dogs (Chu Lai)
Anderson	William Allison	Army	66th Combat Tracker Team Vet. (Chu Chi)
Anderson	Erling	Army	39th Infantry Platoon Scout Dogs (Bien Hoa)
Armstrong	Robert Dale	USMC	Marine Scout Dog
Atkins III	Joshua	Army	Army Scout
Baker	Gary	Army	Army Scout
Baker	Donald Lee	USMC	Marine Sentry Dog
Baldoni	Lindsay David	Army	39th Infantry Platoon Scout Dogs (Bien Hoa)
Banaszynski	Richard	Army	34th Infantry Platoon Scout Dogs (Bien Hoa) (An Khe)
Barkley	Earl	Army	Army Scout
Beauregard	Richard	Army	59th Infantry Platoon Scout Dogs (Duc Pho)
Beaver	James Harold	Army	50th Infantry Platoon Scout Dogs (An Khe)
Beck	Terrence Daniel	USMC	Marine Scout Dog
Beesley	Gary Evans	Army	43rd Infantry Platoon Scout Dogs (Quang Tri, Dong Tam)
Behrens	Peter Claus	USMC	Marine 1st Provisional
Belcher	Robert Winslow	USMC	Marine Scout Dog
Bell	Mark Wayne	USMC	Marine Scout Dog
Bennett	John	Army	Army Scout
Berge	James Maynard	Army	50th Infantry Platoon Scout Dogs (An Khe)
Best	Billy Howard	USMC	Marine Scout Dog
Beuke	Dennis Arthur	Army	Combat Tracker Team 8 (CTT)\
Bevich Jr.	George Michael	USAF	377th SPS (Tan Son Nhut)
Blaauw	James	Army	Army Scout
Blair	Charles Douglas	Army	64th Combat Tracker Team-CTT
Bost	Michael James	Army	42nd Infantry Platoon Scout Dogs (Phan Rang & Camp Eagle)
Bowman	Stephen Wesley		
Boyd	James	USAF	3rd SPS (Bien Hoa)
Boyer	James Roger	Army	Combat Tracker Team 2 (CTT)
Bozier Jr	Willie	Army	Army Scout

Last Name	First Name	Branch	Unit I
Brede	Robert William	Army	Combat Tracker Team 2 (CTT)
Brophy	Martin Earl	Army	41st Infantry Platoon Scout Dogs (Lai Khe & Phu Loi)
Brown	Charles Paul	Army	40th Infantry Platoon Scout Dogs (Pleiku)
Browne	Walter D	Army	41st Infantry Platoon Scout Dogs (Lai Khe & Phu Loi)
Buckingham	Keith Charles	Army	43rd Infantry Platoon Scout Dogs (Quang Tri, Dong Tam)
Bullwinkel	Alden John	Army	61st Combat Tracker Team-CTT (Di An)
Burdette Jr	Hilburn	Army	Army Scout
Burk	Jimmy Rea	Army	43rd Infantry Platoon Scout Dogs (Quang Tri, Dong Tam)
Burlock Jr	Kenneth	Army	25th Infantry Platoon Scout Dogs (Bien Hoa)
Burnette Jr	Archie	Army	Army Scout
Cabarubio	James	USMC	Marine Scout Dog
Cain	Douglas Michael	Army	43rd Infantry Platoon Scout Dogs (Quang Tri, Dong Tam)
Camp	Anthony Lorin	USMC	Marine Scout Dog
Campbell	William Ladd	Army	49th Infantry Platoon Scout Dogs (Long Binh)
Carinci	Joseph A	USMC	Marine Mine & Boobytrap
Carrillo	Melvin	Army	48th Infantry Platoon Scout Dogs (DaNang)
Carter	Merle Keith	Navy	Navy Sentry
Castle	Russell Leonard	Army	40th Infantry Platoon Scout Dogs (Pleiku)
Chisholm	Ronald Lee	USMC	Marine Sentry Dog
Clark	Walter	Army	Army Scout
Clokes	Robert	Army	40th Infantry Platoon Scout Dogs (Pleiku)
Colford	Darrell Lee	Army	38th Infantry Platoon Scout Dogs (Chu Chi)
Collier	Steven	Army	Army Scout
Conklin	Michael	Army	Army Scout
Conner	Jack William	Army	557th Combat Tracker Team-CTT (Camp Eagle)
Conners Jr.	Ralph Wilson	Army	41st Infantry Platoon Scout Dogs (Lai Khe & Phu Loi)
Connors	Jack Lee	Army	557th Combat Tracker Team-CTT (Camp Eagle)
Cox Jr.	Edward Erlin	Army	76th Combat Tracker Team-CTT (Long Binh)
Crawford	Bobby Dean	Army	43rd Infantry Platoon Scout Dogs (Quang Tri, Dong Tam)
Crawford	Gordon	Army	Army Scout
Creaghead	Clarence	Army	49th Infantry Platoon Scout Dogs (Long Binh)
Cumbie	William Thomas	USMC	Marine Scout Dog
Currier Jr.	Gordon Leroy	Army	212th MP (Long Binh)
Czarnota	Christopher	Army	Army Scout

Last Name	First Name	Branch	Unit I
Davis	Alan	Army	48th Infantry Platoon Scout Dogs (DaNang)
Davis	Eligah	USMC	Marine Mine & Boobytrap
Davis	Abron	USMC	Marine Scout Dog
Deitrick	George Douglas	Army	41st Infantry Platoon Scout Dogs (Lai Khe & Phu Loi)
Dell	Kenneth John	Army	49th Infantry Platoon Scout Dogs (Long Binh)
Detrick	Gary Gene	Army	47th Infantry Platoon Scout Dogs (LZ Sally & Phu Bai)
Dillinder	Randy Eugene	Army	34th Infantry Platoon Scout Dogs (Bien Hoa) (An Khe)
Doria	Richard Albert	Army	48th Infantry Platoon Scout Dogs (DaNang)
Doyle	John Francis	Army	59th Infantry Platoon Scout Dogs (Duc Pho)
Drobena	Michael James	USMC	Marine Scout Dog
Drum	Thomas	Army	62nd Combat Tracker Team-CTT (Bien Hoa)
Drysdale	Charles Douglas	USMC	Marine Scout Dog
Ducote Jr.	Lonnie Joseph	Army	34th Infantry Platoon Scout Dogs (Bien Hoa) (An Khe)
Duff	Phillip	Army	Army Scout
Duke	Douglas Ovyle	Army	Veterinarian-Army
Dunning	William Martin	Army	66th Combat Tracker Team Vet. (Chu Chi)
Elliott	Robert William	USMC	Marine Mine & Boobytrap
Erickson	Russell Martin	Army	59th Infantry Platoon Scout Dogs (Duc Pho)
Esterly	Lawrence Alan	USMC	Marine Scout Dog
Eubanks	George F	Army	25th Infantry Platoon Scout Dogs (Bien Hoa)
Evans	Ronald Lee	Army	44th Infantry Platoon Scout Dogs (Chu Chi)
Farley	Marshall Colin	Army	44th Infantry Platoon Scout Dogs (Chu Chi)
Fisher	Thomas William	USMC	Marine Sentry Dog
Ford	Bernard	USAF	35th SPS (Phan Rang)
Fox	Gary Wayne	Army	25th Infantry Platoon Scout Dogs (Bien Hoa)
Fraley	Eugene Thomas	Navy	Navy Seal Team
Fraser	William George	USMC	Marine Scout Dog
Freeman	David Michael	Army	34th Infantry Platoon Scout Dogs (Bien Hoa) (An Khe)
Freeman	Jeffrey	Army	39th Infantry Platoon Scout Dogs (Bien Hoa)
Fritz	Gerald W	USAF	56th SPS (Nakhon Phanom) Thailand
Fuller	Stanley Carl	Army	76th Combat Tracker Team-CTT (Long Binh)
Fuller	Gary Leroy	USAF	366th SPS (DaNang & Phan Rang)
Gaspard Jr.	Claude Joseph	Army	33rd Infantry Platoon Scout Dogs (Pleiku)
Giberson	Jerry Guy	Army	Army Scout
Glenn	Livingston	Army	57th Infantry Platoon Scout Dogs (Chu Lai)
Goudelock	William Roger	Army	57th Infantry Platoon Scout Dogs (Chu Lai)
Green	Billy Monroe	Army	Army Scout
Grieve	Michael A	Army	Army Scout

Last Name	First Name	Branch	Unit I
Griffin II	William Donald	Army	63rd Combat Tracker Team-CTT (DaNang)
Groves	William E	Army	Army Scout
Grundy	Dallas	Army	33rd Infantry Platoon Scout Dogs (Pleiku)
Gyulveszi	Theodore Louis	Army	42nd Infantry Platoon Scout Dogs (Phan Rang & Camp Eagle)
Hales	Raymon Draper	Army	58th Infantry Platoon Scout Dogs (Camp Evans)
Harding	John H	Army	557th Combat Tracker Team-CTT (Camp Eagle)
Harris	Jessie Earl	Army	212th MP (Long Binh)
Hartsock	Robert Willard	Army	44th Infantry Platoon Scout Dogs (Chu Chi)
Hartwick Jr.	Floyd Wayne	USMC	Marine Scout Dog
Hatcher	David	Army	63rd Combat Tracker Team-CTT (DaNang)
Henshaw	Patrick Lee	Army	Army Scout
Hernandez	Victor Reyes	Army	57th Infantry Platoon Scout Dogs (Chu Lai)
Hicks	Larry David	Army	Army Scout
Hilerio-Padilla	Luis	Army	Army Scout
Hilt	Richard Michael	Army	57th Infantry Platoon Scout Dogs (Chu Lai)
Holland	Wayne Bizzle	Army	Army Scout
Holley	Glynn Byron	Army	Army Scout
Holt	Herschel Cyle	USMC	Marine 1st Provisional
Hoppough	Dennis Karl	USMC	Marine Scout Dog
Howard	James Ray	Army	44th Infantry Platoon Scout Dogs (Chu Chi)
Howard	Mark Thomas	Army	Combat Tracker Team 2 (CTT)
Huberty	William M	Army	44th Infantry Platoon Scout Dogs (Chu Chi)
Hughes III	Edward Cowart	Army	44th Infantry Platoon Scout Dogs (Chu Chi)
Hurksman Jr.	Wilhelm S	Army	43rd Infantry Platoon Scout Dogs (Quang Tri, Dong Tam)
Ilaoa	Faleagafula	USAF	56th SPS (Nakhon Phanom) Thailand
Ireland	Elmer Glenn	Army	42nd Infantry Platoon Scout Dogs (Phan Rang & Camp Eagle)
Jenkins	Steven Lee	Army	981st MP
Jenkins	Clayton Dean	USMC	Marine Sentry Dog
Jenks	Robert James	Army	45th Infantry Platoon Scout Dogs (Dong Tam)
Jesko	Stephen Edward	Army	Army Scout
Joecken	Richard Kenneth	Army	44th Infantry Platoon Scout Dogs (Chu Chi)
Johnson	Carl Irving	Army	34th Infantry Platoon Scout Dogs (Bien Hoa) (An Khe)
Johnson	James Allen	Army	39th Infantry Platoon Scout Dogs (Bien Hoa)
Johnson	Freddie Lee	Army	1st Combat Tracker Team-CTT (Cu Chi)
Johnson	Arnold Edward	Army	Combat Tracker Team 2 (CTT)
Johnson	Larry	Army	44th Infantry Platoon Scout Dogs (Chu Chi)

Last Name	First Name	Branch	Unit I
Johnson	Herbert Burton	Army	Army Scout
Karau	Ronald Dean	Army	Army Scout
Kiefhaber	Andrew John	Army	65th Combat Tracker Team-CTT (Kong Tam)
King	Alexander	Army	557th Combat Tracker Team-CTT (Camp Eagle)
Kobelin II	John	Army	40th Infantry Platoon Scout Dogs (Pleiku)
Koon	George Kenneth	Army	Combat Tracker Team 2 (CTT)
Kuefner	John Alan	Army	35th Infantry Platoon Scout Dogs (Dian See)
Kuehn	Lloyd Martin	Army	40th Infantry Platoon Scout Dogs (Pleiku)
Kunz	Anthony Edmond	Army	Army Scout
Lagodzinski	Roger Thomas	Army	57th Infantry Platoon Scout Dogs (Chu Lai)
Land	David Alfred	USMC	Marine Scout Dog
Lane	Richard Arthur	Army	Army Scout
Lawton	Edward Lester	Army	75th Combat Tracker Team-CTT (An Khe)
Lebrun	Robert Normand	Army	Army Scout
Lee	Edward Gilbert	Army	44th Infantry Platoon Scout Dogs (Chu Chi)
Levins	Frederick Richard	Army	76th Combat Tracker Team-CTT (Long Binh)
Lindholm	Dan Victor	Army	Army Scout
Lindsay	Stephen Lee	USMC	Marine Scout Dog
Lipton	Joseph Price	USMC	Marine Scout Dog
Lockhart	Harlan Nathan	Army	35th Infantry Platoon Scout Dogs (Dian See)
Loftis	Joel Conrad	USAF	35th SPS (Phan Rang)
London	Dennis W	USAF	56th SPS (Nakhon Phanom) Thailand
Lovellette	Gary Vaughn	Army	45th Infantry Platoon Scout Dogs (Dong Tam)
Lumsden	William Wayne	Army	Combat Tracker Team 3 (CTT)
Magruder	David Byron	Army	Army Scout
Mahurin	Elmer Wain	Army	Combat Tracker Team 8 (CTT)
Mansfield	John Montague	Army	Army Scout
Marasco	Joseph Allen	Army	62nd Combat Tracker Team-CTT (Bien Hoa)
Marchant	Paul	Army	59th Infantry Platoon Scout Dogs (Duc Pho)
Markey Jr.	James Paul	Army	63rd Combat Tracker Team-CTT (DaNang)
Marrufo Jr.	Rodney Elmer	Army	66th Combat Tracker Team Vet. (Chu Chi)
Marshall	Clifford Wayne	Army	43rd Infantry Platoon Scout Dogs (Quang Tri, Dong Tam)
Marshall	Mark Duane	USMC	Marine Scout Dog
Martin	Kenneth	Army	40th Infantry Platoon Scout Dogs (Pleiku)
Martinez	Juan Patricio	Army	41st Infantry Platoon Scout Dogs (Lai Khe & Phu Loi)
Mason Jr.	Benjamin H	USMC	Marine Sentry Dog
Matel	Ronald James	Army	1st Combat Tracker Team-CTT (Cu Chi)
Mattson	Paul Edward	Army	59th Infantry Platoon Scout Dogs (Duc Pho)

Last Name	First Name	Branch	Unit I
Maurer	Walter Lawrence	Army	Army Scout
May	Robert Walter	Army	34th Infantry Platoon Scout Dogs (Bien Hoa) (An Khe)
Mazzone	Joseph	Army	57th Infantry Platoon Scout Dogs (Chu Lai)
Mc Intosh	Donald William	Army	Army Scout
McCarty	Glenn Weldon	Army	Army Scout
McFall	Gary Richard	Army	34th Infantry Platoon Scout Dogs (Bien Hoa) (An Khe)
McGrath	Edward Charles	Army	43rd Infantry Platoon Scout Dogs (Quang Tri, Dong Tam)
McLaughlin	James Bruce	Army	Army Scout
Merschel	Lawrence James	Army	Army Scout
Meyer	Leo Roland	Army	61st Combat Tracker Team-CTT (Di An)
Michael	James Albert	Army	Army Scout
Miller	Timmy Larry	USMC	Marine Scout Dog
Mills	Rodney Kenneth	Army	Army Scout
Montano	William Andrew	USMC	Marine Scout Dog
Morrison	James	Army	39th Infantry Platoon Scout Dogs (Bien Hoa)
Mugavin	Martin M	Army	48th Infantry Platoon Scout Dogs (DaNang)
Munch	Michael R	Army	57th Infantry Platoon Scout Dogs (Chu Lai)
Munoz	Jose	Army	1st Combat Tracker Team-CTT (Cu Chi)
Murray	Harry Walter	Army	1st Combat Tracker Team-CTT (Cu Chi)
Myers	Richard	Army	39th Infantry Platoon Scout Dogs (Bien Hoa)
Newell	Tim Edwin	Army	47th Infantry Platoon Scout Dogs (LZ Sally & Phu Bai)
Nicolini	Peter Joseph	Army	44th Infantry Platoon Scout Dogs (Chu Chi)
Norris	Robert Norman	Army	42nd Infantry Platoon Scout Dogs (Phan Rang & Camp Eagle)
Nudenberg	David Alan	Army	63rd Combat Tracker Team-CTT (DaNang)
Nurzynski	Joseph Anthony	Army	59th Infantry Platoon Scout Dogs (Duc Pho)
Oaks	Robert Larry	Army	Army Scout
Ohm	David James	Army	Army Scout
Olmstead	John Paul	Army	48th Infantry Platoon Scout Dogs (DaNang)
Orsua	Charles David	USAF	35th SPS (Phan Rang)
Palacio	Gilbert Gonzales	Army	34th Infantry Platoon Scout Dogs (Bien Hoa) (An Khe)
Park	Irving Geon	USAF	12th SPS (Cam Rahn Bay & Phu Cat)
Parker Jr.	Carter	Army	Army Scout
Parrish	Billy Joe	Army	66th Combat Tracker Team Vet. (Chu Chi)
Payne III	Howard David	Army	59th Infantry Platoon Scout Dogs (Duc Pho)
Payne	Terry John	Army	Army Scout
Payne	Robert Paul	USMC	Marine Scout Dog
Pearce	Marvin Robert	Army	47th Infantry Platoon Scout Dogs (LZ Sally & Phu Bai)

Last Name	First Name	Branch	Unit I
Petersen	Harry Thomas	Army	Army Scout
Piasecki	John Michae	Army	Army Scout
Pierce	Oscar Wayne	Army	40th Infantry Platoon Scout Dogs (Pleiku)
Plambeck Jr.	Paul	Army	39th Infantry Platoon Scout Dogs (Bien Hoa)
Plattner	Ernest Melvin	Army	44th Infantry Platoon Scout Dogs (Chu Chi)
Poland Jr.	Leon Lovell	USMC	Marine Scout Dog
Porter	Richard Charles	USMC	Marine Mine & Boobytrap
Pretter	Thomas	Army	38th Infantry Platoon Scout Dogs (Chu Chi)
Pulaski Jr.	Peter	Army	42nd Infantry Platoon Scout Dogs (Phan Rang & Camp Eagle)
Quinn	Thomas Wayne	Army	45th Infantry Platoon Scout Dogs (Dong Tam)
Randolph	Michael James	Army	1st Combat Tracker Team-CTT (Cu Chi)
Rathbun	Gary Allan	Army	42nd Infantry Platoon Scout Dogs (Phan Rang & Camp Eagle)
Ratliff	Billy Harrison	Army	75th Combat Tracker Team-CTT (An Khe)
Ray	William Clayton	Army	58th Infantry Platoon Scout Dogs (Camp Evans)
Rhodes	Robert David	USMC	Marine Scout Dog
Rivera	James	Army	62nd Combat Tracker Team-CTT (Bien Hoa)
Roberts	Virgil Jessie	Army	557th Combat Tracker Team-CTT (Camp Eagle)
Robinson	Charles John	Army	49th Infantry Platoon Scout Dogs (Long Binh)
Rosas	Jose Antonio	USMC	Marine Scout Dog
Roth	John Howard	Army	50th Infantry Platoon Scout Dogs (An Khe)
Rowe	Michael Thomas	Army	Army Scout
Sandberg	Charles H	Army	44th Infantry Platoon Scout Dogs (Chu Chi)
Schachner	David Brennan	Army	40th Infantry Platoon Scout Dogs (Pleiku)
Schmid	Robert Anthony	Army	44th Infantry Platoon Scout Dogs (Chu Chi)
Schossow	Dennis Robert	USMC	Marine Mine & Boobytrap
Schwab	Richard Michael	Army	57th Infantry Platoon Scout Dogs (Chu Lai)
Schyska	Leroy Floyd	Army	46th Infantry Platoon Scout Dogs (Tay Ninh)
Scott	Dave Russell	Army	Army Scout
Segundo	Pete Sprule	USMC	Marine Scout Dog
Selix	James Michael	Army	47th Infantry Platoon Scout Dogs (LZ Sally & Phu Bai)
Severson	Paul Roy	Army	Army Scout
Sheldon	William Charles	Navy	Navy Sentry
Shelton	Bobby James	Army	38th Infantry Platoon Scout Dogs (Chu Chi)
Shepard	Raymond Andrew	USMC	Marine 1st Provisional
Sheppard	Ronald Eugene	Army	49th Infantry Platoon Scout Dogs (Long Binh)
Simpson	Edward Monroe	Army	45th Infantry Platoon Scout Dogs (Dong Tam)
Sims	William Jess	Army	60th Mine and Booby Trap

Last Name	First Name	Branch	Unit I
Smith	Ronald C	Army	212th MP (Long Binh)
Smith	Gary Kenneth	Army	39th Infantry Platoon Scout Dogs (Bien Hoa)
Smith	Michael Francis	Army	59th Infantry Platoon Scout Dogs (Duc Pho)
Smith	Stephen Jay W	Army	Army Scout
Smith	Winfred Lee	Army	Army Scout
Smoot	Robert Gene	Army	557th Combat Tracker Team-CTT (Camp Eagle)
Soto Concepcion	Jose	Army	25th Infantry Platoon Scout Dogs (Bien Hoa)
Southwick	John Paul	USMC	Marine Scout Dog
Spangler	Max Ray	Army	45th Infantry Platoon Scout Dogs (Dong Tam)
Spencer Jr.	Daniel Eugene	Army	Army Scout
Steptoe	Raymond	Army	35th Infantry Platoon Scout Dogs (Dian See)
Sturdy	Alan MacDonald	Army	41st Infantry Platoon Scout Dogs (Lai Khe & Phu Loi)
Sullivan	Jeremiah Joseph	Army	38th Infantry Platoon Scout Dogs (Chu Chi)
Sullivan	Donald Sherril	Army	40th Infantry Platoon Scout Dogs (Pleiku)
Sunday	James Michael	Army	43rd Infantry Platoon Scout Dogs (Quang Tri, Dong Tam)
Sweat Jr.	Herbert Hoover	Army	34th Infantry Platoon Scout Dogs (Bien Hoa) (An Khe)
Sweatt	Theodore A	Army	25th Infantry Platoon Scout Dogs (Bien Hoa)
Tallman	George	Army	Army Scout
Taranto	Robert Joseph	Army	57th Infantry Platoon Scout Dogs (Chu Lai)
Taylor	Mark Randall	Army	42nd Infantry Platoon Scout Dogs (Chu Chi)
Teresinski	Joseph Alvin	Army	557th Combat Tracker Team-CTT (Camp Eagle)
Thibodeaux	Michael I	Army	Army Scout
Tosh III	James C	Army	25th Infantry Platoon Scout Dogs (Bien Hoa)
Triplett	James Michael	USMC	Marine Scout Dog
Truesdell	John Leroy	Army	Army Scout
Van Gorder	William Joseph	Army	57th Infantry Platoon Scout Dogs (Chu Lai)
Vancosky	Michael Anthony	USMC	Marine Scout Dog
Vogelpohl	Rex Alan	Army	57th Infantry Platoon Scout Dogs (Chu Lai)
Waddell	Larry Jonathan	Army	Army Scout
Ward	Danny Edward	Army	43rd Infantry Platoon Scout Dogs (Quang Tri, Dong Tam)
Ward	David James	Army	981st MP
Webb	Howard Lee	Army	42nd Infantry Platoon Scout Dogs (Phan Rang & Camp Eagle)
Whetham	Vernon E	Army	43rd Infantry Platoon Scout Dogs (Quang Tri, Dong Tam)
White	John Oliver	Army	57th Infantry Platoon Scout Dogs (Chu Lai)

Last Name	First Name	Branch	Unit 1
White	Garson Franklin	USMC	Marine Scout Dog
Whitehead	Alfred Evarts	Army	44th Infantry Platoon Scout Dogs (Chu Chi)
Whitten	Robert Eugene	Army	Army Scout
Wickenberg	Erik Bernard	Army	43rd Infantry Platoon Scout Dogs (Quang Tri, Dong Tam)
Winningham	Richard	Army	43rd Infantry Platoon Scout Dogs (Quang Tri, Dong Tam)
Wood	Robert Helm	USMC	Marine Scout Dog
Yeager	Michael Joseph	USMC	Marine Mine & Boobytrap
Yochum	Lawrence Wayne	Army	59th Infantry Platoon Scout Dogs (Duc Pho)
Young	Jon Michael	Army	43rd Infantry Platoon Scout Dogs (Quang Tri, Dong Tam)

Dogs KIA

Name	Tatoo	DOD	Unit
Prince	182X	12/9/65	3SPS
Smokey	1A82	6/15/66	USMC
Kaiser	UNK	7/1/66	USMC/scout
Tiger	3A17	8/9/66	25IP
Ludwick	1X74	8/22/66	377SPS
Lucky	2X37	10/17/66	44IP
Sarge	5X94	11/1/66	42 IPSD
Bodie	M460	11/16/66	USMC/scout
Pirate	8X71	12/2/66	34 IPSD
Cubby	612E	12/4/66	377SPS
Rebel	UNK	12/4/66	377SPS
Toby	UNK	12/4/66	377SPS
Duke	9X60	1/3/67	41 IPSD
Frico	0H67	1/13/67	212TH
Sheps	8X63	1/13/67	41 IPSD
Hanno	0H03	2/16/67	33IP
Baron	0X81	2/23/67	25 IP
Reb	21X8	2/23/67	48IP
Blaze	0B54	2/28/67	12SPS
Prince	30X7	3/2/67	48IP
Gallo	28X5	4/13/67	USMC/unk
Rex	8X60	5/25/67	33IP
Kazan	7X51	6/15/67 MIA/KIA	57IP
Bark	5A35	6/16/67	42 IP
Mike	4X64	7/2/67	41 IPSD
Bummer	9X58	7/4/67	USMC/unk
Arko	0K10	7/15/67	USMC/scout
Bruno	26X8	7/16/67	48IP
Gunder	1X07	8/13/67	34IP
Prince	43X3	9/2/67	44IP
Bozo	9X40	9/12/67	377 SPS
Toto	52X8	9/12/67	USMC
Duchess	55X2	9/13/67	USMC/scout
Bootsy	9X64	9/19/67	48IP
Blitz (Possible name Blutz)	X239	10/4/67	43IP
Rip	2X12	10/16/67	USMC
Eric	36X3	11/9/67	44IP
Shadow	9X00	11/9/67	44IP
Bodie	4A75	11/16/67	CCT #2
Sargent	6X81	11/27/67	44IP
Mitzi	9X43	12/5/67	USMC/scout
Keechie	14X7	12/10/67	34IP
Troubles	1X16	12/30/67	UNK
King	66X5	1/10/68	43IP
Renny	A548	1/11/68	35SPS
Arras	K072	1/12/68	45IP
Suesser	0K81	1/21/68	42IP
Diablo	X313	1/31/68	3SPS
Satch	M164	1/31/68	212 MP
Ringo	X700	2/6/68	USMC
Rex	X306	2/7/68	43IP
Rex	0K11	2/7/68	43IP
King	334X	2/10/68	981ST MP
Prince	0X99	2/20/68	USMC/scout
Hunde	M145	2/28/68	3SPS
Caeser	5X56	3/4/68	39IP
Reggie	3A57	3/10/68	981ST MP
Irish	1A56	3/20/68	USMC/sentry
Machen	2X99	3/21/68	39IP
Duke	5A23	4/7/68	35IP
Sam	76X2	4/11/68	USMC/scout
Rex	4A85	5/4/68	40IP
Ming	X528	5/11/68	45IP
Buckshot	23X9	5/13/68	44IP
Thunder	4A45	5/15/68	42IP
Caeser	3A55	5/19/68	38IP
Wolf	150X	5/22/68	USMC
Smokey	0X16	5/27/68	USMC
Smokey	X121	6/1/68	43IP
Duke	3A15	6/13/68	25IP
Kurt	6A92	6/22/68	34IP
Baron	1X33	6/30/68	USMC/scout
Bodo	X041	7/1/68	USMC/scout

Name	Tatoo	DOD	Unit
King	0K87	7/1/68	43IP
King	49X0	7/4/68	57IP
Rinny	185E	7/4/68	212 MP
Prince	3X92	7/10/68	USMC/sentry
Silver	X101	7/24/68	59IP
Willie	6M11	7/27/68	47IP
Cracker	60X1	8/19/68	49IP
Lux	0K29	8/19/68	3SPS
Chase	98X6	8/20/68	57IP
Shadow	B387	8/26/68	62CTT
Rover	M075	9/7/68	57IP
Tim	19X2	9/11/68	44IP
King	8X87	9/13/68	34IP
Ago	0H28	9/20/68	49IP
Anzo	0H79	9/23/68	USMC/sentry
Cookie	41X5	9/28/68	49IP
Polo	808M	9/28/68	58 IPSD
Savage	M263	9/28/68	49IP
Fritz	X740	10/18/68	57IP
Jack	130M	10/18/68	57IP
Sargeant Bilco	8X00	10/25/68	59 IPSD
Mac	X083	11/5/68	USMC/unk
Fritz	2M97	11/7/68	57IP
Feller	03X5	11/8/68	39 IPSD
Thea	5A99	11/8/68	USMC/sentry
Husky	48X4	11/11/68	USMC/scout
Bo Bear	025M	11/12/68	58 IP
Stark	071X	11/16/68	USMC/sentry
Gretchen	3M32	11/18/68	44IP
Buck	61X2	11/24/68	47IP
Britta	0X47	11/27/68	25IP
Silber	1M57	11/27/68	25IP
Saber	X547	11/30/68	USMC
Arko	K094	12/12/68	45IP
Buddy	80X5	12/15/68	43IP
King	58X3	12/23/68	41IP
King	58X3	12/23/68	41 IPSD
Wolf	0K43	1/7/69	49IP
Apache	9M46	1/11/69	USMC/scout
Prince	69X7	1/15/69	USMC/scout
Kaizer	6M91	1/18/69	USMC/scout
Bruno	8M05	1/20/69	35IP
Money	32X3	1/24/69	50IP
Shep	48X8	1/24/69	50IP
Fritzie	763F	1/26/69	35SPS
Rex	3X06	1/26/69	USMC/scout
Shep	45X8	1/27/69	USMC/scout
Smokey	X817	1/27/69	57IP
Shack	9X28	1/28/69	43IP
Arry	912X	1/29/69	USMC/scout
Baron	385M	1/30/69	USMC/scout
Princess	45X9	2/2/69	39IP
King	2A15	2/15/69	48IP
Lobo	58M4	2/15/69	43IP
Rex	5A77	2/22/69	35SPS
Crypto	8M63	2/23/69	45IP
Duke	409M	2/23/69	49IP
Oaf	1X29	2/23/69	38IP
Fritz	999F	2/28/69	12SPS
Prince	703M	3/15/69	37IP
Ranger	787M	3/16/69	37IP
Blitzer	5X32	3/17/69	USMC/sentry
Brutus	46M2	3/17/69	43IP
King	245M	3/20/69	33IP
Bizz	16M6	3/21/69	47IP
Blackie	03X7	3/21/69	49IP
Deno	7M28	3/30/69	41IP
Baron	53X9	4/7/69	39IP
Ziggy	2M78	4/10/69	41IP
Axel	8X57	4/13/69	USMC/scout
Peanuts	3M56	4/13/69	USMC/scout
Princess	1M20	4/13/69	47IP
Chief	5A67	4/17/69	USMC/sentry
Storm	01M3	4/23/69	39IP
Butch	38M6	4/25/69	33IP
Com-mander	X482	4/26/69	41IP
Smokey	36M0	5/13/69	57IP
Hector	X459	5/14/69	40IP
King	8M51	5/18/69	49IP
Socks	X889	6/1/69	47 IPSD

Name	Tatoo	DOD	Unit
Arko	0K13	6/5/69	USMC/scout
Claus	K024	6/18/69	40IP
Hasso	0K55	6/18/69	41IP
Egor	751M	6/23/69	41 IPSD
Cookie	42M2	6/24/69 MIA/KIA	46IP
Paper	684M	6/26/69	42IP
Ikar	X682	7/2/69	40IP
Kelly	5M52	7/2/69	39IP
Dugan	X322	7/18/69	USMC/scout
Rebel	X202	7/19/69	58IP
Bo-Bo	7M25	7/24/69	40IP
Flare	X272	7/26/69	42IP
Prince	9A38	7/27/69	USMC
King	390M	8/1/69	USMC/scout
Princess	49A1	8/3/69	39IP
King	81M5	8/14/69	37IP
Mesa	103M	8/24/69	49IP
Rusty	6A97	8/30/69	42IP
Alex	0K64	9/16/69	43IP
Fritz	M275	10/6/69	35IP
Aston	K092	10/11/69	39IP
King	9A18	10/13/69	39IP
Fritz	4M69	10/15/69	47IP
Sarge	292M	10/29/69	34IP
Baron	385M	10/30/69	USMC
Blackie	T0O3	11/6/69	66 IPCT
Mike	760M	11/10/69	57IP
Hannabel	740M	11/22/69	USMC/scout
Duke	383M	12/6/69	57IP
Blackie	3A33	12/7/69	USMC/scout
Chief	3M43	12/9/69	57IP
Jack	7X18	12/17/69	34IP
Andy	5A48	1/9/70	50IP
Erich	3M92	1/18/70	35 IPSD USMC?
Toby	T036	1/25/70	63CTT
Shep	69A3	1/29/70	47IP
Joe	X134	2/13/70	USMC/scout
King	7A65	2/13/70	59IP
Dix	M064	2/15/70	57IP
King I	32M8	2/20/70	USMC/scout
Little Joe	223M	2/22/70	47IP
Rex	83X4	3/6/70	48IP
Rebel	94A3	3/8/70	50IP
Gar	789M	3/9/70	37IP
Teneq	T012	3/12/70	62CTT
Duke	230M	3/24/70	57IP
Axel	K059	3/31/70	58IP
Sam	544M	4/6/70	57IP
King	X200	4/8/70	39IP
Ceasar	07A2	4/10/70	50IP
Baron	31A8	4/11/70	58 IP
Princess	764M	4/19/70	37IP
Kat	00M3	4/20/70	48IP
Notzey	X405	4/25/70	33IP
Smokey	7M50	4/26/70	47IP
Chooch	06M3	4/28/70	48IP
Danny	21M2	4/29/70	42IP
Lighting	0M40	5/11/70	981ST
Kelly	UNK	5/18/70	34 IPSD
King	07M6	5/19/70	42IP
Rebel	X820	5/26/70	USMC/scout
Tasso	0K40	5/26/70	25IP
Shadow	X622	5/27/70	45IP
Gretchen	40X7	5/29/70	42IP
Rex	93M9	5/29/70	34IP
Dug	112M	6/1/70	47IP
Buck	7X74	6/2/70	42IP
Charger	416A	6/2/70	47 IPSD
Krieger	65M8	6/2/70	42IP
Thor	335A	6/3/70	42IP
Max	8X18	6/4/70	42IP
Rommell	52X6	6/10/70	50IP
Prince	271M	6/12/70	37IP
Joe	6B54	6/15/70	45IP
Rolf	K086	6/17/70	42IP
Lodo	729M	6/25/70	37IP
Buck	O108	7/12/70	USMC/unk
Stormy	4M33	7/17/70	USMC/sentry
Skipper	288M	7/25/70	USMC
Dusty	724M	7/28/70	37IP
Duke	721M	8/4/70	48 IPSD

Name	Tatoo	DOD	Unit
Tiger	3M78	8/15/70 WIA 8/11/70	57IP
Buddy	6M61	9/2/70	59IP
Gretchen	265A	9/3/70	39IP
Jack	24M8	9/5/70	USMC/scout
Blackie	38A3	9/9/70	47IP
Rover	475A	9/19/70	33IP
Baron	81A3	9/23/70	47IP
Sam	5A84	9/24/70	62CTT
Royal	19X8	9/27/70	48IP
Tye	341M	9/29/70	42IP
Penney	9M96	10/5/70	34IP
Fant	K027	10/22/70	47IP
Prince	288A	10/26/70	59IP
Caesar	25A3	10/31/70	USMC/scout
Heidi	18A6	10/31/70	58IP
Butch	6M36	11/8/70	38IP
Buddy	898M	11/12/70	48IP
Heidi	T031	11/12/70	63CTT
Arras	K015	11/27/70	42IP
Artus	K012	12/11/70	42IP
Sam	66A7	12/16/70	57IP
Bobo	66A5	12/26/70 mine	43IP
Duke	461A	1/3/71	48IP
Sarge	934M	1/12/71	57IP
Tempo	50A7	1/19/71	48IP
Country Joe	7K31	1/23/71	USMC/mine
Kelly	55A0	1/23/71	USMC/scout
Lance	82A6	1/26/71	42IP
Sissy	441A	1/26/71 mine	43IP
Axel	84A6	1/29/71	39IP
Prince	74X1	1/30/71	47IP
Bounce	494A	2/14/71	43IP
Heidi	0030	2/19/71	43IP
Wolf	7X03	2/26/71	57IP
Spike	M004	3/1/71	981 MP
Thor	326M	4/9/71 mine	63CTT
Heidi	X017	4/23/71	57IP
Dusty	62M6	4/27/71	58IP
Blitz	56A4	5/31/71	59IP
Brandy	323M	6/25/71	42IP
Cap	4K87	6/27/71	34IP
King	72M4	6/28/71	47IP
King	72M4	6/28/71	47 IPSD
Johnny Reb	3M77	8/27/71	40IP
Sheba	7X54	8/27/71	58IP
Taro	287M	8/30/71	59IP
Casey	13M7	9/17/71	58IP
Black Jack	498M	9/23/71	48IP
Dusty	23M8	10/17/71	48IP
Duke	84A2	1/21/72	59IP
Blitzen	07A5		USMC/unk
Brutus	2M96		37 IP
Brutus	44M9		981 MP
Caesar	165A		scout?
Chief	700M		USMC/scout
Dagger	150F	KIA 1967?	CTT #4
Duke	M827		USMC/scout
Fritz	499A		scout?
King	61A0		43 IPSD
King	7M79	mine?	34 IPSD
Major	3M74		USMC
Max	7X72		USMC/scout
Pepper	94A2		44 IPSD
Pinke	UNK		25IP
Prince	0X02		USMC/scout
Prince	7X56		UNK
Prince	8M34		33 IPSD
Rennie	7K34		USMC/mine
Rusty	3X22		39 IPSD
Sam	80A0		40 IPSD
Sheba	824M		39 IPSD
Sugar	A953		315SPS
UNK	7K25		USMC
UNK	7K37		USMC
Woody	0078	KIA 5/71? mine/tunnel	43 IPSD

BIBLIOGRAPHY

Burnam, John C., MSG (USA ret.) *Dog Tags of Courage*. Fort Bragg, California: Lost Coast Press, 2000.

Clark, Colonel William H.H. *The History of the United States Army Veterinary Corps in Vietnam 1962-1973*. Ringgold, GA: Author, 1991.

Dickson, Paul. *War Slang*. New York, NY: Pocket Books, 1994

Eggenberger, David. *An Encyclopedia of Battles*. New York, NY: Dover Publications, 1985

Fox, Lieutenant Colonel Roger P. *Air Base Defense in the Republic of Vietnam 1961-1973*. Washington, D.C.: Office of Air Force History, 1979.

Gardner, Toni. *Walking Where The Dog Walks: An Interspecies Odyssey in Vietnam, 1968-69*. Baltimore: Minou Press, 2006.

Haran, Peter. *Trackers: The Untold Story of the Australian Dogs of War*. Sydney, Australia: New Holland Publishers, 2000.

Lemish, Michael G. War Dogs: Canines in Combat. Washington, D.C.: Brassey's, 1996

Lubow, Robert E. *The War Animals*. New York: Doubleday and Co., 1977.

Morrison, Wilbur H. *The Elephant & the Tiger*. New York: Hippocrene Books, 1990.

Millan, Cesar *Cesar's Way – The Natural, Everday Guide to Understanding & Correcting Common Dog Problems*. New York, NY: Harmony Books, 2006

Putney, Captain William W. D.V.M., USMC (RET.). *Always Faithful: A Memoir of the Marine Dogs of WWII*. New York, NY: The Free Press, 2001

Rosser-Owen, Davis. *Vietnam Weapons Handbook*. Wellinborough, England: Patrick Stephens Limited, 1986

Stanton, Selby. *U.S. Army Uniforms of the Vietnam War*. Harrisburg, PA: Stackpole Books, 1989.

Tucker, Spencer C. Editor. *Encyclopedia of the Vietnam War*. New York: Oxford University Press, 1998.

Young, Rick. *Combat Police: U.S. Army Military Police in Vietnam*. New Jersey: Senbraak's Writings, 1994.

ENDNOTES

CHAPTER ONE – THE SEEDS OF A 10,000-DAY WAR

1. Documents declassified in 1997 indicated that President Kennedy may have wanted a withdrawal from Vietnam by 1965. Among the documents was a key memo written on October 3, 1963 by General Maxwell D. Taylor, chairman of the Joint Chiefs stating, "All planning will be directed towards preparing RVN forces for the withdrawal of all U.S. special assistance units and personnel by the end of the calendar year 1965."

2. President Franklin D. Roosevelt created the office in 1941 and was headed by William Joseph "Wild Bill" Donovan. The OSS favored Vietnam independence from France throughout the war and immediately afterwards. The 12,600 member organization was disbanded by President Truman on October 1, 1945. In early 1946 Truman replaced it with the Central Intelligence Group and in 1947 with the CIA.

3. "Atlantic Charter," World Book Online Reference Centre, http:www.aolsvc.worldbook.aol.com/ar?/na/ar/co/ar035860 html, September 22, 2003.

4. Initially MAAG was to provide direct assistance to the Vietnamese people. The French threatened to reject any aid and essentially MAAG worked for the French and their objectives. MAAG would continue to funnel aid and assistance throughout our involvement in the Vietnam War.

5.Ronald H. Spector, After Tet: The Bloodiest Year in Vietnam (New York: The Free Press) p. 314

6. The one year rotation was known as DEROS (date of estimated return from overseas). The idea was to increase the morale of combat troops by giving them a date when they could get out of Vietnam.

7. Slang names and racial slurs for the enemy or foreigners, in general, appeared in every war. Gook is probably derived from the Korean word *kuk* (meaning nationality) and pronounced "kook" and "goo" meaning slime or dirt. The word would surface in 1912, with the Marines in Nicaragua and as a description of noncombatants in the Pacific during World War II. It gained widespread popularity during the Korean War before hitting the big time in Vietnam. In 1951, Ralph Reppert reported in the *Baltimore Sun* about the use of gook: "Probably the most widely used slang term of this war [Korea]. Now it is a popular term for any native, soldier, or civilian; allied or belligerent. The word was even heard in the States, used by garrison soldiers to indicate residents of the nearest town."

8. Fighting still continued in the southern Philippines against the ferocious Moros tribesman. It took another decade before the American army finally subdued them.

9. Downey, Fairfax, *Dogs For Defense* (New York: Daniel P. McDonald 1955), p. 11.

10. E.B. Gregory, Major General, The Quartermaster General to Office of the Under Secretary of War, Legislative Branch, 23 February 1944, Subject: Request for Legislation Authorizing Return to the Original Owners of Dogs Donated to the Government for Use in the Armed Forces and Now Found Surplus. Dave Arts located this memo at NARA while working on his thesis "Loyalty Betrayed: Comparing the Fates of the American Military Working Dogs That Served In World War II and the Vietnam War." Arts stated there were several memos supporting the return of K-9 veterans by both civilians and military personnel.

11. Reina Lt. Col. David J., "The 26th Infantry Scout Dog Platoon," Project No. MHD-5, Military History Detachment, 15 February, 1953, p.10.

12. Military Review, "War Dogs," July 1953, p. 57

13. In August 1967, the Air Force secured responsibility for the sentry dog training in Wiesbaden, Germany under the auspices of the 7100th Security Police Squadron, 7101st Air Base Wing.

14. The prices have risen over the years. A top notch German shepherd or Belgian Malinois could fetch $4,000 easily on today's market.

15. Based on the records available at the time, it appears that the trainers were Air Force T/Sgt. Pitts and MSgt. Pate.

16. Just where these dogs originated from is a matter of speculation. Several years earlier, the French had departed and it is hard to believe that the Vietnamese with no formal military working dog program could adequately maintain these animals for a long period of time. Five months later, USMC Colonel T. W. Brundage purchased and accepted two Doberman Pinchers from Willy Necker's Training School and Boarding Kennels in Wheeling, Illinois. What these dogs were purchased for is not known. But what is known is that Brundage was the Acting Director for the Policy and Planning Division for ARPA. APRA was an acronym for Advanced Projects Research Agency, which effectively was a clandestine operation and the motivating force behind Project 19. Brundage himself gave the OK to purchase the male and female dogs (named Bullet and Jessy) for $752.29. Since they were Dobermans, was Brundage planning on some type of war dog program for the Marine Corps based on the World War II model?

17. Chilson, Colonel Virgil R., memo Chief of Staff, Subject: Utilization of War Dogs, 9 October 1961.

18. Clark, The History of the United States Army Veterinary Corps in Vietnam 1962-1973, p. 8.

19. How MAAGV arrived at these figures is anyone's guess. There was no way over 1,000 dogs could be acquired in such a short period of time. These figures would later be amended and lowered. Even at the lower figure, the ARVN could not properly support (medically) the number of dogs provided by the United States.

20. Patterson (ret.), Maj. Pat. First Dogs to Nam, *DogMan*, May 1994.

21. Ibid.

21a. Brooks, Jr., Colonel William P., memo to Chief, OSD/ARPA, R&D, 28 May 62.

22. The hookworm is a small parasitic nematode worm, about 7 to 13mm long, of the family Ancylostomatidae. The worms have hooked mouthparts with which they fasten themselves to the intestinal walls of various hosts, including humans. If not treated, hookworm infection can lead to abdominal pain and iron-deficiency.

23. Memo from Capt. Alvin W. White, USAF, VC, to HQ USAF (AFCSG-3), Subject: Report as requested by classified message AFCG-3 68602, October, 1962.

24. Millan, Cesar, Cesar's Way (New York: Harmony Books, 2006), p. 66.

25. Press clipping, New York *Times*.

26. MACV was the joint service headquarters structured to coordinate military activities during the Vietnam War. The MACV commander worked closely with the U.S. Ambassador and the Joint Chiefs of Staff at the Pentagon 25. TWX, UPI AS1, 3 Sep: Year not listed but TWX received at OTSG, 10 Sep 64.

27. Memo, by unknown source, "Confidential-Norforn," 11 Feb 1963, p. 43.

28. Ibid. p. 44.

29. In March 1964, President Johnson replaced Harkins with General William Westmoreland.

30. Memo: Pedone to Robert C. Phelps, Advanced Research Projects Agency, Office of the Secretary of Defense, the Pentagon, 1 June 1963.

31. It appears that no one in the United States military bothered to monitor, evaluate, or record the exploits of ARVN dog teams after 1966 to any degree. Scraps of information float about like feathers in the wind.

An attempt has been made to gather these and find a home for them within this book, but they are few and far between. Finally there is the conclusion of the war in 1975. Unfortunately the victors in such a conflict do not retain the historical material of those vanquished to help us with our story. When Saigon fell, it was a time when no one asked, and perhaps rightfully so, what had happened to not only the dogs turned over by the Americans but those that were in ARVN control to begin with. Whatever conclusions we draw are strictly speculative and with few facts to build our story on.

Chapter 2 – American Boots and Paws on the Ground

1. http://www.forbes.com/fyi/1998/0504/031_print.html

2. Among the photographs taken during and immediately after the landing of the Marines, none showed Karch smiling. When asked about this he replied "...if I had to do it over, that picture would have been the same. When you have a son in Vietnam and he gets killed, you don't want a smiling general with flowers around his neck as leader at that point." Karch received his second Legion of Merit honor for his efforts during this landing.

3 .Operation Starlite took place between 18-24 August 1965. The plan was for the 7th and 4th Marines to eliminate the 1st Viet Cong Regiment.

4. The name is derived from the French word "sappe" (trench) which became connected with military engineering in the seventeenth century.

5. Just where and with whom the implementation of Top Dog 45 originated is a matter of conjecture. The program officially began on 3 July 1965. John Weaver, an E-4 at the time and one of the original Top Dog 45 handlers, provided his DD-214 for inspection. The DD-214 is the official discharge papers used by all the services and may give a bit of information as to where the whole sentry dog program in Vietnam originated. Under the section titled "Decorations, medals, badges, commendations, citations and campaign ribbons awarded or authorized" are two designations: SOG-66, and SOG-27. It is possible that these designations refer to Tan Son Nhut and Da Nang, locations where Weaver served. SOG refers to Studies and Operations Group. This ubiquitous name refers to a host of clandestine activities carried out in the Republic of Vietnam, inside Laos and Cambodia, and where no American was meant to walk, North Vietnam. SOG reported directly to the pentagon via MACV and was an army unto its own in Vietnam.

6. Allen K. McIntosh, Coke L. Westbrook, A Review of the Military Dog Program, CORG memorandum, 1968, p. 13.

7. This also flies in face of the statement by Roger Fox in his book *Air Base Defense in the Republic of Vietnam 1961-1973* when he states, "The dogs had no trouble in adjusting to the weather and working conditions." For every dog that did adjust easily there was another one that had difficulties. Even dogs well acclimated could succumb to heat stroke at any given moment if precautions were not taken.

8. Gas operated and using the 30-06 round, the M1 was great in WWII but was outdated for Vietnam. Over 4 million of the rifles were made during their production run.

9. Dick Bachmann, "Toby – The Best "Top Dog," *DogMan* (May-June 1995), p. 6.

10. Fogle, Bruce, *The Dog's Mind: Understanding Your Dog's Behavior,* New York: MacMillan, 1990 p. 38.

11. Even today we do not truly know the full capability of the olfactory ability of dogs. Dogs can sense chemical changes in people about to have epileptic seizures and warn their masters. Recent studies also indicate that canines can smell different types of skin cancers in humans. Exactly what canines can be expected to do still needs to be explored.

12. The dogs that did not return to their handlers or owners were quickly adopted by American citizens that applied to the War Department for a K-9 veteran.

13. Holt, along with USMC dog handler Raymond Andrew Shepard, were killed 3 August 1966. During a rain storm they ran inside a Vietnamese pagoda where the VC had planted a mine. The explosion killed Holt,

Shepard, and six other Marines. Holt was 23 years old and was from Nashville, TN. Shepard was 24 years old and was from Chicago.

14. Naval Message, 11 July, 1965, From COMUSMAC to CINPAC. Since this message was sent via teletype, indicating even a more urgent requirement, the entire communication was entirely in capital letters.

15. When known, the dog's identification number will accompany the dog's name when first mentioned. Dogs did not wear metallic identification tags like human soldiers. This ID number is tattooed either in the left ear or inside the skin fold of the left flank. It is known as the Preston Brand System and first began with military horses and mules. The tattoo (7/16" in height) consists of one letter and two or three digits. This system makes it possible to provide individual identification of 4,000 dogs with a single letter and combination of numbers. So the very first dog would be marked as "A000" and the four-thousandth as "999A."

16. This would contrast dramatically with the troops that participated in future conflicts well distanced from Vietnam. Perhaps it was one major lesson that was taken away from the Vietnam experience – that the men and women who participate in our country's battles be respected and honored regardless of how unpopular the foreign engagement might be. Unfortunately this basic premise of supporting the troops took decades to evolve. For many Vietnam veterans it came too late. This is one reason why many veterans from that period will often greet each other with a handshake and a "Welcome home" to symbolize something that they never received when it was needed the most.

17. Some anti-war activists purportedly went so far as to send Western Union telegrams to parents of soldiers in Vietnam informing them that their son was killed, when in fact they were alive and well.

18. Morrison, Wilbur H. *The Elephant & the Tiger*. New York: Hippocrene Books, 1990.

19. Fox, Roger P. *Air Base Defense in the Republic of Vietnam 1961-1973*. Washington, D.C. 1979.

20. Risse, John "Pleiku Air Base – 1965, *DogMan* (November-December 1994, p.1. On 12 April 1966 Risse was off post when a mortar attack took place about 0200 hours. Duke was alone in his kennel, while Risse was nearby "off base," hunkered down in a bunker during the attack. Spooked from the assault, Duke literally ripped down his kennel fence and escaped. No one could get the dog under control and Risse returned as fast as he could. Risse was able to round him up and collar him but soon noticed that his rear legs were badly torn up. The dog had lost quite a bit of blood and was in tough shape. Duke was transported to the 9th Medical Center in Saigon but his handler was not allowed to accompany him. Duke never returned and Risse is not sure, but believes he was put down due to his injuries. Forty years later he would later state, "I will never forget Duke. He was a great dog and sometimes I wonder what would have happened if we had been together that night so long ago."

21. Some recent reports claim that mines accounted for sixty-three percent of the casualties in Vietnam. This is a fabricated figure, dished out as an expedient by proponents attempting to ban the use of land mines around the world in recent years. There is little doubt that the millions of mines left over from numerous conflicts around the globe is a very real and sad commentary of current affairs. However historical evidence should not be altered to enable any effort – even the extraordinary humanitarian effort for the disposal of mines seeded around the world.

22. In December 1968 the status of the 197th was deemed "unsatisfactory" by military auditors. They were not alone. Four divisions along with the 194th Armored Brigade and the 6th Armored Calvary Regiment all earned the dubious distinction.

23. Bair, letter to Tom Mitchell 13 October 1998.

24. The USMC system for Military Occupation Specialty (MOS) was a bit different from the Army's. The men were assigned a primary MOS of 0311 (Basic Rifleman) and often a second and third. In no case was the primary MOS designation that of a dog handler. 8671 is the secondary MOS for a sentry dog handler and 8672 for a scout dog handler. USMC Mine and Booby Trap Detection dog handlers never

received a secondary MOS as the program was considered experimental. The MOS for an Army sentry dog handler was 95B4D.

25. The story of the Montagnards and how they were exploited is a story within itself. By the end of the war eighty-five percent of their villages were abandoned or destroyed and more than 200,000 Montagnards had died. For many of them, their war did not end with the fall of Saigon in 1975. In 1993, about 400 of the mountain people were found in Cambodia still carrying on the fight. They were eventually demobilized peacefully and most of them were resettled in the United States.

26. Entire books have been written about the Ho Chi Minh Trail. It is more than just military actions to interdict the flow of traffic, but the thousands of stories from those who were part of it on both sides. By 1970, more than 70,000 North Vietnamese defended the trail in the area where it passed through Laos. Truck convoys that ran at night could stretch for 50 to 75 miles in length. Over time, the route took on the same mystique as the Burma Road did during World War II. There was no romanticism attached to the trail. Although never completely eradicated, consider that more than 9,000 enemy trucks were destroyed during 1970. The chances of being blown up while driving a truck were pretty good. So good in fact, that the North Vietnamese even handcuffed their drivers to the steering wheels of their trucks so that they would not desert during an American bombing run.

Chapter 3 – Joe, the Dog, and Charlie

1. This was a sarcastic description for the daily briefings delivered at 5 P.M. by the U.S. Public Affairs Office for the benefit of reporters in Saigon. The information provided was always positive for the allies and led to what was known as a "credibility gap" by the journalists that began as early as the Kennedy Administration.

2. WP is an incendiary device that can be used as a smoke screening agent or as an anti-personnel flame compound. It was often referred to as "Willie Pete" or "Willie Peter."

3. Monthly Report of Activities, From 1st Lt. Robert V. Wilder To: Commanding General III MAF, 10 May 1966.

4. Smokey (1A82) was a Marine dog killed on 15 June 1966 a month earlier than Kaiser. Although no further information was available, he was probably a sentry dog.

5. I've never found any evidence to suggest that those in command encouraged the use of dogs to interrogate prisoners – this was true in Vietnam as it was in the infamous scandal of Abu Grahib prison in Iraq. In Vietnam, the United States basically maintained the commitments made in the Geneva Convention in the treatment of prisoners and the enemy did not. This is a well documented fact. How operations were conducted on a day-to-day basis in the bush can sometimes be questioned. Yet it is too easy for someone to make a judgment unless we walk in the same boots as those on an obscure and dangerous jungle trail. And those boots could have encountered a firefight a few minutes earlier with an unseen enemy and might have stepped on a booby trap after leaving a "peaceful" village and taking several prisoners.

6. The Hawk is a medium range, surface-to-air guided missile that provides air defense coverage against low-to-medium-altitude aircraft. It is a mobile, all-weather day and night system. The Marine Corps' "B" Battery of the 1st Light Anti-Aircraft Missile Battalion deployed with HAWK, marking the first surface-to-air missile system to be placed at the front in the Vietnam War. They were initially positioned on the DaNang airfield and were then placed atop Hill 327 west of the airbase. They were never fired during the course of the war.

7. Marine Sentry – 1966 Anthony Giorgi *DogMan,* May-June 1996 page 8.

8. Ibid.

9. Atwell, Bill "We Don't Salute," *DogMan*, March-April 1996, p. 6.

10. "Operation Safeside – USAF Scout Dogs", *DogMan* Vol. 2, No.6, November 1995, p2.

11. Email, Mitchell to Lemish 22 November 1995.

12. The eleven dogs that returned to the United States were Auggie (UNK), Blitz (UNK), Goldie (0H27), Kurt (6A03), Major (5A46), Muggs (4A58), Nipper (4X26), Rex (113X), Sabre (0H31), Samantha (3A93), Scout (2X55).

13. A Guidron is a small flag or pennant carried as a standard by a military unit.

14. Renamed DARPA for "Defense" in 1972, back to ARPA in 1993, and then back to DARPA in 1996. The agency was formed in 1958 in response to the Soviet launch of Sputnik with the overall mission to keep United States military technology ahead of its enemies. Over the years its diverse activities included mobile robots, development of GPS, and Apranet, which evolved into today's Internet.

15. In May 1966, ARPA also looked into employing Catahoula hog dogs, also known as Catahoula Leopards. Catahoulas are bred to go and find livestock in swamps, hilly canyons, thickets or forests, or mountains. Fairly primitive psychologically compared to other dogs, they are not easy to train and are distantly related to the Australian Dingo. It appears this breed was dismissed quickly and no further attempt was made by the military to investigate their potential.

16. Technically speaking, the Labrador retrievers were trailing dogs and not tracking dogs. A tracking dog locates each of an individual's footsteps, and seldom varies from the trail more than two feet, regardless of wind direction. Bloodhounds are the traditional picture of a tracking dog. The trailing dog is scenting to a person's cells that have fallen along a particular route. The dog may work some distance away from the actual footsteps and may sniff at leaves or other vegetation several feet off the ground. The dog will work a boundary of cells along a trail and may zigzag back and forth to acquire this scent picture.

17. Sambo acquired a U.S. derived number while the other two had British assigned numbers. It is not known if these dogs were tattooed the same as American dogs.

18. Craddick, Steve, "Trackers Jungle Trained" *DogMan,* October 1994 p.4.

19. These were operations Orange, Georgia, Liberty, Swanee, Jay, Napa, Hot Springs, Buck, Triton, El Paso.

20. Johnson, Stan, "A GI Named K9" *DogMan,* November-December 1994, p.7

21. At this time civilian dogs were typically fed a mix of table scraps. Packaged dog food was just starting to become popular with the public.

22. "Nutrition of military dogs under stress," McNamara JH, Vet Med Small Anim Clin 1972; 67(6): p. 615.

23. Browning, J. Pinoake, Frederick News Post, unknown date.

24. Hurley, PFC Tom, Heroic Scout Dog Retires, *Stars & Stripes*, undated. Hurley states in his piece that Castle died while Turk was returning to the states. Since his piece was written sometime in 1968, well after Castle died, it is probable that he did not get the full story. Turk would continue to have quite a career, but once he returned to work, he never left Vietnam again.

25. "Scout Dog Goes To States To Rejoin Wounded Master," The Army Reporter, 8 April 1967.

26. Different accounts place Rex at several locations after Bevich's death. Rex has been reportedly attached with his leash next to Bevich's body, nearby running loose, and on the other side of the base near the kennel in different accounts.

27. After his death, Nemo's memorabilia was forwarded to the Air Force Museum at Wright Patterson in Dayton, Ohio but was lost at some point along the way. Unfortunately so was his grave site. According to Bill Cumming, a VDHA unit director, it is believed to be at a small grove of trees near the old training kennels, but no one can confirm the exact location.

28. Research paper, Carr, C. Jelleff, Meiselman, Sumner, and Lamanns, Carl "Concept for a Superior Ambush Detection Dog," 11 May 1966

29. Massey, Tom (as told to Tom Mitchell), "Vietnam Navy Dog Handlers," *DogMan*, May-June 1997, p. 1.

30. Navy SEAL member ADR2 Eugene Fraley was also killed in Vietnam on 21 January 1968. Even though he worked with Rinnie, Fraley's did not have a MOS as a dog handler and it was not his prime occupation. Also, Fraley was killed in an accident in the Dinh Toung Province and was not acting as a dog handler at the time.

31. Haran, Peter. *Trackers: The Untold Story of the Australian Dogs of War*. Sydney, Australia: New Holland Publishers, 2000.

32. Dees was assigned to the Special Forces and was involved with civic affairs and not the canine program.

33. John C. Burnam, MSG (USA ret.), *Dog Tags of Courage*, Fort Bragg, CA: Lost Coast Press, 2000), p. 150-151.

34. Burnam, ibid. p. 177.

35. Phone conversation with author, 8 August 2000.

36. Small, Pvt., Vet Tech, letter to Mendez, 21 June 1967.

37. The bodies were recovered a day later and this is the date of the reported deaths.

Chapter 4 - Is This Any Way To End a War?

1. The battle that took place at Khe Sanh as a prelude to the Tet Offensive was actually the second major battle to take place there. The first confrontation took place between April and October of 1967. Just who won the second battle is still open to speculation. General Giap claimed victory and stated it was never the intention of the NVA to overrun the firebase. If that was the case, then 10,000 to 15,000 North Vietnamese were sacrificed for the ruse. Entire books have been written on this one battle and there are probably more to come. Two books worth mentioning are: Head, William, and Lawrence Grinter, eds. *Looking Back on the Vietnam War: A 1990s Perspective on the Decisions, Combat, and Legacies* (1993) and Pisor, Robert, *The End of the Line: The Siege of Khe Sanh* (1982).

2. Nam: The Vietnam Experience 1965-1975. Page, Tim and Pimlott, John, eds.Mallard Press 1988

3. "1968 Tet Offensive – Personal Remembrances", *DogMan*, February 1998, p. 2.

4. The shooting was also captured on moving film, just like the flag raising on Iwo Jima during World War II was shot on movie film. It is the still photo of the Iwo Jima flag raising by Joe Rosenthal that reached epic proportions. What the two had in common was the power of a still picture. Both events captured in motion are relegated to the dustbins of history while the still photos remain potent images of two very different wars.

5. A forward air controller was typically flying a light single or twin-engine aircraft and would direct airborne bombing, strafing, or artillery and mortar fire.

6. Kollar, Robert, letter, 15 November 15 1968.

7. Nearly half of Ben Tre was destroyed during the Tet Offensive. Purportedly an unidentified U.S. Army officer later stated, "It became necessary to destroy the town to save it." In 2003 columnist Mona Charen and Vietnam War researcher B.G. Burkett concluded that Ben Tre had been destroyed by the Viet Cong as they retreated. The pair also believes Peter Arnett was the source of the quote. But Arnett remembers it as "It was a shame the town was destroyed."

8. Phone conversation with author, 15 February 1999.

9. Alphonse-Marie-Louis de Prat de Lamartine, 21 October 1790 – 28 February 1869, was a French writer, poet, and politician.

10. Lubow, Robert E. *The War Animals*. New York: Doubleday and Co., 1977, pp 177-178.

11. The unit designation is a little confusing since there were no scout dogs involved. In the evaluation's conclusions this was noted.

12. It should be noted that no training ever took place on "old" buried material while at Fort Gordon. In a combat environment the dog is searching for active scents and under quite harsh conditions. Even if this type of training took place, it is doubtful that finding long buried ordnance would be very productive while out on patrol.

13. The four dogs were Topper (3A36), Bear (unk), Pete (72M8), and Jet (unk).

14. Letter, Otis Archives, Washington, D.C.

15. El Cajon News, Students' Threat To 'Napalm' a Dog, 8 November 1968.

16. 62nd IPCT Operational Report – Month of August, 1 Sept. 69.

17. Endy, Mary Ann, "The story of war dogs and handlers" *DogMan*, February 2001, pg. 5.

18. Department of the Army, The Center of Military History, letter to the author 12 April 1995. In an undated note by Major Bruce F. Kay he noted, "... deployment in early 1970 to an undisclosed location." There has been speculation the 55th IPSD might be used in covert operations in Laos or Cambodia. It's a remote possibility that deploying the 55th IPSD may have been discussed, but eventually dismissed.

19. Apparently a serviceman who returned home inquired about the awards in a letter and the St. Louis Post Dispatch newspaper had picked up on it. It is still quite possible that these dogs did perform a heroic action and should have been properly recognized.

20. MacRobbie, Steve, *DogMan*, March-April 1996, p. 3.

21. Senior officer debriefing report: Colonel W. H. Brandenburg, USARV Provost Marshall and CO, 18th Military Police Brigade, Period 30 Aug 68 through 22 Dec 69. 26 January 1970. Department of the Army, Office of the Adjutant General, Washington, D.C. Report No. AD 707208.

22. Senior officer debriefing report: Paul M. Timmerberg, Commander, 18th MP Brigade and Provost Marshall, Vietnam, 17 June 71 through 30 May 1972. 6 December 1972. Department of the Army, Office of the Adjutant General, Washington, D.C. report No. A.D. 523511.

22. McIntosh, 1Lt. Donald K., Monthly Report of Scout Dog Operations, 57th IPSD, 3 October 1969.

23. Lunkenheimer, memo, Subject: Evalutaion of Off Leash Scout Dogs, 9 May 1969. Cobb would later earn a Bronze Star with "V" for saving a patrol from a VC ambush.

24. Little Joe was KIA 22 February 1970.

25. According to Perry Money, one of the original USMC mine dog handlers, one dog was not read and shipped out at a later date. Email, Perry Money to author, 30 November 2007.

26. http://www.capmarine.com/cap/rex.htm

27. Unit history, 43rd IPSD, 27 October 1970.

28. Canine dentistry was a relatively new endeavor at this time. Dogs would have their teeth scaled routinely but this was performed by veterinarians while the dog was under anesthesia or with a special muzzle that permitted the teeth to be cleaned without the loss of any fingers.

29. "Dentist finds a way to hide 2 ounces of gold – inside sentry dog's mouth," *DogMan,* June 2005, p. 3, Robert L. Engelmeier, Col USAF – Ret.

30. Xuan Loc, about 20 km north of Saigon was the last big battle for the ARVN against the NVA in 1975. Twenty-five years later, the scars are still quite visible, with the bombed out buildings and the impact of artillery and small arm rounds still visible in walls and fences. The biggest difference is probably the number of television antennas pointed south toward Ho Chi Minh City.

31. Charlie Cargo, interview with author, April 1995.

32. Zika, Richard, letter to author 28 December 1997.

33. Ibid.

34. Memo, Office of the Chief of Information, Army Fact Sheet No. 54, 10 April 1952.

35. Letter, Bush K.B. Major General to Ramsden, Mr. A., 29 April 1952.

36. Can't Go Home, Page 2 of 3 http://vdha.us/content243.html 3 November 2007.

37. The letter is shown as it appeared in an API publication.

38. With the media today and the use of the Internet, millions of people would have known about the plight of the dogs in Vietnam. In 1970, the majority of information was still delivered via newspapers. Email did not exist and communication was either over the phone or through written letters. One wonders how this same situation would play out today in our media driven world that we live in.

39. Rumors about what happened with the dogs still persist to this day. Among them are that Trajan was passed on to an American school teacher and that Marcian was later run over by a vehicle and killed. Caesar's last owner was Air Comander Bill Connaughton who evacuated in 1975 and passed him on to an Austrlian Civil Aid worker in Vung Tau. Peter Haran returned to Vietnam in 2008 and reportedly located the great-great-great grandson of Caesar in Saigon.

40. Arts, Davis Jay, "Loyalty Betrayed: Comparing the Fates of the American Military Working Dogs That Served In World War II and the Vietnam War," p. 30.

41. Ibid. pg 31.

42. The sheer number of variables is huge, especially when an evaluation is conducted under combat situations. Another aspect not even discussed is that American forces were in a state of withdrawal from the battle. If this same evaluation was done a couple of years earlier, say in 1966 or 1967, the results might have been quite different.

43. From the apparent documents, no consideration seemed to be given to the dogs handed over to the Vietnamese (i.e., sentry, scout, or mine detector). Based on the information available, the Vietnamese would not be able to differentiate the dogs' abilities gifted to them.

44. http://www.pbase.com/vdha/635thsps_history

45. http://www.pbase.com/vdha/635thsps_history

46. Lt. Col. William T. Ashby, USAF, VC and Lt. Colonel Hubert E. McKinney, USAF, VC, "Canine Ehrlichiosis in the Retrogradation of United States Forces Military Working Dogs From Thailand," p. 17.

47. Interview, George Negus Tonight, Australian Broadcasting Corporation, 26 April 2004.

48. In October 2002, Budda and his first handler Bob Brown were recognized by the Special Operations Association at their annual meeting. In March of 1967 the pair was assigned TDY to a classified all-volunteer unit of the U.S. Special Forces. The twosome led six clandestine expeditions into neutral Laos.

49. Peters, Pete, "If Only I Could Talk" unpublished.

Chapter 5 - In Our Hearts, We Did Bring Them Home

1. *Time* 22 Nov 82, http://www.bartleby.com/63/31/1231.html

2. Condensed from Northeast Magazine, Hartford Daily Courant, 14 May 1995.

3. Further research indicates that Phillips passed away in 1996 and in a very brief phone conversation his sister said no dog was ever returned home. In a 2001 *Dog World* article, "From Homefront to Home Life," author Mary Elizabeth Thurston mentions a Vietnam medic, named Tom Johnson, as having smuggled home a scout dog that lived to be 17 years old. However this information has never been corroborated or confirmed.

4. "From Camelot to Kent State: The Sixties Experience in the Words Who Lived It," by Joan Morrison and Robert K. Morrison, New York, Times Books, 1987.

5. Ibid.

6. I attempted to contact the editors of the book in 2003 and forwarded a letter to the publisher asking for an interview. Although the letter was never returned as undeliverable, neither was it ever answered.

7. Greene also went on to write a fictional account of his dog in the book *A Star For Buster*, University Editions, 1994. It tells of the dog's exploits during WWII and a boy's attempt (successfully) to have his dog enshrined on the town's Board of Honor for veterans killed-in-action.

8. *Dogs of War*, The Dog Museum, brochure, p.2

9. www.schombergerstudios.com

10. Benge, Laura, War Dog Memorial Fund continues effort; Nearly a million dollars has been raised, *DogMan*, December 1999, p.1.

11. Ibid.

12. *DogMan*, October 2000, p. 2. As president of the VDHA, Kimler had to walk a fine line. Many members of the VDHA were upset with the fact that it appeared that the memorial project was "hijacked" by Nature's Recipe and that the company was profiting from the events and that the original location, Washington, D.C. was never to be realized. Other members reasoned that without Jeff Bennett and Nature's Recipe, there would never be any memorial, much less two of them. Also, there would never have been a documentary aired nationally, that would bring so much recognition to the war dogs. Nonetheless, a wedge would forever be introduced between the two organizations and among many of the members. It is for that reason that purportedly the third memorial, matching the other two, remains in storage.

13. Email to author, 9 April 2008.

14. **SEC. 2877. ESTABLISHMENT OF NATIONAL MILITARY WORKING DOG TEAMS MONUMENT ON SUITABLE MILITARY INSTALLATION.**

(a) Authority to Establish Monument- The Secretary of Defense may permit the National War Dogs Monument, Inc., to establish and maintain, at a suitable location at Fort Belvoir, Virginia, or another military installation in the United States, a national monument to honor the sacrifice and service of United States Armed Forces working dog teams that have participated in the military operations of the United States.

(b) Location and Design of Monument- The actual location and final design of the monument authorized by subsection (a) shall be subject to the approval of the Secretary. In selecting the military installation and site on such installation to serve as the location for the monument, the Secretary shall seek to maximize access to the resulting monument for both visitors and their dogs.

(c) Maintenance- The maintenance of the monument authorized by subsection (a) by the National War Dogs Monument, Inc., shall be subject to such conditions regarding access to the monument, and such other conditions, as the Secretary considers appropriate to protect the interests of the United States.

(d) Limitation on Payment of Expenses- The United States Government shall not pay any expense for the establishment or maintenance of the monument authorized by subsection (a).

15. Thurston, Mary Elizabeth, "From Homefront to Home Life," *Dog World*, June 2001, p. 60.

16. Ibid. Robby was put down on 19 January 2001.

17. Ibid.

18. Moore, George E. DVM, MS, DACVPM, DACVIM, et al, "Causes of death or reasons for euthanasia in military working dogs: 927 cases (1993-1996)" JAVMA, Vol 219, No. 2 15 July 2001, p. 209-213.

19. Emlock, Erin, R.I. Veteran opens his home, heart, The Providence Sunday Journal, 20 October 2002, p. C-5.

20. Kandoll, Debbie, email to author, 24 March 2008.

21. Kandoll, Debbie, email to author, 2 April 2008.

22. The website is www.militaryworkingdogsadoptions.com. As with everything else on the Internet, websites and email addresses come and go. Like most things having to do with the government, should you consider adopting a K-9 veteran several items are available that will help you in the process. If you are knowledgeable and persistent, and respect the person you are dealing with, the reward at the end will justify the time and effort. It should also be understood that those who work in the government and who are involved in the adoption process are not callous or indifferent about the situation at hand. Often they are limited by what they can do based on the structure of the organization they are working within.

23. Unfortunately, producer William D'Angelo passed away several years ago and I was never able to determine how the idea for the series evolved. Also the series star for the first season, Arch Whiting, passed away in May 2007. NBC has also been unable to provide any information about the series development.